To the Teachers and hundreds of Pupils in the schools of Caroline County who willingly secured data which is herein presented this volume is respectfully dedicated.

INTRODUCTION.

The continual need of the children, teachers, and officers of our public schools having some historical data concerning the home county of Caroline has led to the publishing of this book which is here presented to the public.

The constant neglect of a citizenship to compile facts concerning its growth and history must inevitably lead to an almost total ignorance of the same and subsequently to a lack of appreciation of the local heroes.

Having read of the struggles of the colonial troops during the Revolutionary War, how many of us are conscious of the fact that our county then only in its infancy furnished not only its quota of soldiers and supplies, but the leader of the troops of the Eastern Shore—Colonel William Richardson?

Have we fully realized that the immortal Declaration of Independence was made possible by just such assemblages of determined citizens as the one held in this county in June 1774?

Has it ever occurred to us that our county furnished one subject of the cause for the War of 1812—the impressment of American Seamen?

Generally may it be said that Caroline's worthies of the past and present have held and still hold an honored place among the leaders of the State. To give due credit to these is one valid reason for such a volume. Perhaps, a more important reason, however, for such an effort is the necessity of the pupils in our schools acquiring a fundamental knowledge of the organization and earlier history of our county (1) to teach an appreciation of home and local environments and (2) to furnish a proper basis for state and national history.

Assuredly, Caroline County has a rich background which adds dignity to the present, for out of the early days step stately personages who add charm to every scene; stirring events that warm the blood; and spots hallowed by the acts of brave ones; yes, changing persons and events—moving pictures so to speak.

In the "History of Caroline County" an attempt has been made to record in simple form the substance of facts gleaned from reliable sources by the pupils, teachers, and officials of the public schools through talks with the older residents, county officials, by means of old manuscripts, deeds, wills, newspapers, church and court records, and from the several volumes of history and novels pertaining to our county and state.

Our appreciation is here extended to those principals, teachers, and children of our schools who have contributed material as well as to that large host of parents and friends who have answered the questions of children from day to day with such uniform courtesy and cooperation. Especially are our thanks due to Capt. Chas. W. Wright, Edward T. Tubbs, Zebdial P. Steele, J. Kemp Stevens, James E. Hignutt, officials of the Clerk's office, and others who either through personal knowledge, memory, data or help of records aided us greatly in this publication.

To the Editors of the County newspapers—*Greensboro Enterprise, Denton Journal, American Union, Federalsburg Courier* and *Caroline Sun*, as well as to Swepson Earle, author of the Colonial Eastern Shore, we desire to acknowledge our gratitude for the use of valuable engravings and etchings loaned us.

While conscious of the laborious efforts and painstaking care bestowed, we fully realize that a work, so largely one of original research, is inevitably not without imperfections and some errors. In submitting it, therefore, to the public, it is with the hope that generous readers will appreciate the difficulties attending the undertaking and will accord consideration and justice to the motive which has animated this humble tribute.

EDWARD M. NOBLE.

Denton, Maryland, October 10, 1920.

SOURCES AND REFERENCES

Consulted in the Preparation of

THE HISTORY OF CAROLINE COUNTY.

Public Records:

Congressional Library, Maryland State Library, Maryland Land Record Office, Maryland Historical Society, Enoch Pratt Library, Peabody Library, Land and Will Records of Caroline County, Land and Will Records of Dorchester County, Land and Will Records of Talbot County, Records of Bethesda Church, Preston; Tennessee Historical Society, Third Haven Meeting, Easton.

Newspapers:

Maryland Gazette, Annapolis; *Easton* (Md.) *Gazette*; *Denton Journal*; *American Union,* Denton; *The Pearl,* Denton.

Books and Pamphlets:

American Archives, Washington; Maryland Archives; History of Maryland Conventions 1774-1776; Senate and House Journals, Annapolis; Atlas Landholders Assistant; *McSherry's* History of Maryland; Makers of Methodism; Asbury's Journal; Hanson's History of Kent County; Tilghman's History of Talbot County; Earle's Colonial Eastern Shore; Wright's History of the Wright Family; Federal Census of 1790; The Tory Maid; Maryland Historical Magazine; Maryland in Prose and Poetry.

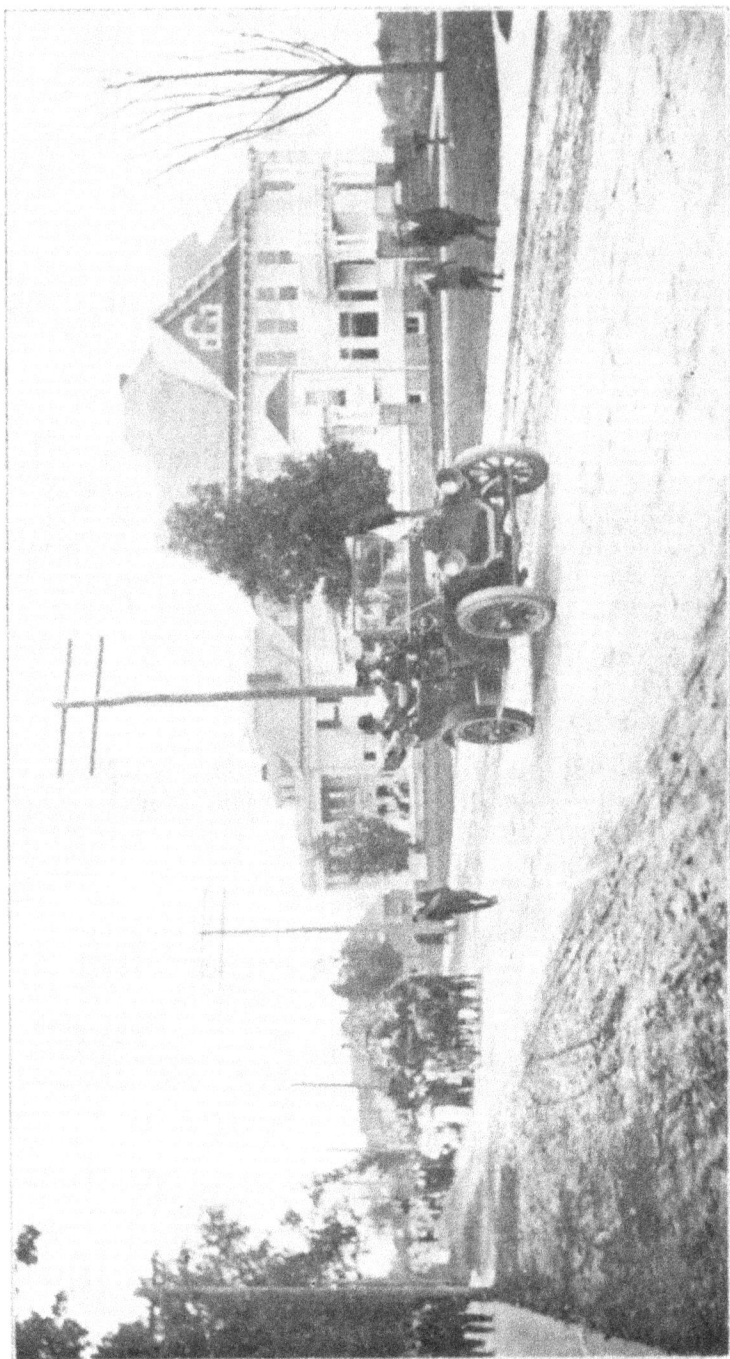

FIFTH AVE.. DENTON. SHOWING COUNTY ATHLETIC DAY PARADE.

CONTENTS.

xvi

FORMATION OF CAROLINE COUNTY.

Up until 1774 there was no Caroline County. The land where we now live belonged to Dorchester and Queen Anne's counties. Large tracts were uncleared and roads poor. When people living here had business at court, they had to make a long, rough journey either to Cambridge or Queenstown. Far-seeing men decided to petition the General Assembly of the province to make a new county out of parts of Dorchester and Queen Anne's, which they felt would result in a more rapid development of this section as well as prove a great personal convenience.

The petition was granted (in 1774) creating the new county and giving to it the name of Caroline. This was in honor of Caroline Eden, a sister of Frederick Calvert, the last Lord Baltimore, and wife of Sir Robert Eden, then English governor of Maryland.

The same Assembly provided that the new county be divided into hundreds. This was an English term for what we would call districts. A map given elsewhere in this history shows these divisions and you can readily find in which of the original hundreds you live.

The Assembly also appointed seven commissioners for Caroline county, namely: Charles Dickinson, Benson Stainton, Thomas White, William Haskins, Richard Mason, Joshua Clark, and Nathaniel Potter. These men were to buy four acres of land at Pig Point (now Denton) have it surveyed and recorded in the county records. Upon this land the court house and jail were to be built.

In the meanwhile, court was to be held at Melvill's Warehouse. This was a small settlement about a mile and a half above Pig Point, consisting of a tobacco warehouse, wharf, store, and a few houses. Elections were to be held there as well as other business transactions. As a result Melvill's Landing, the temporary county-seat, became a place of considerable importance in the early history of Caroline. A prominent man at the Landing was James Barwick, who kept the inn, was jailor, provided the necessary rooms for court use, and kept the ferry which ran from Melvill's Warehouse to the causeway opposite. An old store house belonging to Edward Lloyd of Talbot was rented for a jail. It was evidently not in good condition, for the court ordered it put in better repair by placing logs under the sills and that these logs be sunk in the ground. The warehouse was a more substantial brick structure built previous to 1763 situated a little back from the river. Here the great hogsheads of tobacco were received from planters, weighed, stamped and stored for shipment.

The first session of court was held March 15, 1774 at Melvill's Warehouse. It continued being held there twice a year in March and October until 1777, when Bridgetown (now Greensboro) succeeded in having it moved there. Later, however, it was decided for the convenience of public business, Melvill's Warehouse being most central, that court be held there as usual. Notwithstanding this fact, records prove that sessions were held at Bridgetown in August and November of '78 and June, October, and November of '79.

Feeling was strong concerning the permanent location of the county-seat. The people in the upper part of the county insisted upon Bridgetown, while those in the lower section were quite as insistent for Pig Point. In 1785 a compromise was effected by the General Assembly authorizing the purchase of two acres of land at Melvill's Landing. Matthew Driver, the owner of the Brick House Farm which extended nearly to the Landing, promptly deeded the required amount of land to the justices of the county to be used as a site for the court house and jail. All that happened within the next five years regarding this compromise we do not know, but in 1790, all the belongings of the county court were moved to Pig Point. A house was rented there, and used until the completion of the court house about 1797, for the court sessions.

ORGANIZATION OF THE COUNTY.

I. Introduction.

The early government of Maryland was modeled after the Palatinate of Durham in England, with a few added "powers" which made the Governor scarcely less than a king.

Of all the Colonial organs of government—The Hundred, the Manor etc.—the County had more functions and more powers than any other, especially in the executive and judicial lines.

II. Why Caroline?

What was the need that led to the organization of Caroline? The inland sections of Dorchester and Queen Anne Counties had developed and were now rich and productive. Trade as well as population had increased and as a whole this section had become somewhat prominent in the respective counties much on account of the fertile soil in this inland section.

Crime too had increased, due in a great degree to the cosmopolitan nature of a new and rapidly growing population. The carrying of prisoners from this section to Queenstown in Queen Anne County or Cambridge in Dorchester County naturally became a problem. With these points in view.—

1. Needs of increased population,
2. Needs of increased trade,
3. Need for increased crime,

a more central government began to be discussed.

Then too because of distance and difficulties of travel in that day the right of suffrage was in a sense practically denied many free-born citizens.

Having in mind these needs of the people the colonists in this section presented a petition to the General Assembly of Maryland, which met at Annapolis, Nov. 1773, praying that the right to organize a new County be granted them.

Below is given the Act passed by this Assembly.

"WHEREAS, a considerable body of the inhabitants of Dorchester and Queen Anne's Counties, by their petition of this General Assembly, have prayed that an Act may be passed for the division of the said counties, and for erecting a new one out of the parts

—3—

thereof; And whereas it appears to this General Assembly, that the erecting of a new county out of such parts of Dorchester and Queen-Anne's will conduce greatly to the ease and convenience of the people thereof: Be it therefore enacted, by the right honorable, the Lord Proprietary by and with the advice and consent of the Governor and the Upper and Lower Houses of Assembly, and the authority of the same, that after the Monday of the second Tuesday in March next such parts aforesaid two counties, Dorchester and Queen-Anne's, as are contained within the bounds and limits following to wit:

Beginning at a point on the north side of the mouth of Hunting Creek in Dorchester County, and from thence running up and with the said Creek to the main road at James Murray's Mill, thence by that road by Saint Mary's Chapel Parish church to Northwest Fork Bridge, thence with the main road (that leads to Cannon's Ferry) to Nanticoke River, thence with said river to and with the exterior limits of Queen-Anne's County to intersect the main road that leads from Beaver-dam Causeway to Dovertown, in Kent County upon Delaware, thence with the said road to Long Marsh, thence with said Marsh and stream of the branch of Tuckahoe Creek to Tuckahoe Bridge, thence with the said creek to Great Choptank River and with the said river to the first beginning at the mouth of Hunting Creek, shall be and is hereby erected in a new county by the name of Caroline County."

The land approximately was as follows: From Queen Anne County that part of Caroline lying west of the Choptank River. From Dorchester County that part of Caroline County lying east of the Choptank River with a somewhat indefinite boundary along what is now the Delaware line. Of this section there was yet some question as to Maryland's valid title and probably for this reason the land was largely uncleared.

In addition to the two parts above given Caroline has now a small portion of land—probably a few square rods—included within her boundaries that was in the early surveys a part of Talbot.

III. Naming the County.

The new county was named Caroline in honor of Caroline Calvert, sister of Frederick, last Lord Baltimore, and wife of Robert Eden, last colonial governor of the Province of Maryland.

IV. Completion of Organization.

While these enactments were all in 1773, the actual organization of the county did not take place until 1774 at which time it was necessary to make some changes in the Eastern boundary line as laid out by Assembly in 1773, owing to the fact that although a map had been made and the "vistor" run by the surveyors completed

—4—

yet the exact location of the "division" seemed indefinite in the minds of the legislators.

V. The Finances.

The Assembly, too, in the Acts at time of organization secured to the county the greater part of the monies for a Court House. Besides authorizing assessments the following was ordered by Assembly:

Some time prior to the organization of Caroline County the taxpayers of Dorchester County were assessed for the purpose of constructing a Court House at Cambridge. The taxpayers residing in that portion of Dorchester County which subsequently became a part of Caroline County, had been assessed in a similar manner, and paid to the commissioners of Dorchester County, 70,000 pounds of tobacco.

When arrangements were made for organizing Caroline County, the justices of Dorchester County were authorized to pay to the commissioners of Caroline County, 70,000 pounds of tobacco, this quantity to be credited to the taxpayers residing in that section of Caroline County which formerly was known as part of Dorchester County. The taxpayers of that section of Caroline County formerly a section of Queen-Anne's County, were assessed in proportion to the amount received from Dorchester County. This was to be placed to the credit of the previously mentioned former taxpayers of said section and to be used towards building the Court house and prison in Caroline."

VI. Final Sealing of Boundaries.

The first difficulty about boundaries has been mentioned before—namely the Maryland-Delaware line. Beside this, other changes were made in the line which separates Caroline from Dorchester. These changes were three in number and below we give them quoted from Wright.

1 **Alteration of 1793.**

"The first alteration took place in 1793, when John Smoot, Eccleston Brown, and Thomas Nichols of Dorchester County, with James Summers and Edward Wright Sr. of Caroline County were authorized to have a new bridge constructed to span the Northwest Fork River, about 150 yards or 19½ perches below the site of the old bridge that had been washed away; they were also to have the road (that led from Hunting Creek Church to Cannon's Ferry) altered, to traverse across the new bridge and thus annex to Caroline County a stretch of land formerly in Dorchester County."

2 **Alteration of 1878.**

"The second and less important alteration was made during 1878, in the dividing line and road leading from Hynson to Federalsburg, and it was in reference to straightening the road for a short distance between the lands of William A. Noble and S. Frank Pool residing in the opposite adjoining counties. The expense incurred in making this alteration was borne by these two enterprising gentlemen."

"The third and most important alteration of the boundary line occurred in 1880. Early in that year each of the seventy voters of the section that was proposed for alteration, petitioned the General Assembly of Maryland, that whereas Federalsburg standing upon the dividing line between Dorchester and Caroline County, hence causing divers difficulties; therefore the boundary line between these counties should be altered; beginning at a dividing line approximately one and a half miles north-west of Federalsburg, between the lands of Wm. H. Alburger and Mrs. Ann Noble; then with the same reversed through the lands of Robert McCrea, A. W. Flowers, and others, until the North-west fork of the Nanticoke River is reached then along the river to Miles' Run; along Miles' Run to the road leading from Johnson's Cross Roads to Federalsburg."

By this survey lands lying between the new and the old boundary became part of Caroline County. Then a census of all voters within this limit was taken. With one exception the voters were in favor of Alteration and as a final matter Caroline paid Dorchester $600 for the land.

CAROLINE COUNTY COURTS.

I. *Importance of Courts of that Day.*

As has been mentioned the Palatinate of Durham was the model for Maryland government and accordingly much power was vested in the county unit—the court. The following list of court powers of that day gives an idea of their jurisdiction.

Court powers:
1 To divide Counties into Hundreds.
2 To appoint a constable once a year for each Hundred.
3 To divide the county into highway precincts.
4 To appoint once a year an overseer for each highway precinct.
5 To hear and consider petitions for new highways.
6 To let contracts for keeping ferries.
7 To let contracts for erection and repair of county buildings.
8 To appoint inspectors of weights and measures. (Later for tobacco.)
9 To provide county with standards of weights and measures.
10 To require tobacco inspectors to render them accounts.
11 To remove inspectors from office for misbehavior.
12 To (through Justices) levy taxes.
13 To exempt paupers from poll tax.
14 To exempt superannuated slaves from tax.
15 To (through sheriff) collect taxes.
16 To grant rights to keep ordinary.
17 To establish rates of ordinary as to eating, drinking, etc.
18 To advise sheriff as to day of election of "delegates." (The justices sat with sheriff during election.)
19 To (in some cases) direct the sheriff to sell insolvent debtors into servitude.
20 To pay annual prizes amounting to several thousand pounds of tobacco for the best pieces of linen manufactured in the county.
21 To train and organize Militia.
22 To (in cases of poverty)—
a Bind out orphan children as apprentices.
b Engage physicians for sick paupers.
c Levy tax for the support of the poor and needy.

II. *Establishing the Courts.*

The same assembly—1773—which gave us Caroline, enacted various laws relative to the new County Courts.

1 The Assembly appointed seven Commissioners.
2 These Commissioners were authorized to purchase "A quantity of land, not exceeding four acres of land, at or adjoining Pig Point on the east side of the Choptank River, below Melvill's Warehouse."
3 The Justices of Caroline County were authorized to secure a place for court and gaol.
4 Ordered court to be held at Melvill's warehouse until Court and gaol at Pig Point were complete.

5   Authorized Justices to levy a tobacco assessment sufficient
    to pay for land on which to build court house and gaol—
    plus 5% sheriffs fees for collecting.
6   The commissioners were authorized to contract and agree
    for the building of the Court house and gaol.

III. Places of Holding Court.

1   Melvill's Warehouse.   March 1774 to August 1778.
2   Bridgetown (now Greensboro).   August 1778 to March
    1780.
3   Melvill's Warehouse.   March 1780 to March 1790.
4   Pig Point (now Denton).   March 1790 to present.

IV. Court at Melvill's Warehouse.

By order of Assembly (1773) Melvill's Warehouse
became the temporary county seat and court convened
there for all trems from 1774 to 1778. The following is
the official record of the same.

Court organization—

Maryland at a County Court of the Right Honorable Henry
Harford, Esq. Absolute Lord and Proprietary of the province of
Maryland held for Caroline County at Melvill's Warehouse in the
County aforesaid, the third Tuesday in March, Anno Domini 1774
beginning the 15 day of the said month and continued by several
adjournments until the 17th day thereby. Lordships, commissioners and officers authorized and employed to hold the said court
were

Present

The Worshipful
    Mr. Charles Dickinson
    Mr. Benson Stainton
    Mr. Thomas White
    Mr. William Haskins
    Mr. Richard Mason
    Mr. Joshua Clark
    Mr. Nathaniel Potter

The said Lord Proprietary
his Justices

Wm. Hopper Esq. Sheriff   George Fitzhugh, Clerk.

The following commission and Writ of Dedimus Potestatem
thereon indorsed to the Justices of Caroline County directed are
openly read (viz) the Right Honorable Henry Harford, Esq.; absolute Lord and Proprietary of the Province of Maryland to Richard Lee, Benedict Calvert, Daniel Dulany, John Ridout, John Beale
Boardley, George Stewart, William Fitzhughes, William Hayward,
Daniel of Saint Thomas Ienifer, George Peter, Benjamin Ogle and
Philip Thomas Lee, Esquires, Charles Dickinson, William Haskins,
Thomas White, Richard Mason, Joshua Clark, Benson Stainton,
Nathaniel Potter, William Richardson, and Matthew Driver, Junior
men of Caroline County, Gentlemen Greeting, Know ye, that we
have assigned you and every one of you jointly and severally, our
Justices to keep our peace within our County of Caroline and to do
equal law and right to all the Kings subjects, rich and poor, according to the laws, customs and directions of the acts of Assembly

of this Province, so far forth as they provide, and where they are
silent, according to the laws, statutes and reasonable customs of
England, as made and practised within this Province for the conservation of the peace, and quiet rule and government of the
King's subjects within our said County, and to chastise and punish
all or any persons offending against the said acts, laws, statutes
and customs, or any of them, according to the directions thereof,
and to call before you, or any of you, those who in our County
aforesaid shall break our peace and misbehave themselves; to find
sufficient security of the peace and good behaviour to us and the
said subjects, and if they shall refuse to find such security that
then you cause them to be committed into safe custody, until they
shall be delivered by due course of law from thence; also we have
assigned you, and every three or more of you—(then an enumera-
tion of all crimes and misdemeanors follows) .... and none
others to be Judges. Also by these presents we do command the
Sheriff of our said County of Caroline that at the several Courts
to be held for our said county, he give his attendance and cause to
come before you, or any three or more of you (as aforesaid) such
and so many good and lawful men of his Bailiwick out of every
hundred thereof, by whom the truth of the matter may be better
known and inquired of. Lastly, you shall cause to be brought before you at your said Courts, all Writs, Precepts, Process, and In-
dictments to your Courts and Jurisdiction belonging, that the same
may be inspected and by due course of law determined. Witness
Robert Eden, Esq. Lieutenant General and Chief Governor of our
said Province of Maryland, this twenty eight day of February, in
the third year of our Dominion.

Robert Eden. (Seal)

This first court made appointments and issued Orders of Court but no "trials" were held until August,
1774 at which time the Commissioners and other officers
were the same as those present in March.

V. Court at Bridgetown (Greensboro).

Troubles concerning the location of the seat of Justice began. Jealousy no doubt was the basis of the entire dissention. During the Revolutionary period the
County Treasury had become depleted by general conditions as well as by the depreciation of currency so that
the monies therein had almost reached zero. Wright
says, "Each year that this great and glorious conflict
continued, depreciated Caroline's finances until they had
almost if not quite reached the vanishing point." With
keen political acumen the Northern part of the County
made a heroic effort to have the County Seat removed to
Bridgetown (now Greensboro). The down County poli-
ticians offered vigorous opposition claiming that Edenton (now Denton) the place chosen by the 1773 Assembly was more centrally located and making protest
against "The Bridgeers" lacking dignity of name. The
upper county retaliated in kind by reference to "Pig

Point" and the impropriety of the name Edenton because of its relation to Governor Eden.

And so the war waged. Mass meetings were held and committees from both sections with the fastest local craft obtainable flew "hither and to" across the bay to Annapolis trying to impress the law-makers of their needs. That they created some contention among the law-makers there is shown by the following enactments of 1786 when:

1 "An Act was passed suspending the erection of public buildings in Caroline, and a petition was presented to the Assembly, signed by many inhabitants of the County praying that the public building be erected at Choptank Bridge."

2 "A counter-petition signed by many other inhabitants of the County and preferred to the same Assembly prayed that the said building be erected at or near the center of the County."

3 "The Assembly then passed an Act deferring the erection of public building until the next Assembly, any law to the contrary notwithstanding."

That Court convened in Bridgetown a number of times during this altercation is proven by the Court records. The orders are as follows:

1777

"The Court appoints Messers Richard Mason, Henry Downes, Thomas Hardcastle, Matthew Driver and Nathaniel Potter, or any three or more of them, to agree with some person or persons in Bridgetown, for a house to hold Court in; a good and safe temporary place, and that the same be put in order, fit and proper for the purpose aforesaid, and that they return an account of the same to the next Court."

1778

Ordered by the Court that Caroline County Court be held at Bridgetown for the future.

1778

Ordered by the Court that the Sheriff remove the prisoners now in the public jail at Melvill's Warehouse to Bridgetown as said there shall be a jail fit to receive them.

The Court minutes give the following dates on which Court "set" in Bridgetown, in Aug. 1778 and Nov. 1778, but at the November session the opposition to Greensboro was so strong that the following order was passed:

1778

On motion to remove this Court from Bridgetown to Melvill's Warehouse from whence it was removed at March term, 1778, the Court on mature deliberation is of the opinion that the removal from Melvill's Warehouse was unwarranted by any power in the Court by the Act of Assembly for fixing a place of holding the Court, and that at the convenience of the public business, and as

Melvill's Warehouse is most central, and the place appointed by
the commissioners of the peace under the Act of Assembly entitled "An Act for the division of Dorchester and for erecting a
new house by the name of Caroline" for transacting the public
business for Caroline County and the public buildings which be
erected; therefore it is reported that this Court be held there as
usual, and the Clerk is directed to make on his precepts return-
able to that place, and the Commissioners of the peace with respect to recognition are delivered to attend to the same.

Court adjourned to meet at Melvill's Warehouse,
where the sessions of Dec. 1778 and Mar. 1779 were held.
Then once more the "Bridgeers" gained the ruling power and Court was once more removed to Bridgetown
where it remained during the sessions of June 1779,
Oct. 1779, and March 1780.

The plan of holding Bridgetown Court has been indefinite but recently it has been established that at that
period a Colonial Alms House stood on the east bank
of the Choptank River, about one quarter of a mile
above the present bridge and one hundred yards or more
back from the river's bank, and here Bridgetown held
her Court.

From 1780 to 1790 the contention was continued but
finally with the true Spirit of Democracy which was ever
the inspiration of Caroline the matter was made an
election issue and put before the citizens to be decided
by ballot. The question was submitted to the suffrage
of the people at the election of delegates to Assembly,
1790. Then Bridgetown met her final defeat for when
the "count" was in the vote stood two to one in favor of
Pig Point and made it the permanent seat of Justice.

VI. Denton as County Seat.

"BE IT ENACTED, That the clerk of Caroline County for the
time being shall, at some convenient time before the first day of
March next, remove, from Melvill's Warehouse, all the books, rolls,
papers and other records, belonging to the said County Court, to
Pig Point aforesaid, and there safely deposit, keep, and preserve
the same in some convenient house and the justices of the said
Court shall direct and cause a list of all the said records and books
to be signed by the clerk of said county, and entered upon record
among the proceedings of said county."

The above Act of Assembly, 1790, officially provides
for the passing of Melvill's Warehouse as County seat.
This the Assembly further stated was done for the benefit of the people of the County. The Commissioners
were directed to secure four acres of land at Edenton
before June 1, 1791, on which a Court House and gaol
were to be erected. These Commissioners were William

Richardson, Zabdiel Potter, Jos. Richardson, Peter Edmondson, and Joshua Willis. These men secured the four acres—practically same as now in use—by the "condemnatory" process and paid 30 sh. (a little more than $7) per acre for it. The Court was authorized to meet at Pig Point in such building as the Judges thought most convenient for holding Court and elections. There is no authentic record of the place of meeting during the four years 1791 to 1794. Wright plans it at the old brick mansion which once stood near the present location of the Brick Hotel but there were some half dozen other houses in the town at that time which were equally suitable for such meeting which may be held as probable meeting places.

VII. The First Court House.

In locating the court house the law had also provided the name Eden-Town but until the erection of the building, 1791, the place remained Pig Point in local parlance. Previously, when used, the name had been abbreviated to Edenton, now the E was dropped and henceforth we have Denton.

The Commissioners at this time, 1792, were Christopher Driver, William Robinson, Philemon Downes, Thomas Lockerman, and Jos. Richardson, and through their energy the Court House was begun in 1793. It was a brick building, colonial style, modelled after and much resembling Independence Hall, Philadelphia. Its builder was William Benson of Talbot County, and the total cost was £1800.

And now having secured the building after 20 years of effort, true to the perversity of mankind, the office holders, in part, were both to take up their abode there. A law was enacted by the Assembly compelling Clerk, Register of Wills, and Sheriff as well as deputies to move into the Court House or within one quarter mile of the same before June 1, 1795 the penalty of refusal being a fine of £15 current money. Needless to say they all complied with haste.

VIII. Changes of 1895.

A century run was given the first Court building and during that time, without the building withstood the ravages of time showing little sign of decay. Its permanency bore testimony to the builder as well as for the Commissioners of 1795.

However, with the growth of the County, the citizens demanded a larger and more modern building, so in 1895 the old one was razed. For the new Court House Joseph H. Bernard of Greensboro was selected as Architect and Chairman of the building commission, consisting of Messrs. Wm. E. Lord, George M. Russum, Thos. L. Day, John W. Clark, Bayard Nichols, Alex. Noble, Thomas R. Green and Henry Irwin. This Committee contracted with Slemmons & Lankford of Salisbury, Md. to erect a brick building for the sum of $21,000 which stands today (1919) on the Denton Court House Green.

The boundaries of the "green" have been somewhat changed since 1790 but the location remains the same. Someone has aptly said,

"The once ancient looking Denton is no more but has passed within the brief period of a score of years. In the substantial growth of Caroline's County town, it has done so conforming to the ideals of the townsmen that have not only built well, but have a knowledge of the value of civic pride in the rejuvenating of an old town, or in building a new one."

ORDERS OF COURT.

I. Related to Court.

1774

James Barwick agrees to find a room to hold Court in, a room for the Clerk of this Court to the end of November Court, for which the Court agrees to allow him the quantity of one thousand pounds of tobacco to be levied at November meeting.

1774

The Court appointed Messrs Benson Stainton and Richard Mason to try the Scales and Weights at Choptank Bridge and Melvill's Warehouse, and take an account of what repairs are wanting to the said house, and report the same to Court.

Ordered by the Court that James Barwick put the County jail in better repair than at present, by placing the logs, good and sufficient, under the sills of the same, that the logs be sunk in the ground and that he be paid and allowed for the same in the next levy.

1774

The Court appoints the several persons Constables for the ensuing year: Joshua Willis, of Great Choptank Hundred, Christopher Driver, for Bridgetown Hundred, James Cooper for Northwest Fork Hundred, Davis Robinson for Tuckahoe Hundred, and Solomon Mason for Choptank Hundred; WHEREUPON, the said Joshua Willis, Christopher Driver, James Cooper, David Robinson and Solomon Mason are qualified in open Court by taking the oaths of the government, the oath of constable, subscribing the oath of abjuration and repeating and signing the test.

—13—

John Cooper and Francis Stevens are appointed Sub-Sheriffs who thereupon take the oaths to the government, oath of abjuration and repeats and signs the test.

1774

On application made by Messrs. Robert Goldsborough, Thomas Goldsborough, James Tilghman, Nicholas Thomas, Jacob Moore, Richard Bassett, Solomon Wright, Matthew Browne, they are admitted to practice as attorneys of this County, thereupon they respectively take the oaths of the government and the oath of attorney, and subscribe the oath of abjuration and repeat and sign the test.

1774

The Court agrees to pay Edward Lloyd, Esq., the sum of five pounds current money in dollars at 7 shillings, 6 pence, (about $13) for the use of the old store house at Melville for the purpose of a jail for use in Caroline County until the end of November Court next, to be then levied.

1774

The Court agrees to allow Johannah Bennett the sum of 4 shillings, 1 pence for keeping the Court House in class.

1774

Ordered by the Court that the clerk attend Melvill's Warehouse on Wednesdays every week, which day is by the Court appointed office day.

1774

(Note the time these cases were pending, 1774-1782.)

Webster Case: Richard Andrew, Fork, Special Bail. Judgment
against on award filed under the hands of Messrs. Nathaniel
Hughes Potter, John Stevens and Zabdiel Potter, Arbitrators in
the cause, that the plaintiff recover against the said Defendant, the sum of six pounds, fifteen shillings, Debt and two hundred nineteen pounds of tobacco and fourteen shillings and seven pence half penny, costs and charges.

William Richardson, Clerk.

1774

Court fined Wm. Richardson, Clerk, 7½ shillings for not being present at the time when Court ought to have been called.

II. *Orders Relating to Ordinaries.*

1774

On application of William Haslett he is admitted to keep an ordinary and house of entertainment for one year at his house near Choptank Bridge on payment of 4£ ($20) current money of Maryland, (which John Cooper, sub-sheriff receives) for a license, whereupon the said William Haslett together with Matthew Bell and Matthew Driver, Jr., his securities, acknowledge themselves to owe and stand justly indebted unto the Right Honorable the Lord Proprietor of this province in the sum of 40£ current money of Maryland of their bodies, goods and chattels, lands and tenements, separately to be made and levied to the use of the said Lord Proprietary, his heirs and successors upon condition that if the said Mr. Haslett shall keep good rules and orders in his Ordinary at his dwelling house and do not suffer loose, idle or disorderly persons to tipple, game or commit any disorders or other irregularities in his Ordinary and that he also will and truly observe, fulfil and keep the several matters and things by an Act of Assembly entitled, An Act for licensing Ordinary keepers, hawkers, pedlers, and petty chapmone particularly specified and enjoined and in every respect conform himself thereto, then this recognizance to be void, otherwise of force.

1774

Other licenses for keeping Ordinaries and houses of entertainment were granted as follows:

Levin Bell, near Tuckahoe Bridge; Eleanor Montgomery, at Marshy Hope Bridge; John Fisher, on road from Choptank Bridge to Marshy Hope Bridge; James Barwick, at Melvill's Warehouse.

In addition to the above list ordinaries were also licensed at the following places: Tuckahoe Bridge (Hillsboro), Murray's Hill (Linchester), Nine Bridges (Bridgetown), Potter's Mill (Williston), Chapel Branch (Piney Grove), Cross-Roads near Kingston (Smithson).

Thus it will be seen that the county was well equipped with hotels to take care of the travellers on horseback as well as provide liquid refreshments so common and cheap at that time.

1774

On application of Alexander Widougall (1774), he is license for one year as hawker and pedlar on payment of four pounds money of Maryland (which John Cooper, sub Sheriff receives for a license). License delivered, Clerk records 4£ current money.

The Court agree to the following rates of liquors (and tavern rates) until August Court of 1775:

West India Rum 13s. 4p. per gallon.
Country Brandy 8s. per gallon.
Strong Beer, Country Brewed 4s. per gallon.
Every gill of New England Rum or Country Brandy with Muscavada sugar to make same into Punch and so pro rata 8p.
Every Lemon or Seville Orange 6p.
Hot Diet with small Beer or Cider 1s.
Cold Diet with Ditto 10p.
Horse Stablage with sufficient fodder for one horse one night 6p.
Oats and Indian Corn each 4s. per bu.

III. *Miscellaneous Orders.*

1774

The following order is among the first of the Caroline County Court: Henry Swigate of Caroline County came and prayed to have the mark of his son William Swigates hogs recorded, which is as follows; to wit: crop and under bitt in right ear and the left under sliced and a hole in it.

—15—

The Court agrees to give James Barwick 2500 pounds of tobacco on condition that he keep a public ferry from causeway opposite to Melvill's landing, and keep the causeway and bridge in passable order until November Court next, to be then levied.

1774

Maryland Know all men by these presents that we Michael Lucas, Edward White and Jacob Rumbley Lpd. and County of Caroline, are held and bound unto his Lordship the Lord Proprietary, his heirs and successors in the full and just sum of 1800 pounds of tobacco, to be paid unto the said Lord Proprietary, for his heirs and successors.

To the payment will and true to be made and done we bind ourselves, and each of our heirs, executors and administrators jointly and severally and firmly by the present. Sealed with our own seal and dated this 26th day of December 1774. The Conditions of the above obligations are such that if the above bound Michael Lucas shall truly and faithfully perform the duty of Inspector at Melvill's Warehouse according to the directions of the late account of Assembly, in such case make and provide then the above obligations be void of full force and virtue in law.

Michael Lucas   (Seal)
Edw. White   (Seal)
JACOB RUMBLEY (SEAL)

"Mr. Richard Mason delivers the annual value of Richard Lockerman's lands, which said annual value is as followeth, to wit:

We the subscribers being duly appointed and sworn by Richard Mason, Esq., one of his Lordships' Justices of the peace for the count aforesaid, that we will to the best of our skill and judgment make a true estimation of lands and improvements belonging to said Richard Lockerman, a minor, and now under the guardianship of said William Tripp of Talbot County. As is to say his part of Talson Manor said to be five hundred and eighty five acres. We therefore duly certify that on the second day of April 1774, we met on said lands and did find thereon:

One dwelling house 25ft. by 16ft. with a 10ft. shed.
A kitchen 25 ft. by 17½ ft.
A smoke house 12 ft. by 12 ft. built of logs.
A barn 25 ft. by 25 ft.
A corn house 16 ft. by 18 ft.
A milk house 10 ft. by 6 ft.
Two small hen houses.
Two corn houses.
A Garden 100 ft. square.
An apple orchard of 65 trees.
Four small English Walnut trees.
A nursery of peaches, cherries, quinces and plums.
About 40 acres cleared land, etc."

The following item (Sept. 1775) is interesting in its provision.

. The Court binds William ...., orphan son of William ...., deceased, by the consent of his mother, to Henry .... until he obtains the age of twenty one years, he being twelve years old November twelfth next, to teach him the trade of cart-wheelwright, and to find him in sufficient meat, drink, washing, lodging and clothing and at the expiration of his servitude to give him a suit of clothes of broadcloth or drugget, white shirt, a pair of shoes and stocking, a hat, a set of tools, a broad axe, a saw, a drawing knife, and three augers, one ½ inch, one 1 inch and the third 1½ inches, two chisels, a gouge, a rule, a scale, and a pair of compasses and gives bond with Thomas Hardcastle and Henry Sharpe his sureties, in the sum of forty pounds current money for due performance.

At the December session of the Court an estimate of goods and chattels of Alford, deceased, included

"One negro fellow named Peter aged 38 years, 48£; One negro woman named Phillis aged 44, 32£; One negro girl named Esther age 4, 20£."

THE HUNDRED—ELECTION DISTRICTS.

I. Introduction.

The Hundred is a division antedating the county, the town, the manor or the parish. When the Angles and Saxons landed on English soil more than one thousand years ago, they formed bands of one-hundred for their protection and government. When the necessity arose in the colonies the early settlers adopted the Hundred as a civic division best suited to their isolated colonies. It was not in the same form as that of the Anglo-Saxon for the personal Hundred—one hundred families or one hundred soldiers—was unknown here. Maryland's division was made geographically.

The necessity for this civic division came with the issuing of legal writs to freemen to meet as representatives in Assembly. Thus you see Maryland's Hundred was originally a governmental district whose chief executive was the constable.

Later when counties were formed and writs of election were issued to the sheriff, instead of the constable of the Hundred, this division remained under the constable who attended to many civic duties in his division.

II. Caroline's Hundreds.

At the time when the Assembly granted the organization of Caroline County, they also passed an act that the new county be divided into Hundreds. In accordance with this Act the November Court, 1774 divided the county into five hundreds as follows:

1 Fork Hundred beginning at the Northwest Fork Bridge and running with the main county road that divides Caroline County from Dorchester County, to Cannon's Ferry on the North East Fork (Nanticoke) River, and from the said Ferry up the said river and branch to the head thereof, and so round and as far as is inhabited by the people of the Province of Maryland until it intersects the head of the main branch of the Northwest Fork River, and then down the Northwest Fork Branch to the Northwest Fork Bridge.

2 Great Choptank Hundred beginning at the mouth of Hunting Creek and running up said creek to the bridge over James Murray's Mill Dam and from thence with the main county road that divides Caroline County from Dorchester County to the North West Fork Bridge and from thence up the said North West Fork Branch to Marshy Hope Bridge and from thence with the main road that leads to Nathaniel Potter's Landing on Great Choptank River and from thence down the said river to the mouth of Hunting Creek.

3   Choptank Hundred beginning at Nathaniel Bradley's in Choptank Hundred, and runs with the first line to Tuckahoe Hundred, so as to include Francis Orrell's in Choptank Hundred and from thence up Choptank River, and the main branch of the said river to the Dover road and down with the said road to Long Marsh to the head of Tuckahoe Creek and down with the said creek to the said beginning.

4   Bridgetown Hundred beginning at Nathaniel Potter's landing on Great Choptank River and running from thence with the main county road that leads to Marshy-Hope Branch, and from the said branch up the said Northwest Fork branch and stream as far as is settled by the inhabitants of the Province of Maryland, and all around as settled as aforesaid, until it intersects the main branch of the head of Great Choptank River, and from thence down the said river branch to Nathaniel Potter's landing on Great Choptank River.

5   Tuckahoe Hundred beginning at Nathaniel Bradley's upon Tuckahoe Creek, and from thence with a straight line to Francis Orrell's on Charles Nichol's plantation on Choptank River, and down with the said river to Vincent Price's and up with Tuckahoe Creek to the said beginning.

The court also appointed in 1774 the following constables for the Hundreds as below:

Miscellaneous Orders and Business of the Court:
"The Court (1774) appoints Christopher Driver constable of Bridgetown Hundred, Joshua Willis of Great Choptank Hundred, James Cooper of Fork Hundred, and Solomon Mason of Choptank Hundred who respectively took the oath of Government, the oath of Constable, and subscribes the oath of abjuration and repeats and signs the test."

Owing to the indefinite boundaries of the Fork Hundred a change was found necessary as Cannon's Ferry proved to be in Delaware. This change made the Fork Hundred so small that the part remaining was in 1776 incorporated in Great Choptank Hundred.

Then the Great Choptank seemed large and unwieldly for civic purposes, and again, in March, 1780, another change was made separating this Hundred into two parts. The Eastern part became Fork Hundred while the Western part retained the name of Great Choptank Hundred.

While the names of many of the boundary places have been changed they may be identified by reference to the map of Hundreds.

ELECTION DISTRICTS.

While the hundreds continued as subdivisions from 1774 to about 1800 all elections for county officers in Caroline County and members of the Assembly of Maryland were held at the county seat, and every voter who had the required qualifications, fifty acres of land, or forty

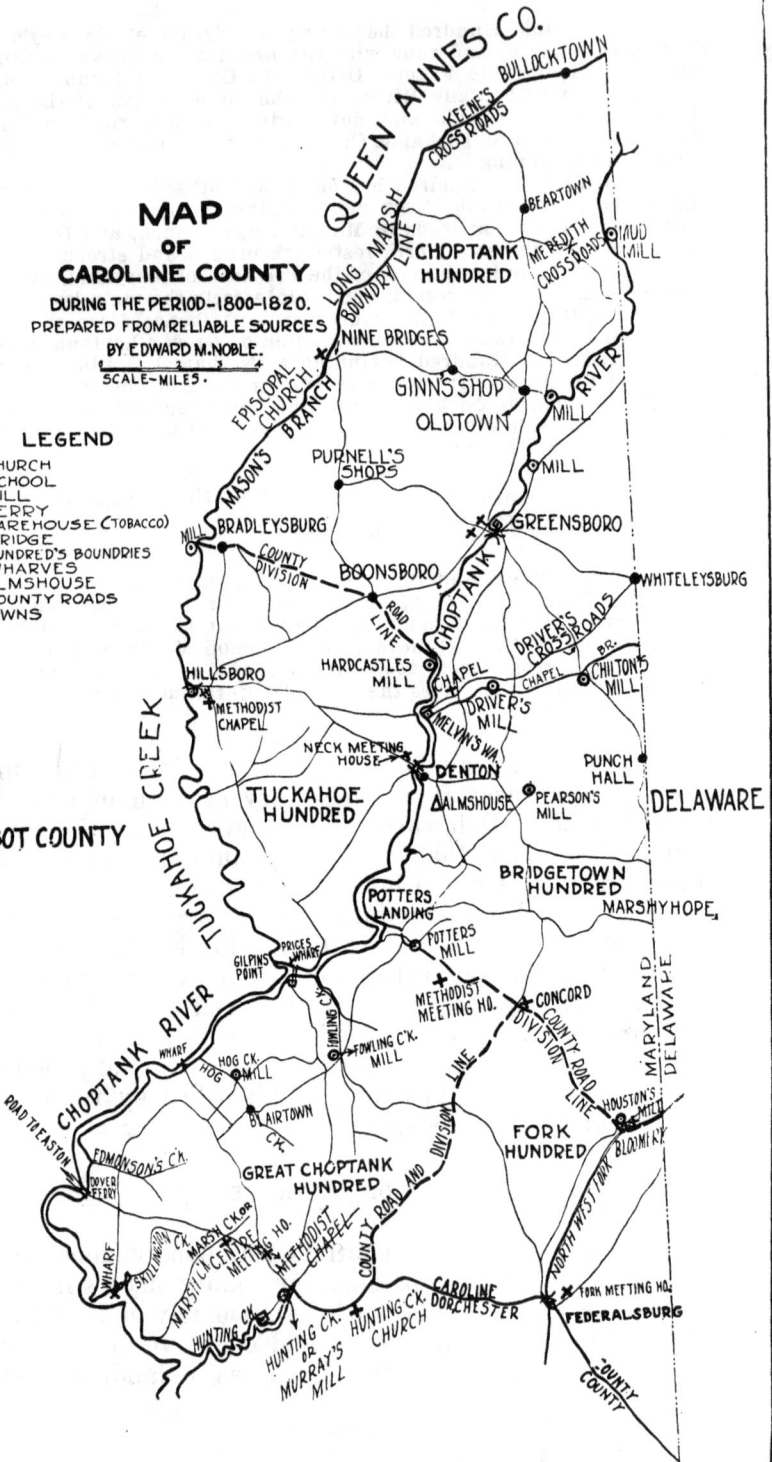

MAP
OF
CAROLINE COUNTY
DURING THE PERIOD—1800-1820.
PREPARED FROM RELIABLE SOURCES
BY EDWARD M. NOBLE.

SCALE—MILES.

LEGEND

+ CHURCH
# SCHOOL
⊙ MILL
— FERRY
▣ WAREHOUSE (TOBACCO)
✕ BRIDGE
-‑- HUNDRED'S BOUNDRIES
X WHARVES
△ ALMSHOUSE
— COUNTY ROADS
• TOWNS

QUEEN ANNES CO.

BULLOCKTOWN

KEENE'S CROSS ROADS

BEARTOWN

MEREDITH CROSS ROADS

MUD MILL

CHOPTANK HUNDRED

LONG MARSH BOUNDRY LINE

NINE BRIDGES

GINNS SHOP

OLDTOWN

RIVER

MILL

EPISCOPAL CHURCH

MASON'S BRANCH

PURNELL'S SHOPS

MILL

BRADLEYSBURG

COUNTY DIVISION

BOONSBORO

ROAD LINE

GREENSBORO

WHITELEYSBURG

DRIVERS CROSS ROADS

CHOPTANK

HILLSBORO

METHODIST CHAPEL

HARDCASTLES MILL

CHAPEL

CHAPEL

CHILTON'S MILL

BR.

DRIVER'S MILL

MELVYN'S WA.

NECK MEETING HOUSE

DENTON

ALMSHOUSE

PEARSON'S MILL

PUNCH HALL

DELAWARE

TUCKAHOE HUNDRED

TALBOT COUNTY

TUCKAHOE CREEK

BRIDGETOWN HUNDRED

MARSHYHOPE

POTTERS LANDING

POTTERS MILL

PRICES WHARF

GILPINS POINT

METHODIST MEETING HO.

COUNTY DIVISION LINE

CONCORD

COUNTY ROAD LINE

MARYLAND DELAWARE

FOWLING CK.

WHARF

HOG CK.

HOG CK. MILL

FOWLING CK. MILL

ROAD TREASTON

BLAIRTOWN

CK.

EDMONSON'S CK.

DOVER FERRY

GREAT CHOPTANK HUNDRED

FORK HUNDRED

HOUSTON'S MILL

BLOOMERY

CHOPTANK RIVER

WHARF

SMITHVILLE CK.

MARSH CK. or CENTRE MEETING HO.

METHODIST CHAPEL

HUNTING CK.

COUNTY ROAD AND DIVISION LINE

NORTH WEST FORK

CAROLINE DORCHESTER

HUNTING CK. or MURRAY'S MILL

HUNTING CK. CHURCH

FORK MEETING HO.

FEDERALSBURG

COUNTY

pounds sterling in money or personal property, who decided to vote was obliged to go there to exercise his rights, not by casting a ballot but viva voce; that is, the voters told the Judge or Judges of the election, the names of the persons for whom they proposed to vote. The Sheriff of the county was then judge of the election and made the official returns of the result. At some period of this method of elections, the polls were kept open four days in succession for the convenience of voters who lived in remote parts of the county.

Finding that the great inconvenience in getting to polling places kept many from voting, the General Assembly in 1798 enacted a law dividing the counties of the state into election districts of which Caroline County was to possess three. The following year a commission named by the legislature divided Caroline County into the Upper, Middle and Lower Election districts which superseded the several hundreds then in existence. Greensboro and Denton were the polling places for 1st and 2d districts while the 3rd or Lower district voted at Hunting Creek. In 1805 the voting place of the 3rd district was removed to "The Walnut Trees" near Hynson and in 1816 returned to Hunting Creek.

Harmony became the election place of the Lower district in 1852, an honor evidently coveted with much eagerness.

The Legislature of 1854 erected district No. 4 which included about all of the territory which is now embraced in the Federalsburg district.

In 1861 the provision was made for dividing Election district one into two precincts but this Act was repealed the following year at which time the county was divided into 5 election districts with Henderson, Greensboro, Denton, Harmony and Federalsburg as the respective polling places. This arrangement continued until 1880 when the sixth or Hillsboro election district was organized.

Preston which had been known for some time as Snow Hill became the voting place of the southern portion of the Fourth district in 1880 while Harmony continued only as the polling place for the 1st precinct of said district.

In 1894 the section around and including Ridgely having developed rapidly it was found necessary to erect the Seventh or Ridgely election district while at the same session the Eighth district was formed from parts of the 3rd, 4th and 5th districts and American Corners designated as the polling place.

Somewhat later the 3rd election district having become rather unwieldly for voting it was decided to divide the same into two polling precincts, an arrangement which still continues.

LAND GRANTS.

Originally all of Caroline County which lies north and west of the Choptank River lay within the bounds of Kent.

When Talbot county was organized from Kent about 1662 this territory was included. Again in 1707 this part of Caroline was again transferred when Queen Anne county was formed. Within 23 years after surveys began on Kent Island, Thomas Skillington of Talbot had a survey made on the east side of the Choptank River in the Frazier Flats section. This was about March 4, 1663. Shortly thereafter surveys were made on Fowling and Hunting Creeks as well as farther on up the river. Cedar Point the site of Melvill's Warehouse and the first Court House was surveyed for John Edmonson of Talbot in 1665. Likewise were surveys made about the same time in the Oakland neighborhood then designated as the "Forest of Choptank" and the Marshy Hope section between Smithville and Federalsburg. As indicated elsewhere lands were taken up slowly north east of the Choptank because of the uncertainty of the state boundary line.

On all lands granted in Maryland by the Lord Proprietor to settlers in his province under his "condition of plantation," he reserved an interest in each grant and stipulated an annual land rent to be paid by the grantee for two purposes; the first was to make the free-holders feel a bond of allegiance to his Lordship, and the second though small in separate changes, yet large in the aggregate,—was his source of personal revenue. The rent was about one shilling (25c) per year on each 50 acres of land granted. These rents called quit-rents were exacted by the Lord Proprietor's government and paid until 1776.

Patent or Land Grant, or How Land Was Originally Given Out By the Proprietor.

Charles, Absolute Lord and Proprietor of the Provinces of Maryland and Avalon, Lord Baron of Baltimore, Etc. To the Persons to whom this Present shall come, Greetings in our Lord God Everlasting. KNOW YE, that Whereas in pursuance of our Instructions to our Govenor and Judge in Land Affairs for the Granting of our Back Lands on the Borders of this our Province, bearing date the fourteenth day of June, Seventeen hundred and thirty three, and Registered in our Land Office, Henry Ennalls, deputy surveyor of the county of Dorchester, that by his certificate returned into our Land-Office certified, that he hath laid out for a certain .... Moore, of said county, a tract of land in said county, on our said borders containing one hundred and thirty acres of said county, a Tract called Calf Path, ... and for which land the said .... Moore has paid the sum of Two pounds, and nine pence half penny sterling.

We therefore hereby Grant unto him, the said .... Moore all that the aforesaid Tract or Parcel of Land called Calf Path, lying and being in the county aforesaid, and on our said Borders, beginning, (then follow a description of the land) according to the certificate of surveyor thereof, taken and returned into our Land-Office, bearing date nineteenth day of October, seventeen hundred and forty three, and there remaining, together with all Rights, Profits, Benefits and Phivileges thereunto belonging, Royal Mines excepted. TO HAVE AND TO HOLD the same unto him, the said .... Moore, his heirs, and assigns, foreevr, to be holden of us and our heirs, as of our Manor of Nanticoke in free and commons Soccage, by Fealty only for all manner of services.

Yielding and paiyng therefore, yearly, unto us, and our heirs, at our receipt at our City fo St. Mary's .... the rent of five sihllings, three pence and half penny sterling, in silver or gold; and for a lne upon every alienation of the said land, or and Part or Parcel thereof, one whole years rent, in silver or gold, or the full value thereof, in such commodities as we and our heirs, or such officer or officers as shall be appointed by us and our heirs, from time to time, to collect and receive the same, shall accept i ndischarge thereof, at the choice o fus and our heirs, or such officer or officers, aforesaid; Provided that if the said sum for a fine or alienation, shal lnot be paid unto us and our heirs, or such officer or officers aforesaid, before such alienation, and the said alienation entered upon record either in the Provincial Court, or County Court where the same Parcel of land lieth, within one month next after alienation, then the said alienation shall be void and of no effect.

GIVEN under our Great Seal of our said Province of Maryland, this eighteenth day of March, Anno Dom. seventeen hundred and forty six.

WITNESS our trusty and well-beloved Samuel Ogle, Esquire, Lieutenant General and chief Governor of our said Province of Maryland, Chancellor and Keeper o fthe Great Seal thereof.

THE MASON AND DIXON LINE.

What is meant by this line? Why does it concern Caroline County? Read and learn. The Mason and Dixon line with its stone markers is the visible record of the treaty made in a territorial war between Penn and Calvert in Colonial days. One historian says, "This dispute had an even date almost with the original grant to Lord Baltimore." This grant it was held covered all the land from the 38° to the 40° parallels and extended to Delaware Bay and the Atlantic Ocean. Such being the case it included all the present state of Delaware as well as a strip 15 miles wide along the southern boundary line of Pennsylvania.

In the present state of Delaware the Swedes settled first, then the Dutch wrested it from them. Later, in

1682 a special grant was made from the Duke of York to William Penn giving him the Delaware section. In 1685 this grant was duly confirmed. Proprietary Maryland refused to submit so that up to the year 1732 there was ceaseless litigation as well as an occasional outrage along the border.

Reverting to the earlier contention we find that in 1681 the "Three Lower Counties," (now Delaware) settled the northern boundary separating them from Pennsylvania as follows: With New Castle for a centre and using a 12 mile radius the arc of a circle was drawn, the line thus made forming the northern boundary then as now.

But the Maryland-Pennsylvania dispute continued and finally in 1750 it was settled by "map," but on real land the location of the boundary was indefinite. Both Penn's heirs, and Frederick, Lord Baltimore, wanted it settled in a manner that would last for all time. The following survey of the Eastern boundary was made locating it definitely.

Recognizing the 38° parallel as the Southern boundary of Maryland it was then decided to find on this the middle point between Delaware and Chesapeake Bays and from this run a North line which should form a tangent with the New Castle "arc" at its most westerly point. This was done and the line forms the Eastern boundary of Caroline County as well as of the state.

Many interesting facts are connected with the running of this line by the surveyors, most of which are recorded in a series of letters written by Gov. Sharpe of Maryland to Lord Baltimore.

In a letter dated June 22, 1761, Gov. Sharpe states that the surveyors, running the Maryland-Delaware line from the "middle point" before mentioned found that on reaching a distance of 25 miles north they were unable to take further observations because they could find no star by which to set their transits. Moreover at the same time they became sickly with Maryland fever from having been so long a time in a dismal part of the country abounding in swamps. [They were in the Hickman and Smithville section]. As a result of the letter the surveyors were instructed to discontinue for a time.

As a conclusion of the above, Sharpe writes Aug. 17, 1761 stating that on Aug. 9 the surveyors, evidently recovered from Malaria, were able to make observations by Alioth and the Polar Star, accordingly were proceeding up the peninsula with the line, believing they would not again be interrupted until they reached Newcastle. On Sept. 5 they found themselves 44 miles to the north and were hoping to reach Newcastle in October, but it was a case of hope deferred for again on October 22 Sharpe writes that they had been often interrupted by wet and cloudy weather and had not yet extended the line more than 77 miles but believe they lack only 5 or 6 miles of the distance necessary, hence, imagine the remaining distance can be run in 10 or 12 days. The exact day of completion is not given but the account states that, Nov. 12, 1761, the north and south line has been completed, and they are preparing the tangent ready for the west line.

The fact of 12 days being necessary for the running of a 6 mile line shows the difficulty of the work at that time. Instruments were scarce, and less perfect than now and mayhap surveyors less expert. Moreover in this case the direction of extra work devolved on the surveyors. To proceed through the forest it was necessary to open a way. This was done by cutting a roadway or "vista" 8 yards wide along the line to be surveyed, as well as the setting of the stone line marks.

While not connected directly with Caroline County it might be well to here mention the Mason and Dixon line as Maryland's Northern boundary. It was on this line that Charles Mason and Jeremiah Dixon put their personal work, and for them the entire line was named. Coming over in 1763, they had perhaps even more trials than the surveyors of the North and South Line, for the Indians of Southern Pennsylvania added to their danger.

The East and West Line began 15 miles south of Philadelphia, connecting with the North and South Line at its point of tangency with the Newcastle arc, west along the entire southern boundary of Pennsylvania.

And so the historic Mason and Dixon Line was run. It is marked from the "middle point" to the Newcastle tangent and thence to the western limit of Pennsylvania by square mile stones, four successive having on one side M and on the other P, while on the fifth stone on the Maryland side has the coat of arms of the Baltimore's and the reverse side that of the Penn's. Such is the story of the Mason and Dixon Line which someone has said, "Next to the Equator is the most widely known line in the world."

ROADS, FERRIES, BRIDGES, FENCES AND GATES.

Roads.

Even before the formation of Caroline County, roads and bridges lying within her bounds, had been provided for by this Act passed in September 1704, which was for the benefit of the entire province.

"WHEREAS it is thought convenient, and very much for the benefit of the inhabitants of this province, that roads and paths be marked, and the heads of rivers, creeks and branches, be made passable.

"BE IT THEREFORE ENACTED, by the Queen's most excellent majesty, by and with the advice and consent of her Majesty's Governor, Council and Assembly of this province, and the authority of the same, that all public and main roads be hereafter cleared, and well grubbed, fit for traveling, twenty feet wide; and good and substantial bridges made over all heads of rivers, creeks, branches and swamps, where need shall require, at the discretion of the justices of the county courts.

AND, for the better ascertaining what is or shall be deemed public roads, be it LIKEWISE ENACTED, by the authority aforesaid, that the justices of the county courts shall set down and ascertain in their records, once every year, what are the public roads of their respective counties, and appoint overseers of the same; and that no persons whatsoever shall alter or change any such public roads, without leave or license of the Governor or Council, or justices of the county courts, upon penalty of five hundred pounds of tobacco.

AND, that all the roads that lead to any ferries, courthouse of any county, or to any church shall be marked on both sides of the road with two notches. And the roads that lead to any county Court house, shall have two notches on the trees on both sides of the road as aforesaid, and another notch a distance above the other two. And any road that leads to a church, shall be marked at the entrance into the same, and at the leaving any other road, with a slip cut down the face of the tree, near the ground. Any road leading to a ferry, and dividing from other public roads shall be marked with three notches of equal distance at the entrance into the same."

In one of these Acts overseers of plantations were required to fell "all dead trees on each side of the main roads, whose limbs hang over the road, to prevent any danger that may happen by falling on travelers."

In November 1798 the Assembly enacted that,

"WHEREAS the present mode of repairing the public roads in Caroline County is found by experience to be expensive, and inadequate to the purpose intended; and it has been found necessary that proper regulations should forthwith be made for keeping the roads of the said county in due repair; therefore, overseers, not exceeding five in any hundred, shall be appointed."

"AND BE IT ENACTED, that it shall be the duty of the said overseers to keep all the public roads in the said county well and sufficiently cleared and grubbed, fit for traveling, twenty feet wide at the least, and to make and keep good and substantial bridges over all the heads of rivers, creeks, branches and swamps, where the same shall be necessary for the convenient and easy passage of travelers, with their wagons, carts, carriages, horses and cattle, and to remove all nuisances which may obstruct or annoy their passage, and well and sufficiently to causeway, all and singular such places in and upon the said roads as shall require the same, at the discretion and by the direction of the said justices; and for this purpose the said justices, or some one or more of them, in their respective neighborhoods, shall be and they are hereby authorized and required, from time to time, to superintend the making and repairing of the said roads, bridges and causeways, and to direct and advise the overseers in the execution of this Act."

These overseers had the right when roads needed repair to call upon the inhabitants of the county for the necessary labor. Should those called refuse to go, they must send a substitute or pay a fine of one dollar for each day's absence. That there might be no shirking of work the same fine was imposed if the person attending did not perform a reasonable amount of labor. The owners or overseers of slaves were responsible for their attendance and work.

An Act to build a bridge and open a road in Caroline County.

January, 1802.

"WHEREAS it is represented to this General Assmbly, by the petition of sundry inhabitants of Caroline County, that they labor under many inconveniences for want of a bridge over a branch of the Northwest Fork River, at a place known by the name of The Old Bloomery, in said county, and a road to lead from Douglasses mill across the said bridge, until it intersects the main road leading from the Northwest Fork Bridge to Marshyhope bridge; and the prayer of the said petitioners appearing reasonable, therefore,

BE IT ENACTED, by the General Assembly of Maryland, that George Collins, Charles Ross and James Houston, be, and they are hereby appointed commissioners for the purpose of building and completing a new bridge at the same place where the old bridge now stands, over said branch, and the said commissioners, or a majority of them, are hereby empowered to agree and contract with any person or persons, upon the best and cheapest terms they can, to finish and complete the said bridge in a good substantial and workman like manner."

The one hundred and fifty dollars needed for building the bridge was obtained through assessments.

"AND BE IT ENACTED, that the said commissioners, or a majority of them, are hereby authorized and empowered, to lay

EARLY STEAMBOAT ON THE CHOPTANK.

out, open and clear, a road at the expense of the petitioners, or any part of them particularly interested therein, or any other persons who may voluntarily offer their assistance, not exceeding twenty four feet in width, to commence at or near Douglass mill aforesaid, and to run from thence in the most convenient direction over the Old Bloomery, aforesaid, and through James Houston's lane, or by James Wright's mill, as the said commissioners, or a majority of them, may think most expedient, until it intersects the main road leading from the Northwest Fork bridge to Marshyhope, provided, that the said road shall not go through the garden or meadow of any person or persons without his, her or their consent."

Ferries.

In early Caroline County there were only three bridges of much size—the ones at Greensboro, Federalsburg, and Hillsboro, hence the crossing of the Choptank River below Greensboro had to be made by ferries of which there were about four, as follows: From Melvill's Warehouse across to a point near the Dunning Farm, one from Denton across a little later, from Gilpin's Point to Prices' Landing (Tuckahoe Neck) and from Hog Island (below Dover Bridge) to the Talbot side.

The Court appointed persons to keep these ferries and charge in accordance with the regulated amounts. Tobacco was for a while the chief article of payment as per the following: Court order of Talbot County in 1760: Ordered that if Deborah Nichols doth not keep sufficient boat and hands to transport the inhabitants of this county from Barker's Landing to Hog Island or from Hog Island to Barker's Landing, and give a good attendance to the said ferry that her allowance next November Court shall be reduced to one-half. (Allowance of 4000 lbs. of tobacco per year.) This amount was paid by the County in addition to the fees paid by everyone outside the county travelling by said ferry.

The rates of non-residents in crossing the Denton Ferry in the year 1800 were as follows: Foot passengers 08c, horses 16c, two wheel carriage, horse and passengers 35c, four wheel phaeton, horses and passengers 75c, black cattle 12c. Persons that owned land in the county but not residing therein were not charged for ferriage.

Bridges.

The three bridges in the County were evidently constructed very early as evidenced by some legislation concerning these structures as follows:

November, 1794.

"WHEREAS the inhabitants of Talbot, Queen-Anne's and Caroline counties by their petition to this General Assembly have set forth that the bridge over Tuckahoe creek is in a ruinous and almost impassable condition and have in their petition stated their advantages that would result by the erection of a new bridge over said creek, about three hundred years below the place of the old bridge, and it appearing that by building the new bridge, as prayed for, and altering part of the public road as may be necessary so as to pass over the same, will shorten the distance for travelers, and add to the convenience and advantage of the said three counties; And whereas the bridge heretofore built was done and kept up at the expense of the said three counties, the said petitioners have prayed for a new one to be erected, and that the sum of one hundred and fifty pounds may be levied on the said counties respectively for the purpose aforesaid; wherefore to carry the same into effect,

BE IT ENACTED, by the General Assembly of Maryland That for Talbot county John Roberts, for Queen-Anne's county Henry Pratt, for Caroline county Philemon Downes, shall be and they are hereby appointed commissioners, for the purpose of building and completing the said new bridge; and the said commissioners, or a majority of them, are by this act authorized and empowered, as soon as it may be conveniently in their power, to cause the said new bridge to be built over the said creek, opposite a place formerly known by the name of The Old Rolling House, lying on the east side of the said creek, ... which said new bridge shall be built and completed in the best and most substantial manner it can for the money hereby to be granted; and the said commissioners, or a majority of them, are by virtue of this act, fully authorized and empowered, as they in their discretion shall think best, to agree for the said work with a contractor or contractors, for the whole, or in parcels, or they may purchase materials and hire workmen and laborers to complete the said work; and the said commissioners, or a majority of them, are also empowered to open and lay out, on the east side of said creek, from some fit and convenient part of the old road, a new road to lead to and across over the said new bridge to the Talbot side."

An Act to erect a new bridge over Great Choptank River, in Caroline County, passed January 15, 1808.

"WHEREAS the old bridge over the Choptank river, at the village of Greensboro, in said county, is in a ruinous condition, and nearly impassable, and as it is found absolutely necessary that a new one be built at, or near, the place where the old one stands, therefore,

BE IT ENACTED, by the General Assembly of Maryland, that George Reed, Nehemiah Townsend and William Whitely be, and they are hereby appointed commissioners for the purpose of building and completing the new bridge as aforesaid, at or near the place where the old one now stands; and the said commissioners, or a majority of them, are by this Act employed to agree and contract with any person or persons, upon the best and cheapest terms, to finish and complete the said new bridge."

In 1810 inhabitants of Talbot and Caroline counties living near Dover Ferry petitioned and Assembly "for the convenience of the public" to incorporate a company for erecting a bridge over the Choptank river at that point. The bridge was built and is commonly known as Dover Bridge.

An Act to incorporate a company for building a bridge over Choptank river at or near Denton Ferry (about 1812).

"WHEREAS it is represented to this General Assembly, by the petition of sundry inhabitants of Caroline county, that the convenience of the public would be greatly promoted by erecting a bridge over Choptank river at, or near, Denton Ferry, and that sundry persons, by articles of voluntary association have contracted and agreed each with the other, to erect a bridge at the place aforesaid, and have subscribed and paid considerable sums of money towards the same, and pray that a law may pass to incorporate the said association; and it appearing reasonable, therefore,

"BE IT ENACTED by the General Assembly of Maryland, that the subscribers or proprietors of shares for building said bridge, as well as those who may hereafter become stockholders, their successors and assigns shall be, and are hereby created and made a corporation and body politic, by the name and style of The President and Directors of the Denton Bridge Company.

"AND BE IT ENACTED, that the capital stock of said Company is hereby declared to be the sum of three thousand dollars, to be divided into six hundred shares of five dollars each."

It seems that the Denton Bridge was not built for several years after 1812, probably about 1820, until which time a ferry was used.

In 1849 the people of the county tiring of the disadvantages arising from a privately owned bridge, had the General Assembly enact a measure which provided for the Levy Courts buying and making it a public bridge. Soon after this it was either thoroughly overhauled or rebuilt and stood until about 1875 when the new iron bridge was erected.

After many years of use and inconvenience on account of the narrowness of the draw this bridge was in 1913 replaced by the modern concrete structure now in use.

Fences and Gates.

To protect the property in the county from damage done by live stock the General Assembly enacted,

"That from and after the first day of August 1824, corn fields, and all grounds kept for enclosure in Dorchester and Caroline counties, shall be fenced, (here followed a description of fences required) and if any live stock of any kind or description whatsoever, shall break into any person's enclosure, the same being of the height and sufficiency aforesaid, then the owner or owners of such live stock shall be liable to make good all such damages to the owner or owners of such enclosure, as shall be found and awarded by two or more judicious persons who may view the same under their oath or affirmation, made before some justice of the peac ein said counties."

AN ACT relating to gates on the public roads in Caroline County.

BE IT ENACTED, by the General Assembly of Maryland, that from and after the passage of this Act, it shall and may be lawful for any of the citizens of Caroline county to keep on the public roads in said county all such gates as are now erected on the public roads, for their own private use and convenience, upon the express conditions following: all and every owner or owners of a gate or gates hung on good and sufficient iron hinges, and shall keep the same and that part of the said road which they occupy in good order and repair, so as to impede as little as possible persons traveling with carriages of pleasure or burden."

"AND BE IT ENACTED, that if any person or persons after the passage of this Act, shall cut down, destroy, wilfully leave fixed open, or remove any of said gates, they shall, upon conviction thereof before a magistrate, forfeit and pay to the owner of such gate a sum not less than one, nor exceeding ten dollars for every such offence, to be recovered as small debts are out of court."

"AND BE IT ENACTED, that if any slave shall cut down, destroy, injure, or wilfully leave fixed open, any gate upon the public roads, such slave shall be punished for every offence on conviction of a justice of the peace by the oath of one or more witnesses, by whipping on his or her back, in the discretion of the said justice, not exceeding for each offense the number of ten lashes; Provided always, that the master or mistress of such slave, or any other person in their behalf, may redeem said slave so convicted from punishment by the payment of the fine to the owner or owners of such gate, imposed by this Act, upon free persons for like offenses."

"AND BE IT ENACTED, that on all gates authorized by this Act to be kept on the public roads, the owner or owners thereof shall pay annually a tax of one dollar for each and every gate by him, her or them kept on the public roads in said county."

Gates on public roads were abolished between 1860-1870, much to the relief of travelers.

INDIANS OF THE EASTERN SHORE.

I. Origin.

Whence came they? No written language exists to tell the story of their race and only a few specimens of "picture writing" are preserved to throw light on the Indian's past, hence our present day knowledge is based chiefly on legendary lore which like most traditions is not always authentic.

The historians of early days would seem to have been possessed of vivid imaginations. Note for example the record of Captain John Smith who explored on the Eastern Shore in 1608. "They were noble warriors. One was like a giant the calf of whose leg was three-quarters of a yard about, and all the rest of his limbs so answered to that proportion, that he seemed the goodliest man we ever beheld. His hair, the one side was long, the other shaved close, with a ridge on his crown like a cock's comb. His arrows were five-quarters long, headed with the splinters of a white crystall-like stone, in the form of a heart, an inch broad and an inch and a half more long. These he wore in a wolf's skin at his back for a quiver, his bow in one hand and his club in the other." Reading this we can only say "And there were giants in those days."

II. Tribes.

The chief tribe of the Eastern Shore was the Algonquin. They covered a vast area and from them sprang the sub-tribes such as Delaware, Nanticoke, Choptank, etc. These tribes were shore Indians and lived by fishing. Generally speaking they were peace-loving, gentle, and noted for making and selling weapons, or bowls of soapstone to the neighboring tribes who prized them highly.

The Delawares were the branch of the Algonquins from which sprang the Netego or Nanticokes and from this tribe the Nanticoke River gets its name. Indians figured extensively in Eastern Shore history because of all the Algonquins they were the most warlike. Their fighting spirit was probably developed in part both before and during Colonial days through frequent attacks on the Algonquins by the fierce Susquehannoughs, a branch of the more northern Six Nations which had wandered south from New York and Pennsylvania and had become separated from their people. In colonial days these warlike Susquehannoughs not only massacred the whites but swooped down on the gentle Algonquin tribes with death dealing attacks.

Again, in the heart of the savage might makes right. The Nanticokes were the most numerous sub-tribe of the Algonquins hence the desire for power may have developed their savage instincts. This aggressiveness of the Nanticokes extended not only toward the weaker camps of their own people but reached out to the white man as later events will prove.

III. Policy of Maryland.

The policy of this colony as shown by the attitude of the Governors was one of "justice, moderation and kindness." Land acquired from the natives was, if possible, paid for by giving hoes, broadcloth, axes, etc., thus maintaining peaceful relations between the white and red men.

Self protection, too, was a strong incentive on both sides. The Indians outnumbered the white settlers and this same justice, moderation and kindness was the best means of self-protection from the savage, while through their friendship for the whites, the Algonquin hoped safety from the Susquehannough.

The chief business relation between the whites and Indians was the bartering of guns or ammunition for hides.

To avoid any possible difficulty in trading with the Indians, a privilege was granted every white inhabitant of Dorchester County to trade with them without license, only at Captain Henry Trippe's house, in 1680. Previously the Governor had issued special licenses to individual traders who could go to the Indian camps and there trade, often selling them guns and ammunition, in violation of the trading regulations, which caused much trouble between colonists and the native Indians.

This privilege was during the time when Caroline was in part included in Dorchester County.

IV. Indian Wars.

Maryland as a whole was comparatively free from Indian incursions and the history of the Eastern Shore gives record of only two organized expeditions to repel the savage,—one active and one incipient. They were as follows:

The first expedition came in 1639 when various Indian troubles on Eastern Shore led Lord Baltimore to send an expedition across the Bay. McSherry says, "The armament consisted of two pinnaces and a skiff manned with thirty good shot or marksmen who were drafted or pressed, and several volunteers. To equip and victual this force the Governor was under the necessity of sending a shallop to Virginia to procure a supply of arms, ammunition and food."

The second or incipient expedition was 1642 when Indian outbreaks were rumored. The Nanticokes had planned to cross the bay to Western Shore and attack the white settlers there.

Governor Calvert anticipated their actions and appealed to the Governor of Virginia, to join him, as previously, in raising a force of approximately 200 men to repel the Indians. He also declared that we might call martial law, and establish a "dead-line" extending from the Pawtuxent River to the Potomac. Hearing of this preparation for their reception the Nanticokes weakened and a truce was declared before active warfare began.

V. Continuation of Peace Policy.

The original peace policy is shown throughout the remainder of this account. At Saint Mary's, April 13, 1669 the following act was passed for the "Continuance of peace with the protection of our neighbors and confederate Indians at Choptank River."

CHARLES CALVERT, ESQUIRE, *Governor.*

It being most just that Indians, the ancient inhabitants of this province, should have a convenient dwelling place in this their native country, free from the encroachments and oppression of the English, and more especially such who are in danger to be destroyed by their neighbor nations our enemies, and whereas Ababco Hatsawapp and Tequassimo have of late given large testimonies of their fidelity towards us in delivering up the murderers of Captain John Odber for which they are in danger to be cut off and destroyed by the Wiccomesses and their confederates, the Matwha Indians. Be it enacted that all the lands lying within a certain district shall be unto said Ababaco Hatsawapp and Tequassimo and the people under their government, under the yearly rent of six beaver skins, to be paid to the lord Proprietary of this province.

VI. *Treaties.*

There is recorded but one official treaty with the Indians, namely, The Treaty With Nanticokes, 1704.

"It is agreed upon that from this day forward there be an Inviolable peace and amity between the Right Hon'ble and the Lord Propry of this Province and the Emperor on Nanticoke upon the articles hereafter in this treaty to be agreed upon to the worlds. end to endure and that all former acts of hostility and damages. wnatsoever by either party sustained be buried in perpetual oblivion.

"That the said Emperor of Nanticoke shall deliver up all Indians that shall come into his dominion that are, or shall be, enemies to the English and further that if any Indian subject to the said Emperor shall hereafter kill an English man that the said Emperor shall be oblidged to deliver such Indian up to the Governor of this Province as a prisoner.

"Forasmuch as the English can not easily distinguish one Indian from another, that no Indian shall come into any Englishmans plantation painted and that all the Indians shall be bound to call aloud before they come within three hundred paces of any English mans cleared ground and lay down their arms whether Gunn, Bowes or Arrows or other weapons, for any English man that shall appear upon his call to take up, and in case no one appears, that he shall leave his arms if he come nearer, and that afterwards by calling aloud endeavour to give notice to the English of his nearer approach, and if any English man shall kill any Indian that shall come unpainted and give such notice, and deliver up his arms as aforesaid, he shall die for it as well as an Indian that kills an English man, and in case the English and Indians meet in the woods accidentally every Indian shall be bound immediately to throw down his arms upon call, and in case any Indian so meeting an English man refuse to throw down his arms upon call shall be deemed as an enemy.

"The privilege of hunting, crabing, fowling, and fishing shall be preserved to the Indians inviolable.

"That every Indian that killeth or steleth an hog or calfe or other beast or any other goods shall undergo the same punishment that an English man doth for the same offence.

the marke of Vnnacok Casimon."

VII. *Migration.*

By harassing the Nanticokes the Six Nations had brought them into subjugation; also in a treaty with the white had stipulated that these Indians be permitted to leave Maryland. About 1750 the majority of the Nanticokes migrated north, carrying with them the bones of their fathers, as was their custom. Part of the tribe went to Canada West, near Lake Erie, part to Wyoming Valley. Pa., and part to Otsiningo (now Binghampton), New York.

Following this migration we find that in 1761 those Nanticokes in Wyoming Valley appealed through the Governor of Pennsylvania to Maryland for permission to return for a remnant of their tribe yet remaining in that state. The appeal was granted and the remaining Indians permitted to migrate.

Two appeals were made by Nanticokes for land monies. That part which had withdrawn to Canada West petitioned in 1852 through their chief and headsmen, that the Maryland Assembly grant them certain annuities for which tradition claimed had once been paid their tribe for land rights. The Maryland Assembly declared the claim faulty and the petition was denied.

Again, we find in 1767 the Nanticokes from Otsiningo, New York making a similar appeal through one Ogden, Atty. In this case the appeal was granted but not seemingly for the amount asked, for the records add that, Sir William Johnson, England's chief Indian agent "made up the difference at the expense of the Crown."

So the Indians wandered away, lost their tribal identity and were blighted by civilization. Then with all this in 1761 came small-pox. In the Nanticoke tribe alone from 1763 to 1773 the warriors were reduced from 700 to 300. Soon all that was left on Eastern Shore to mark the home of the Red Man was their camp sites or the relics often found in field and forest.

VIII. Miscellaneous.

A further account of the Nanticoke Indians comes from one of their chiefs—White by name.

"Every Indian being at liberty to pursue what occupation he pleases, my ancestors, after the Lenape came into their country, preferred seeking a livelihood by fishing and trapping along the rivers and bays to pursuing wild game in the forests; they therefore detached themselves and sought the most convenient places for their purpose. In process of time they became very numerous, partly by natural increase, and partly in consequence of being joined by a number of the Lenape, and spread themselves over a tract of land and divided into separate bodies. The main branch of the Nanticokes proper were then living on what is now called the Eastern Shore of Maryland. At length the white people crowded so much upon them that they were obliged to seek another abode and as their grandfather, the Delaware, was himself retreating back in consequence of the great influx of the whites, they took the advice of the Mengroe (mingo's) and bent their course to the large flats of Wyoming, where they settled themselves, in sight of the Shawanos town, while others settled higher up the rives, even as high as Chemenk, (Shenango), and Shummunk, to which places they emigrated at the beginning of the French War.

'Nothing," said White, "equalled the decline of my tribe since the white people came into the country. They were destroyed, in part by disorders they brought with them, 'by the smallpox and by the free use of spiritous liquors to which great numbers fell victims."

"The Nanticoke, the Choptanks and the Metapeake Indians, descendents of the Delawares, were first seen along the bay shores of Talbot county by Captain John Smith and his exploring party from Virginia in 1608 and later by Clayboure and his trading party four or five years before Lord Baltimore's Colonists landed at Saint Mary's, near the mouth of Saint Mary's river. They had a peculiar and sacred respect for their dead. The corpse was buried for some months and then exhumed and the bones carefully cleaned and placed in an 'Osuary,' called manto-kump, (Manito) with the local termination or rather signification, "place of the mystery spirit.' When their tribes moved from one place to another they carried the bones of their dead with them. When they emigrated, about the middle of the 18th century and settled in northern Pennsylvania, they carried their sacred relics with them, in bags on their backs, and buried them near the present site of Towanda. The Indian name literally meant 'where we bury our dear.' "

WHEN INDIANS LIVED IN OUR LAND.

When the Calverts came to America there were two important families of Indians living within the territory granted them. The Susquehannoughs in the northern part of the colony belonging to the Iroquois family were fierce and warlike, while on what is now known as the Eastern Shore lived the Algonquins, of more peaceful disposition. The Nanticoke and Choptank tribes belonged to this family. They were tide water people living along the rivers which now bear their names. Although these Indians were traders rather than fighters, the Nanticokes on several occasions proved hostile to the settlers.

The men of the Choptank and Nanticoke tribes were tall and handsome, but disfigured themselves with paint. The women were short and heavy, lacking the dignity of the men. Like other tribes their cheek bones were high, mouths and noses large, eyes black and beadlike. Such clothing as the men wore was made of finely dressed skins forming a mantle which hung from the shoulders and an apron about the waist. They adorned themselves with as many chains of beads and shells as they could procure. Their straight black hair was tied in a single lock and ornamented with feathers. In winter a decorated robe, leggins and mocassins were worn for protection against the cold. The women wore short-sleeved tunics with leggins and mocassins in one, and the children's dress was much the same as their parents.

Homes. The tents or wigwams of these Indians were made of young saplings set in the ground to form a circle with the flexible ends tied together to form a framework. This was covered with bark or skins. When fire was needed, it was built on the ground in the center of the tent. The wigwam held no furniture, a pile of leaves covered with straw serving as a bed. Except for sleeping purposes the wigwam was seldom used, as the Indians lived almost entirely out of doors.

The Chief's House. The chief's house, though much larger, was built of the same materials. Instead of the circular form it was oblong with holes cut in the sides for windows and an opening at the top to let out smoke from the fire. Grasses or rushes woven into curtains divided the interior. The only furniture consisted of poles laid across four stakes driven in the ground, the whole being covered with leaves and skins and used as a bed. A strong stockade enclosed the chief's house, neighboring wigwams and council-fire around which the men gathered to discuss public matters and hold religious ceremonies.

Outside the villages the land was held in common. Each family had a plot to cultivate, the manual work being done by the women and children. A part of each crop was for the chief, stored by him for personal use as well as for entertainment of guests and reserve in case of famine or siege. The main crops grown were corn, beans, tobacco, melons, and gourds. The men fished, trapped, and hunted small game. They also made weapons and bowls which were greatly prized by neighboring tribes who traded for them. The women, as in all savage races, were the burden bearers and real workers. With bones for needles and sinews for thread they made the clothing for their families from skins they had carefully dressed. With wooden hoes they worked crops they had sown and later must harvest. When camp was to be moved, it was the women who carried the packs upon their willing backs while the men strode along with only their beloved bows and arrows as burdens.

These red men were governed by a chief whose power was absolute over them and whose position was hereditary. Next in rank was a general who had charge of all expeditions, peaceful or hostile. Such men as distinguished themselves in council or battle were given the title of cockarouse. These men, with the chief, general, and medicine man formed the council of the tribe.

The medicine man was looked upon as a person of great importance in the camp. His skill was supposed to be magical as well as medical. The Indians believed sickness a result of offending a spirit and part of their treatment consisted of pow-wowing, wild dancing, and gesticulation to appease the Evil One. Along with this herbs were used, while in case of wounds, the flesh was burned.

Ceremonies and Feast. In religious ceremonies, feasts and rites the medicine man again played a prominent part. These festivals were mostly in connection with seasonal changes, harvests, or return of migratory game. They were celebrated with dancing, singing, and feasting. Not until some time after the coming of the white men did these Indians indulge in any drink at their feasts except water sweetened wtih sugar—maple sap. In later years, drunkenness became prevalent among them as a result of trading valuable furs with the settlers for "fire water," as they called liquor.

Tobacco was a sacred herb among the Indians and used only in the ceremonial pipe. In the council it was lighted by the chief who drew on it a few times, opened the subject for discussion, and passed the pipe to the Indian next in rank. He in turn puffed a while then gave his views on the matter. This was continued until the pipe had gone all around the fire and each man allowed an opportunity to speak. Another use made of the pipe was to determine the attitude of visiting tribes. The chief after smoking it a while passed it to the principal man of the visiting tribe. If he accepted the pipe and smoked it, his errand was understood to be friendly, but if he refused to smoke, it was a sign of trouble between the tribes. The pipes were made of clay and decorated to suit the savage fancy. Several have been found in our county within recent years along with numerous stone hatchets, axes, and darts.

Indian Money. One of the Indian means of exchange was known as peak and consisted of small pieces of clam or mussel shell in purple or white. The purple was known as wampum-peak and had twice the value of the white. Rough bits of shell, rudely shaped, known as "roenoke" was much less valuable. Both peak and roenoke were strung and valued according to measure. The value of a yard of white peak was 9 pence (18c), in trade with the English; the purple, 18 pence (36 cents).

Indian Warfare. The Indians in their attacks upon the settlers used the same form of warfare as when fighting their own race. They delighted in surprise attacks and displayed great skill in this. When an attack was to be made, the chief and his warriors met in council and celebrated the coming events by dancing and pantomine of shooting, tomahawking and scalping of foes. After this they slipped from camp and travelled noiselessly to their destination. Often they went under cover of darkness, in single files, hiding behind trees until at a signal, they burst upon their victims with a war-hoop and began their cruel slaughter.

There are in some of our communities Indian stories and legends which have been handed down for several generations, and while in this way have become altered, still must have had some foundation in fact. One of these stories is of the kidnaping of a child near McCarty's Wharf, in lower Caroline. An infant boy, Richard Willoughby by name, was left alone in his home while his father and mother were engaged in some out-of-door work. An Indian crept up to the house and stole the child. It was not until after six weeks of searching by the distracted parents and neighbors that he was finally found in an Indian camp at Yellow Hill.

Along Hog Creek the remains of an Indian camp and medicine pit were found a few years ago. Indian caves and a large burying ground were located near Blairtown. On the Caroline side at Reliance there was for seventy years a reservation belonging to the red-men. What is now Downes Wharf once bore the name of Indian Landing. On the old Lyford farm in Tuckahoe Neck bones and skulls of savages have been found.

Perhaps some day you, too, may find a relic of those long-ago tribes and treasure it in memory of a fast vanishing race.

FOREWORD TO THE TRIAL OF POH POH CAQUIS.

(Adapted from the Maryland Archives).

On the 18th day of December, 1682 Poh Poh Caquis, Indian of the Eastern Shore, Maryland came to the home of William Troth at Dover Bridge. Troth was absent from home but, the Indian being cold, Mrs. Troth permitted him to sit by the fire.

After an hour had passed Troth returned, accompanied by John Shepherd, a neighbor. A few minutes later as the Indian, Troth and Shepherd conversed together Thomas Bussey came to the door.

As Troth turned to speak to Bussey, Poh Poh Caquis seized his gun and fired directly at Troth, but failing in this attacked him with his tomahawk, then ran away followed by Troth, Shepherd and Bussey. Although he finally escaped Poh Poh Caquis carried with him a load of buckshot from Troth's gun.

Fearing further trouble, on Dec. 22, 1682 Troth went to the home of John Edmonson where Col. Philemon Lloyd, a member of the Governor's Council, was visiting, and made formal complaint against Poh Poh Caquis.

Lloyd at once wrote to the Governor, and later when the Council met definite action was taken. At this meeting only four members of the Council were present, namely:

> The Hon. Col. Thomas Zailler,
> The Hon. Col. Vincent Lowe,
> The Hon. Col. William Burges,
> The Hon. Mr. John Darnall.

The Council appointed as a Special Commission "to go examine and try" the case of Poh Poh Caquis the Honorable Henry Coursey, Esq. and the Honorable Colonel Philemon Lloyd.

The Hon. Henry Coursey, Esq., was President of the Commission which met at Wye River, Talbot Co., March 5, 1683.

TRIAL OF POH POH CAQUIS.

Scene,—Courthouse at Wye River, Mar. 5, 1683.
Characters,

—45—

Special Commission.

President, the Hon. Henry Coursey, Esq.
Gov. Council the Hon. Philemon Lloyd.
Secretary to President.

White men.

The Constable   John Shepherd
The Interpreter   Thomas Bussey
William Troth

Indians.

Poh Poh Caquis   Wasatwahan
King Ababsco   Weenakaman
King Tequassimo   Cha Cha Pohosse
Wewohquak

TRIAL.

Pres. of Court. (Calls order)
    This body has convened today for the trial of one Poh
Poh Caquis, Indian of the Eastern Shore, subject to Ahatsawak
of Assoteaque. Will the constable bring the prisoner into
Court.
Constable. (Retires)
    (Returns immediately with Poh Poh Caquis.)
    Here he is, Your Lordship.
Pres. of Court. (Addressing assemblage.)
    Gentlemen, we have before us today, in the Sub-Court of
King George in the Province of Maryland, a case of much interest to our Red brothers as well as the White man,—that of
an Indian for an evil attack on his white brother.
    Red men, our Rt. Honorable Lord Proprietor gave you a
convenient dwelling place free from the encroachment of the
white man. It is the will of his Lordship, Gov. Charles Calvert that you have such a home.
    . King Abasco and King Tequassimo have in past times
given testimony of their fidelity. Shall that fidelity be broken
now? The charge is that Poh Poh Caquis has placed himself
under the law of the Province of Maryland by attempting
murder. The Secretary has the complaint as made by one
William Troth to Colonel Philemon Lloyd, while at the home
of John Edmonson, Dec. 22, 1682. Let the Secretary read
the Indictment.
Secretary to President. (Reads)
    About the 18th day of December (1682) came an Indian
to my house about two o'clock in the afternoon. I, not being
present in the house and the said Indian pretending to be cold,
my wife bid him go to the fire and there he was about an
houre. By this time my wife sent for me and when I came
into the house the said Indian came from where he had been
sitting by the fire and look'd upon me, but said not a word to
me not I to him; then straight-way returned to the fire again.
I went to where he was sitting by the fire with his Gunn
standing by him. I spoke to him and said, "How is Ketop".
"Howan Pawmen kees", he replied in Delaware.
Governor's Council. (Addressing Pres.)
    Your Lordship, may I address William Troth.
    (Pres. bows assent and Troth rises facing G. C.)
    (Addressing Troth) Do you affirm the truth of this in-
dictment as read in part before this court.

—46—

William Troth.

Your Lordship, I do. (Sits)

Secretary of Pres. (reads)

John Shepherd, sitting by the fire, said, "He tells me he is a Delaware Indian, and that there are two hundred Senni-quox Indians hard by," I said, "Pish, does thou believe him what he talks of. He lies." The Indian make answer he did not lie, for I should see them by and by. I made answer I would not see them if I could help it, but he said I should and forthwith fell ahollowing.

Governor's Council. (Addressing Pres.)

Your Lordship is John Shepherd in Court?

John Shepherd. (Rising)

Yes Your Honor.

Governor's Council. (Addressing Shepherd).

Were you present at the home of William Troth at the time referred to in indictment read?

John Shepherd.

I was your Honor.

Governor's Council

Do you affirm the truth of the indictment as read.

John Shepherd.

I do your Honor. (Sits)

Governor's Council. (To Sec.)

Proceed.

Secretary of President.

Before I could speak any more words to him, comes to the doore Thomas Bussey. I turned me about to speake to the said Thomas; while my back was toward the Indian the said Indian made ready his Gunn; I presently turned about again and seeing the muzzle of the gunn towards me, I endeavored to get hold of it, but before I could she went off, and with the bonding of my body to get hold of the gun, the shott mist. When he saw he had done no execution he took to his Toma-hawke, and followed me about eight or ten yards; and when I saw he followed me I called for my gunn, and as soon as he heard me call for my gunn he ran and when he was about thirty yards from me I discharged my gun at him. (Sec. sits.)

Governor's Council. (Addressing Assembly)

Thomas Bussey, stand.

Thos Bussey. (stands and bows.)

Your Lordship.

Governor's Council. (Addressing Bussey)

Were you present on the 18th of December 1682 when Poh Poh Caquis attacked William Troth as charged.

Thos. Bussey.

I was your Lordship.

Governor's Council

Thomas Bussey do you affirm that this accusation charg-ing Poh Poh Caquis with an attempt on the life of William Troth of Dover Bridge is true?

Thos. Bussey.

The charge is true Your Lordship. (Gov. Council and Bussey sits.)

Pres. Of Court.

The indictment has been read and its truth affirmed by these witnesses. Interpreter will you ask the prisoner why he denied his tribe.

(Mock interpretation)

Interreter. (To Pres. of Court.)

The prisoner says he was drunk and knew not what he did.

Pres. of Court. (To interpreter.)
Ask the prisoner what defense he makes.
(Mock interpretation)
Interpretor. (To the Pres. of Court.)
The prisoner says he was drunk otherwise he would not have shot at William Troth or have done any mischief.
Pres. of Court. (To Interpreter.)
Tell the Indians that it is the English law that if a man do mischief he must suffer. If drunkenness is an excuse then the English might make themselves drunk and kill Indians.
(King Ababscoete confer with Interpreter.)
Interpreter. (To Assembly.)
King Ababsco says that an English man shott at three Indian boyes but they came home not hurt, soe took noe notice.
Governor's Council. (Interrupting.)
Tell him the English were not informed. If they had the English man should have suffered as the law prescribes in such cases.
Pres. of Court. (Ignoring Council's words.)
Tell the Indians we can remember several miscarriages of their people, for which they have not been punished but we came not here to call to mind old differences but rather expect they should be forgot on both sides; but now we have taken this prisoner in fact he ought to suffer. We desire to know whether they justify the prisoner.
(Mock interpretation)
Interpreter.
They say they cannot justify the prisoner, neither did they come to excuse him.
Pres. of the Court.
Tell them that it is the custom of Christian Nations, that, if the peace is broken, he that doeth it must surely die, and this Indian by the law deserves death; but that the English are not desirous to exercise the rigour of the Lawe; therefore Poh Poh Caquis shall be carried to the whipping post and have twenty lashes on his bare back.
Interpreter. (After mock interpretation.)
Your Lordship, the Indians consent and have commanded one of their great men, Weahquap to execute the judgment.
(Constable, prisoner and Indians turn to leave.)
Governor's Council. (With Emphasis) (Indians turn)
Your Lordship the punishment is not sufficient.
(Mock interpretation)
Interpreter.
King Ababsco and King Tequassimo engage their words for the prisoner's good behavior forever hereafter.
Gov. Council.
It is not enough. Poh Poh Caquis may, notwithstandin, doe further mischief. Troth's life may be in constant danger. In what custody will they keep him.
(Pres. Order Interpretation.)
Interpreter.
Your Lordship, the Indians do not know how to secure him. They can say not more than Abatsawok had said formerly,—that they left it to his Lordship.
Pres. of Court.
The order is given that Poh Poh Caquis receive twenty lashes on his bare back. This for his evil attack. Moreover for the future safety of the English the Court decrees that after this punishment Poh Poh Caquis be transported into some part beyond the sea, as a villian not fit to be trusted here without danger of having the peace broken.

The Constable may remove the prisoner and after We-wahquap hath executed the sentence, the sentence of twenty lashes on the bare back, Poh Poh Caquis may be delivered to the High Sheriff of St. Mary's. (Constable leads out Poh Poh Caquis followed by Indians. Conversation and handshaking among men.)

Pres. of Court.

The trial of Poh Poh Caquis being ended this Special Commission has fulfilled its duty and adjourns the Court.

CAROLINE COUNTY'S FIRST COURT HOUSE.

ERECTION OF THE COURT HOUSE AND JAIL.

Perhaps you wonder why over twenty years elapsed between the formation of the county and the building of the court house. Here is the explanation as given in the records of the county court, General Assembly and Convention of Maryland of 1774-97.

Just previous to the establishment of Caroline, Dorchester county had levied a tax for the purpose of building a court house at Cambridge. That part which had been paid by people living in the section included in Caroline (70,000 lbs. of tobacco) was ordered to be given to the new county. The inhabitants of the section taken from Queen Anne's were to be taxed in the same proportion (56,000 lbs. of tobacco) and the monies therefrom used for building a court house at Pig Point (now

Denton). Although this seemed to assure the financial side of the undertaking, the dark days which were ahead for the entire colony caused a delay. With the outbreak of the Revolution, the Convention which now took the place of the late Assembly, suspended all levies until after the war. Dorchester's tobacco had been turned into paper money and at the close of the war its value had so depreciated that it was necessary to cause a new levy to be made upon the county for £1000. The commissioners were ordered to "demand, sue for, recover, and receive all monies previously levied and collected and use it for the same purpose."

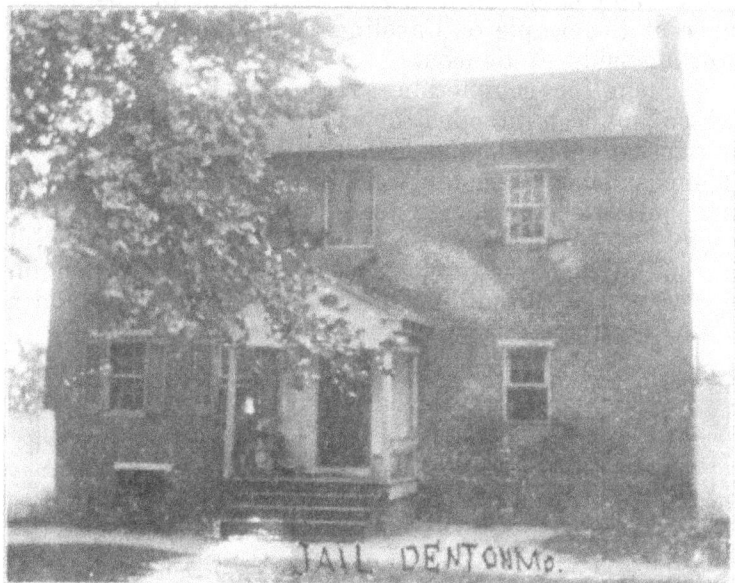

SECOND CAROLINE COUNTY JAIL PRECEDING PRESENT ONE.

While this was being done and things again at a standstill, Bridgetown renewed her plea for the county seat. The compromise spoken of in the preceding chapter occurred at this time and four years elapsed before further decision was reached in the matter. In 1790 it was finally decided that as the removal of court to Pig Point would be for the convenience and advantage of the inhabitants of the county the clerk should move the records, rolls, and books to that place and there, "safely deposit, keep, and preserve the same in some convenient house" before March 1st, 1791.

New commissioners were at this time appointed as follows: William Richardson, Zebdiel Potter, Joseph Richardson, Peter Edmonson and Joshua Willis. These men were to purchase land, have it surveyed, laid out and plotted, collect all monies and tobacco previously levied, and contract for the erection of court house and jail.

On April 27, 1791, they contracted with William Benson of Talbot county to build the court house. The original contract called for £1300 current money, but later, Mr. Benson finding this insufficient, an additional £500 was allowed. In 1797 the building was finally completed and stood until 1895 a tribute to the perseverance of the people of Caroline county and the splendid workmanship of Benson.

Upon the completion of the court house, monies which had been intended for use in building the jail were entirely used. Thomas Hughlett, Zebdiel Potter, and Thomas Allen Sangston were appointed commissioners and authorized to levy a tax of £500 in the years 1797 and 1798 for the purpose of building the prison. Not all of this money was needed, however, and the remainder was used in building a causeway on the east and a wharf on the west side of the Choptank at Denton.

CAROLINE'S PRESENT COURT HOUSE.

A Curl Rendering Shed

Silver Snuffers and Tray

REVOLUTIONARY PERIOD.

The Militia.

I. Introduction.

The story of the Militia of the Eastern Shore is the story of the spirit of the times, and this cannot be more clearly set forth than by quoting from a letter written May 1774, by a Mr. Eddie, officer of the English Government.

"All America is in a flame: I hear strange language every day. The colonists are ripe for any measure that will tend to the preservation of what they call their national liberty. I enclose you the resolves of our citizens; they have caught the general contagion. Expresses are flying from province to province. It is the universal opinion here, that the mother country cannot support a contention with these settlements, if they abide steady to the letter and spirit of their association."

All Maryland was aroused and Caroline County seemed imbued with even more than her quota of enthusiasm, and she was among the first to respond to the call of the nation. Her militia, her minute men, her Flying Camp were the material outgrowth of her spirit of Democracy.

II. Origin of Militia.

The Militia was a provincial organization of a very early date, an Act of General Assembly for such an organization having been passed at their session in 1638.

This Act provided that, under the direction of the Lieutenant General, "The captain of the military band shall use all power necessary, or conducing, in his direction, to the safety and defense of the province."

However at the opening of the Revolutionary period the Militia was only a tentative organization and Caroline as a county had no such military body of which we know.

III. Caroline's Awakening.

In all the colonies the English yoke was becoming heavy and as the spirit of Liberty spread abroad Maryland joined the opposition to England's tyranny with "A stern determination to have it efficient."

Then Caroline came to the fore-front in her state activities when the citizens in 1774 held a large meeting at Melvill's Warehouse, on the 18th day of June, by adjournment from the 8th of the same month, and passed the following resolutions, Charles Dickinson, Esq., chairman:

"1. Resolved, That the inhabitants of this country are by duty and inclination firmly attached to his most sacred majesty, King George the Third, to whom we owe all due obedience and allegiance.

"2. That it is the unanimous opinion of this meeting that the Boston port act is principally grounded on the opposition made by the inhabitants of that town to the tea duty, that the said town of Boson is now suffering in the common cause of British America, and that it is the duty of every colony thereof to unite in the most effectual means of obtaining a repeal of the late act of parliament for shutting up the port of Boston.

"3. That in the unanimous opinion of this meeting that if the colonies came into a joint resolution to forbear all importations whatsoever from Great Britain, (except such articles as are absolutely necessary) until the acts of parliament for shutting up the port of Boston, and for levying a duty in America for the express purpose of raising a revenue, shall be repealed, it will be the means of preserving the liberties of North America.

"Resolved, therefore, That the inhabitants of this county are disposed firmly to unite with the inhabitants of this province and the other colonies of North America, in an association and agreement to forbear the importation of goods and merchandise from Great Britain, during the continuance of the said acts of parliament (except such articles as may be judged proper to be excepted by a general association,) and that all orders for importation, (except the articles before excepted,) ought to cease.

"4. That it is against the opinion of this meeting, that the colonies go into a general non-importation from, or non-exportation, to Great Britain, but should both, or either of these measures be adopted, they will acquiesce therein.

"5. That it is the unanimous opinion of this meeting that the courts of justice be kept open. But should a non-exportation agreement be generally come into, in that case it is the opinion of this meeting that the courts of justice be shut up.

"6. That it is the opinion of the inhabitants of this county, that this province ought to break off all trade and dealings with that colony, province, or town, which shall refuse or decline to come into similar resolutions with a majority of the colonies.

"7. That it is the unanimous opinion of this meeting that delegates be appointed from this province to attend a general congress of delegates from the other colonies, at such time and place as shall be agreed on, in order to settle and establish a general plan of conduct for the important purposes aforementioned.

"8. That Thomas White, William Richardson, Isaac Bradley, Nathaniel Potter, Benson Stainton, and Thomas Goldsborough, be a committee to attend a general meeting at Annapolis. And that the same gentlemen, together with Charles Dickinson, Richard Mason, Joshua Clark, Henry Dickinson, Dr. Wm. Molleson, Charles Blair, Wm. Haskins, Philip Fiddleman, Wm. Hooper, the Rev. Samuel Keene, the Rev. Philip Walker, Henry Casson, and Benedict Brice, be a committee of correspondence to receive and answer all letters, and on any emergency, to call a general meeting and that any seven of the number have the power to act.

"9. That this paper be considered as an instruction to the deputies nominated from this County to meet at the city of Annapolis for the purpose of forming a general association, in which they are not to come into any engagement whatever, but upon condition that the colonies in general shall come into a similar measure.

"10. That a copy of the proceedings be published in the MARYLAND GAZETTE, to evince to the world the sense they entertain of the invasion of their constitutional right and liberties. Signed, per order,

"Henry Downes, Jr., Clerk."

These resolutions show that the intent of the colonists was readjustment of differences, not war. They wanted trade relations changed, not the government. When however April 28, 1774 at 9 A. M. the blood-tidings from Lexington reached Annapolis war became a certainty in the minds of the Assembly.

A letter sent to the State deputies of each county stating the savage massacre of a number of the inhabitants of Lexington, and the movement of the King's troops, numbering 1200, caused great alarm through the colonies; therefore, it became necessary to form some kind of a resistance.

When the convention met at Annapolis in December a resolution was adopted, in substance as follows:

On the eighth day of December, 1774, the deputies from each county met and resolved to form a militia of their respective counties. This militia was to be composed of the gentlemen, freeholders and other freemen. It was further recommended that all persons from sixteen to fifty years of age enroll and form themselves into companies of 68 men; to choose a captain, two lieutenants, an ensign, four sergeants, four corporals and one drummer for each company. These men were to use every means possible to make themselves masters of the military exercise. Each man was to be provided a good fire-lock and bayonet fixed thereon, one half pound of powder, two pounds of lead, and a cartouch box, or powder-horn, and a bag of ball, and be in readiness to act in any emergency.

At the same time it was recommended that the "Committee" of each County raise a solicited subscription or voluntary gift of monies amounting in full to 10,000 pounds of which Caroline's allotment was 358 pounds.

Under the direction of the Committees from the respective counties this money was to be used to purchase arms and ammunition for the use of such county.

The resolves of the convention were immediately carried out; old and young enrolled with the greatest enthusiasm, and money, arms, and ammunition, were everywhere collected to meet the approaching crisis. Maryland was girding herself for the struggle. It broke out in open conflict, just before the meeting of the convention.

To repress toryism, it was enacted that if any inhabitants of the province should, after the 5th of August following, levy war against the United States or should adhere "to any person or persons bearing arms or employed in the service of Great Britain against the United Colonies, _____ or shall afford such persons, _____ any aid or comfort, or shall give them, _____ or any subject of Great Britain any intelligence of the warlike preparations or designs of the United Colonies, _____ such person on conviction thereof by a petit jury, after a presentment by a grand jury, in a court to be erected in this colony by the next convention, for the trial of such offenders, shall suffer death without benefit of clergy, and forfeit all estate which he had at the time of the commission of the crime, to be applied to the use of this colony, unless such convicted person shall be pardoned by the person or persons invested with the power of granting pardon for such offences."

While in all probability the enrollment was not complete on the given date the records state that on September 15. 1775, all persons within the province from sixteen to fifty, subscribed, enrolled and pledged their willingness to bear arms and march to such places within the province, when the convention, or the council of safety commanded.

The militia companies consisted of not more than 74 privates, nor less than 50; each captain of his militia was to submit a muster roll to the committee of Observation. This roll including captains, lieutenants, ensign, number of non-commissioned officers and privates, was forwarded to the Council of Safety, in order that all commissions might be issued in the name of the convention to these officers.

The militia was to meet for exercise weekly; the commanding officer naming the place. Conditions frequently made it necessary that the commanding officer had to have his company divided and exercised at different places. It was necessary that the entire company be exercised once each month.

Every non-commissioned officer and private of the minute-men and militia was to appear at his place of muster with his firelock and other equipments in good order, and to diligently and obediently attend to all instructions, and perform his exercise in arms as commanded. In case he should not appear, or his firearms were not in good order, and having no legitimate excuse, he was subjected to a fine not exceeding the sum of five shillings in common money for every such neglect. Such misbehavior was to be determined by the captain, lieutenants, and ensigns or any two of them.

Every commissioned officer having no reasonable excuse and failing to perform his duty according to his office and station, and for the refusal of duty, shall be fined a sum not to exceed 15 shillings of common money; such misbehavior to be adjudged by other field and commissioned officers, or a major part of them.

The militia continued under the organization until the end of 1775 at which time material changes were made in the military arrangements.

IV. Government.

That the various enactments and organizations pertaining to the government may be understood it might be well to speak of the governing bodies at the close of the provincial organization.

There was a short period between the awakening of the people and the deposing of Robert Eden, last Colonial Governor, when Maryland was really under two governments. The General Assembly was not dissolved, yet the colony resenting their rule sent representatives to Annapolis and formed a "Convention" which first met Nov. 21, 1774. This date was the time of the actual deposing of the Colonial Governor, although his power was gone even before this. It might be well to mention that

Governor Eden still remained in the province after the supremacy had been taken out of his hands by the convention. His easy and affable manner had caused no alarm; for sometime before the change in the governing power he had been apparently neutral. But certain letters were found addressed to him from Lord Dunmore, who was commanding a fleet in the Chesapeake Bay, and was also prominent in stirring up the tories in the lower part of the province, asking Robert Eden to hold himself in readiness to assist the Crown when occasion presented itself. General Charles Lee, into whose hands the letters were placed, immediately forwarded same to the Council of Safety at Baltimore. As the convention was not in session, he advised that the person and papers of Mr. Eden be at once secured.

Captain Smith, company commander under Major Gist, was sent with a detachment of the Maryland regulars for that purpose. The convention afterwards resented this proceeding and reprimanded Captain Smith and ordered him to return to Baltimore. At the same time however, considering the presence of Governor Eden no longer consistant with the safety of the colony, resolved—"That it be signified to the Governor, that he leave his province because the public safety and quiet, in the judgement of this convention is required, and that he is at full power of liberty to depart peaceably with his effects, and that a committee of five persons be appointed to wait on the Governor and deliver him copies of the resolutions together with an address." The house voted on the above resolution; Caroline's vote was as follows: Mr. Richardson, affirmative; Mr. Dickinson, negative; Mr. Mason, negative.

Governor Eden sailed on his majesty's ship Fowey, June 24, 1776. Detachments of militia were placed at convenient posts to prevent any communication with the Fowey man of war together with the ship Defence, which tendered her down the bay to prevent as far as possible any plunder or attack.

After taking the governing power out of the hands of the Governor it became necessary to give this power to some governing body; for this purpose a "Maryland Council of Safety" was chosen by ballot. It was composed of 16 persons, eight of whom resided on the western shore and eight on the eastern shore. This body was to direct and regulate the operations of the minute-men and militia, providing equipment, food, regulating their movements from place to place, and appointing and commissioning field officers, together with the regulation of the rank of all military officers. The Council moreover attended to all matters of state when the Convention was not in session and had the power to call a special meeting of said Convention when they deemed it necessary.

A Local Committee was formed called the "Committee of Observation" whose duty it was to inspect (locally) and report to the Council of Safety on the conduct of any who were suspected of being disloyal, also to investigate direct charges of disloyalty. The term of office of members of this committee was one year, beginning on day of election.

The committee of Observation in each county was held responsible for every able bodied man enrolling, and in case they found those who failed to enroll, their names were forwarded to the State convention which would adopt measures against such persons.

It was further ordered that each committee of Observation, as soon as convenient after their election should choose by ballot five members to act as a "Committee of Correspondence" for their country between the State Council and other counties. One person was named on each committee to act as a treasurer; receiving all sums of money which was given voluntarily; this to be used in encouraging the building of manufactories of any kind for immediate relief in the counties and arming and defending the country.

Their number of elections is shown in the following:

"In September 1775, an election was held at the court houses of the counties for the purpose of electing new members to the committee of Observation. All freeholders in the province, and other freeman having a visible estate of 40 pounds sterling were qualified to vote."

Thus we see that the "Convention" the "Council of Safety," the "Committee of Observation" together with sub-committees formed Maryland's governing body during the Revolutionary period.

Though Caroline county's people were in the main loyal, and did all in their power to carry out the orders of the province, yet Tories and other paid agents of the British Government wrought considerable dissatisfaction in the minds of many well-disposed persons as will be understood from the following extracts from the Maryland Archives.

Caroline County Sept. 17th, 1776.

Sir:

Agreeably to the requisition of the Convention made to the field officers of this county, to endeavor to get a company made up to march to New York, I thought it necessary to convene the 28th Battalion of Militia on Saturday last for that purpose, and after meeting in the usual field of parade, the several Companies were drawn up, except the Company under the command of Capt. John Fauntleroy. I then requested he would draw up his company, who made me for answer, that he had but a few officers in the field and that he should not draw up under me as commander of the field.

Capt. Fauntleroy's reasons for not joining the Battalion I do not certainly know, but after the Battalion were dismissed, I am credibly informed he endeavored to see who would join against me, for what purpose I do not know unless to treat me ill.

As it appears to me, Sir, that he is a disobedient officer and possibly was I to overlook this injury to the common cause, it might prove to be bad consequence, besides under these circumstances my person as well as character may not be altogether safe, and in order sir, that peace and harmony may again take place, I pray that a court marshal may be appointed by your board for the trial of Capt. Fauntleroy in order to find out what I am to be accused with and that he or myself may meet with the instant demerits we deserve.

I am Sir most o'bedt Hble Servt.

Benson Stainton.

(Proceedings of Court Martial.)

Melvill's Warehouse Nov. 16, 1776.

In pursuance to an order from the Council of Safety bearing date of 18th day of September last, for the trial of Capt. John Fauntleroy of the twenty eight Battalion of Militia for this State, I appointed the sixteenth day of November 1776, for holding a Court Martial for the purpose and gave notice of the time and place for holding said Court, to all Persons concerned. And there was present at the time and place,

Vincent Price
Nathaniel Potter
Captains John Mitchell
Peter Richardson
Henry Casson, Sr.

And after fully hearing the allegations of Col. Benson Stainton and the evidence of both sides and considering the same, the Court gives judgment that Capt. John Fauntleroy pay five pounds current money for his offense and breach of duty.

Mat. Driver, President.

V. Reorganization of Militia.

At the meeting of the Convention at Annapolis, Jan. 4, 1776, a reorganization of the militia was effected. A committee had been previously appointed to "Consider what alterations and amendments necessary, in the regulations on the militia of this Province."

The report was in brief as follows: No minute men were to be hereafter enrolled; no companies of minute men were to be continued after the first day of the following March; all arms now in the possession of the "minute men" to be delivered to the Committee of Observation; every able bodied man between the ages of 16 and 50 (with a few exceptions) not yet enrolled in the militia must do so on or before March 1, 1776.

Following was a list of fines, punishments etc. for delay or disobedience and a plan for officering the new organization. After this Convention the "minute men" and "Flying Camp" were disbanded and the entire soldiery became militia.

The convention having been in session on Jan. 1, 1776 resolved that eight companies of troops, to consist of 68 privates under proper officers, to be formed into a battalion, and the remainder of the troops to be divided into companies of 100 men each.

The following Caroline county officers were elected by ballot: East Battalion—Mr. William Richardson, colonel; Mr. Henry Dickinson, lieutenant-colonel; Mr. William Whitely, 1st major; Mr. Matthew Driver, 2nd major; Mr. John White, quartermaster. West Battalion —Mr. Philip Fiddeman, colonel; Mr. Benson Stainton, lieutenant-colonel; Mr. Richard Mason, 1st major; Mr. Henry Dowes, 2nd major; Mr. Thos. Hardcastle, quartermaster. Pay of officers as follows: colonel $50; colonels expenses $30; lieutenant colonel $40, lieutenant-colonels expenses $20; major $33.33; captain $26; drummer and fifer $6; lieutenant $18; ensign $16; surgeons mate $20; sergeant $6.66; corporal $6; surgeon $40; chaplain $20; private $5.33 clerk to colonel $20; pay to other officers was regulated by the Council of Safety.

That a ration consisting of one pound of beef, or three-quarters of a pound of pork, one pound of flour or bread per man per day, three pints of peas at six shillings per bushel per week, or other vegetables equivalent, one quart of Indian meal per week, a gill of vinegar and gill of molasses per man per day, a quart of cider, small beer or rum, per man per day, three pounds of candles for one hundred men per week, for guards; twenty-four pounds of soft soap, or eight pounds of hard soap for one hundred men per week.

Each captain was to enlist his own company and had the following instructions for enlisting men into the service:

1. You are to enlist no man who is not able bodied, healthy, and a good marcher, nor such whose attachment to the liberties of America you have any cause to suspect. Young hearty robust men, who are tied by birth, or family connections or property to this country; and are well practiced in the use of firearms, are by much to be preferred.

2. You are to have a great regard to moral character, sobriety in particular.

3. You are not to enlist any servant imported, nor, without the leave of the master, any apprentice.

4. Those who engage in the service shall be enlisted according to the form prescribed by this convention.

A further order indicating low finance was the following:

"To avoid a needless and insupportable expense, no person after the tenth day of May next, may wear any uniform at exercise, either in single companies or battalions, but hunting shirts, the officers distinguishing themselves from the privates by different feathers, cockades, or the like as fancy may direct."

VI. Meeting the Needs of the War.

The general idea of conservation along all lines seemed to be immediately taken up by the Convention. Early as the meeting of Dec. 8, 1774 we find the following recommendations:

First, that the citizens increase their flocks of sheep for the promotion of woolen manufacturing and to further this they recommended that thereafter no sheep under four years of age be killed.

The second recommendation was that the citizens increase the production of linen and cotton by "planting all they conveniently can" and recommend further that speculators purchase no seed for exportation.

Again in July, 1775 the Council of Safety found it necessary to discourage the killing of lambs, so that more wool might be realized; also to enforce the production of flax.

This year as well as the next two following, meant a period of great conservation on the part of the province. As stated before they were unprepared for war, not having meat, meal, clothing, tents, firearms, or shoes for the soldiers; there was apparently leather in the colonies but it was not made up into shoes, since much of this must be done by hand it was a very slow process.

In 1777 the American Army was so greatly in need of clothing and blankets that collectors were appointed in each county to collect these necessities wherever possible. In Great Choptank Hundred Joseph Richardson was appointed Superintendent of Collections. The Governor and Council limited the prices to be paid as follows: Blankets 13s; a pair of shoes 30d; a pair of stockings 30d; a hat 30d; coarse woolens, fit for soldiers' coats, jackets or breeches ¾ yd. wide 50d; linen, fit for soldiers' shirts, per yard, 16d.

The food question was one of importance. How procure rations for the soldiers?

Nathaniel Potter, whom we remember as one of the first Court justices of Caroline County, and who had bought and packed pork and beef for Caroline County companies under Col. Richardson was (1776) called upon to procure, for the Province, all pork possible at 5 pounds sterling per hundred.

The following letter written by Isaac McHard, Quartermaster to the Council of Safety, brings to us not only food conservation but the necessity of salt.

Caroline County Dec. 30th, 1776.

Gentlemen:

I have contracted with Mr. Potter to buy me all the Pork that is to be had in the county. He had engaged to salt and barrel all that he could get and he thinks it necessary to have salt, therefore hope you will order him fifty bushels, which quantity he thinks he will want. I have likewise engaged with Mr. James Seth, to get for me all the Pork in Talbot and Queen Anne's County if he should want a little salt I hope you will order him a little. I don't know that he will want it for he has contracted to deliver it at Annapolis if possibly he can get it there. If he can not get it there from the badness of the weather it must be salted over here and barreled and brought to Annapolis in the spring. Your granting these orders for the salt will much oblige

Gentlemen, Your hble. Servt.

Isaac McHard.

N.B.   Mr. Crysale will see the salt measured and will take a receipt from the Skipper for the Quantity.

The scarcity of salt threatened the conservation of meat and must be secured for that purpose. Many freeholders were reported as having large supplies of it stored and this led to great dissatisfaction of the people in need of it. Searching parties were organized who went out to search for these stores.

In one case Mr. Colston of Caroline having butchered was in great need of salt; hearing that Mr. Chamberlain of Plain Dealing Talbot, had 100 bushels stored he sent several times to buy it but each time they refused to sell. At last Mr. Colston had his neighbors, seventeen in number, go with him carrying the money and their muskets. They asked again that the salt be sold them, if not to open the door of the house in which the salt was stored. Mr. Chamberlain's wife being the only one at home opened the door of the house; there they found a considerable quantity. They ordered one of Mr. Chamberlain's negroes to measure out 17½ bu. for which they paid $35.00. On their return home they wrote a letter to Mr. Chamberlain explaining the transaction and saying they would pay the price he asked. This matter was brought to the attention of the Council, which took immediate steps to secure 30 bus. from Talbot and Dorchester counties.

War conditions led to other depredations, one of which with its attending civic troubles we give below:

"In great desperation for want of salt, then so scarce, Capt. Richard Andrew and a number of men in November, 1776, entered and searched the dwelling house and outhouses of James Sullivane, looking for salt. As they found only five bushels they did not take any. Then they went to Col. James Murry's on Hunting Creek (now known as the Billup's farm) got the keys from Mrs. Murray and took fourteen and one half bushels of salt. They offered to pay for it, but Mrs. Murray refused payment; however they left $14.50 in the house."

To punish these disorderly people the Committee of Observation summoned witnesses and those active in the affair, but they did not appear and a hearing was set for the following Wednesday, and wholly unexpectedly they came headed by Captain Andrew with more than a hundred armed men. They were so disorderly that nothing could be done in the matter. They declared they would risk their lives in defense of their acts. An appeal was made to the Council of Safety to have Gen. Henry Hooper's brigade of militia sent to arrest them, but considering the need of troops elsewhere and the urgent appeals made by the people on the Eastern Shore for salt, then so scarce that some families had not a pint in months, it seemed that the sending of a militia into a county to suppress local disturbances not regarded as disloyal acts, might lead to serious revolts at this critical period of the Revolutionary conflict.

Scarcity of saltpetre too was giving the government much concern. It was a necessity. Powder must be produced for the man behind the gun. As early as July, 1775 the Council of Safety found it necessary to encourage the manufacture of saltpetre. To do this a sum not exceeding 1000 pounds common money was advanced on proper security for the erection of one or more saltpetre works. This money was to be repaid in good merchantable saltpetre on or before October 1776. The manufacturers were to be paid one half dollar per pound, this rate being fixed by the Council of Safety.

At the same time a similar sum was offered for the erection and working of a powder-mill. Again on Dec. 27, 1775 the Convention appropriated 1700 pounds of common money, each county 100 pounds to be placed in the hands of a discreet and active person in each county, called a supervisor, to be used in procuring and setting up proper kettles, tubs and necessary utensils for the manufacture of rough nitre. That the supervisor show and explain to those who attend to the work the method and process of making crude nitre. To encourage people throughout the county to make nitre they offered the rate of two shillings common money per pound. The following process was recommended by the supervisors: place in open houses, or sheds admitting air, but excluding the rain and sun, the stalks and trashy leaves of tobacco, trodden straw, the sweepings of stables mixed with rich mold collected from floors of barns, and from time to time sprinkled with brine or water; this collection of various substances so as to occasion the fermentation and speedy putrefaction thereof; that the whole mass when properly decayed, may be dug, stirred up and thoroughly blended and thus left without further damping so loose and light as to attract readily and be more plentifully impregnated with nitre for future use. Mr. Joshua Clark was supervisor for Caroline County.

Another necessity for the army was lead. This was conserved to the utmost. From the Archives of Maryland, 1777, the following is quoted showing its scarcity.

"I have been obliged to call upon the inhabitants here for their Clock Weights, and Window Weights; we wanted lead; and as we have here every conveniency for making cartridges and men that understand it I intend to make up all our powder and get all the Lead that I can; We have tradesmen here that understand the making of every military article and they are all at work."

Following in Council of Safety records are letters relating to outfitting of soldiers.

"Resolved that Chas. Beatley of Frederick be empowered to contract for the making and delivering of 650 good, substantial, proved musquets 3½ feet in the barrel and of ¾ of an inch in the bore: With good double bridle locks, black walnut or maple stocks, and plain strong brass mounting, bayonets with steel blades, 17 inches long, steel ramrods, double screws, priming wires and brushes fitted thereto, with a pair of brass molds for every 80 musquets, to cast 12 bullets on one side and on the other to cast shot of such size as the musquet will chamber three of them; for a sum not exceeding $10.66 in bills of credit issued by the Resolutions of the last Convention."

VI. Later Organization of Militia.

In 1777 the militia of Caroline County was continued in two battalions, one east of and the other west of the Choptank River. In each battalion were eight companies, and each company was made up of about 75 men.

William Whitely was commander-in-chief of the militia of the county—both battalions—and had the rank of Colonel. Matthew Driver was next in command as Lieutenant-Colonel and Nathaniel Potter served as Major.

Upon these men, evidently, devolved the important duty of preparing plans for the enrollment of all able bodied men of military age, as well as being directly responsible to the state Council of Safety for the execution of all orders handed down from the Continental Congress and the State Council.

After a close inspection of the names of eligibles, about 1200 men were found to compose the militia of this period. The location of the Captains and men of the various companies was about as follows: *East Battalion*: 1st Company including the Harmony and American Corner's section, Captain Joseph Richardson; 2nd Company, Concord and Smithville neighborhood, Captain John Mitchell; 3rd Company, Chestnut Grove and Federalsburg territory, Captain Nehemiah Andrew; 4th Company, Preston Section, Captain Joseph Douglass; 5th Company, Friendship and Linchester communities, Captain Richard Andrew; 6th Company, Burrsville section, Captain John Stafford; 7th Company, Chilton, Garey's and Denton neighborhoods, Captain Andrew Fountain; 8th Company, Williston and Andersontown communities, Captain Shadrach Lyden. *West Battalion*: 1st Company Boonsboro and Oakland regions, Captain William Hooper; 2nd Company, Lower Tuckahoe Neck section, Capt. Vincent Price; 3rd Company, Hillsboro and Upper Tuckahoe Neck, Capt. Henry Downes; 4th Company, region around Greensboro, east side of river perhaps, Capt. William Haslett; 5th Company, territory around Greensboro, toward Goldsboro and Bridgetown, Capt. Thomas Hughlett; 6th Company, along Tuckahoe Creek and

—67—

Bridgetown, Capt William Chipley; 7th Company, from Jackson's residence near old Town Branch to the Culbreth Section, north east of Goldsboro, Captain Samuel Jackson; 8th Company from Castle Hall toward Bee Tree and Keene's Cross Roads, Capt. John Fauntleroy.

As reported the East Side Battalion consisted of 615 men while in the West Batallion were 585 men.

Somewhat later during the war Henry Dickinson enrolled for the county a company of Light Horsemen, about 15 in number. However, there is no record of this Company having gone into service.

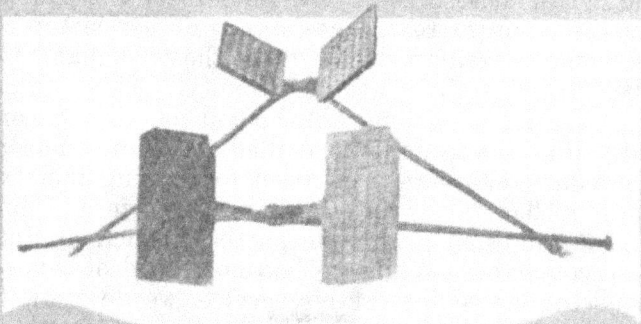

CAROLINE'S MILITARY ACTIVITIES.

In the same year that Caroline county was organized England closed the port of Boston. This greatly incensed the colonists of Maryland, and the counties at once held meetings expressing their indignation at the proceeding. At Caroline's meeting (Melvill's Warehouse, June 18, 1774) resolutions were adopted of which we may well be proud. A full copy of these may be found elsewhere in this volume.

The resolutions provided that delegates be appointed from each colony to meet in a general congress to settle and establish a general plan of conduct. Other counties offering the same resolutions, resulted in the Continental Congress, first proposed by Maryland, which met in Philadelphia, September 1774.

The resolutions named Thos. White, William Richardson, Isaac Bradley, Nathaniel Bradley, Benson Stainton, and Thomas Goldsborough as delegates to attend a general meeting of the province in Annapolis, which meeting, held December 8, authorized the organization of a well regulated militia to be in readiness to act in any emergency. A later meeting (April, '75) gave full power to delegates for the Second Continental Congress to agree to all measures which they should deem necessary and effectual to obtain a redress of American grievances, and the province bound themselves to execute to the utmost of their power all resolutions thus adopted.

It was during this convention that news reached the province of the massacre at Lexington. Maryland, ready to do her part, resolved to organize forty companies of minute-men to go to the assistance of her sister colonies should occasion arise. One of these companies was to be furnished by Caroline County. This company was to consist of strong, able-bodied men living conveniently that they might be drilled together. The men were required to sign a contract expressing their willingness to bear arms and fight in their own and neighboring colonies at such time as the Council of Safety should command. While we find no record of this company being called into active service, we do know that they were organized and drilled for the emergency.

The Council of Safety, formed July, 1775, was composed of sixteen men, eight of whom lived on either shore of the province. The council was to direct and regulate the operations of the minute men and militia, provide equipment and food, regulate their movements, appoint and commission field officers, and regulate the rank of all military officers. During the intermission of the Convention of Delegates, the council was to have authority to act in their place in case of emergency.

Up until this time such fighting arms as were needed in the colony had been purchased from England. That source being cut off, there was difficulty in procuring enough to supply the need. Men having firearms of their own used them, and to supply the remainder of the Minute Men, the Committee of Observation in each county collected those not in use until others could be provided by the province. This lack of equipment caused considerable anxiety and delay in the organization and drilling of troops.

In January, 1776, the convention decided for the better protection of the colony that additional militia be formed and that after March first the minute men be disorganized. In June of the same year Washington's appeal for more men was received and the Maryland Convention ordered the organization of a "flying camp" of 3405 men of the militia. These men, who were to serve with the militia of Pennsylvania and Delaware from Maryland to New York inclusive, now became part of the regular army and agreed to serve until December first. unless previously discharged by Congress.

At this time William Richardson was colonel of the east battalion of the Caroline county militia and a member of the convention from the same county. In August, upon the resignation of James Kent as Colonel of the Eastern Shore Battalion of the Maryland Flying Camp, Richardson was chosen for this important commission. His battalion was composed of seven companies from the various counties with 644 men in all. Captains of these companies were:

John Deen and John Dames—Queen Anne's.
Greenbury Goldsborough—Talbot.
Joseph Richardson and Philip Fiddeman—Caroline.
Thomas Burke—Dorchester.
John Oblevee—Cecil.

These officers were ordered by the Council to organize and exercise their men and report to Colonel Richardson for marching orders. The colonel had orders to march his companies to Elizabeth Town, New Jersey, there to join with other troops under the command of General Smallwood.

In enlisting their men, the captains were given these instructions:

1. You are to enlist no man who is not able bodied, healthy, and a good marcher, nor such whose attachment to the liberties of America you have any cause to suspect. Young, hearty robust men, who are tied by birth, or family connections or property to this country; and are well practised in the use of fire-arms, are by much to be preferred.

2. You are to have great regard to moral character, sobriety in particular.

3. You are not to enlist any servant imported, nor, without the leave of the master, any apprentice.

4. Those who engage in the service shall be enlisted according to the form prescribed by this convention.

Their rations consisted of one pound of beef, or three quarters of a pound of pork, one pound of flour or bread per man per day, three pints of peas at six shillings per bushel per week, or other vegetables equivalent, one quart of indian meal per week, a gill of vinegar and a gill of molasses per man per day, a quart of cider, small beer, or a gill of rum, per man per day, three pounds of candles for one hundred men per week, for guards; twenty-four pounds of soft soap, or eight pounds of hard soap for one hundred men per week.

Lack of tents, clothing and fire-arms delayed the organization of troops. There was also difficulty in transporting the men and supplies, but on September 8, Colonel Richardson and his men joined the army at Elizabeth, New Jersey.

On September 16, Richardson's regiment had a chance to prove their fighting ability. Three hundred of the British having appeared in the plains below the American position at Harlem Heights, Washington ordered an attack. The British were reinforced with 700 men and to strengthen the American forces, Washington ordered up Major Price with three of the Maryland Independent Companies, and Richardson's and Griffith's battalions of the flying camp. These men attacked with bayonet and drove the enemy from their position, pursuing them until the general ordered their recall. (A full account of this encounter will be found in McSherry's History of Maryland, pages 204-210).

Washington in his letter to Congress, dated September 18, 1776, gives the following account of the charge of the Maryland soldiers:

"These troops charged the enemy with great intrepidity, and drove them from the wood into the plain, and were pushing them from thence, having silenced their fire in a great measure, when I judged it prudent to order a retreat, fearing the enemy, as I have since found was really the case, were sent in a large body to support their party."

Colonel Tench Tilghman, one of Washington's staff, in a letter from Harlem Heights, dated September 19th, 1776, says:

"The general (Washington) finding they wanted support, ordered over part of Colonel Griffith's and Colonel Richardson's Maryland regiments, these troops, though young, charged with as much bravery as I can conceive; they gave two fires and then rushed right forward which drove the enemy from the wood into a buckwheat field, from whence they retreated."

General Washington, knowing that he could rely upon the Marylander's in his army, often chose them for posts of danger. He evinced no want of confidence, and often acted as if in command of veteran troops whose resolution he had tried and on whom he could rely. They were the first who met face to face with fixed bayonets, the veteran legions of British regulars; and no troops poured out their blood more freely for the common cause than those of Maryland. No troops behaved more steadily. "The gallantry of the Southern men," as the adjutant-general said, in speaking of these troops, "has inspired the whole army."

On December 1, 1776 the flying camp was discharged in accordance with the agreement upon enlisting. Congress, realizing that men whose enlistments were for so brief a period would never become used to discipline to the degree needed for firmness in action, decided to enlist men as regulars. The colonies agreed to this and Maryland at once started raising her quota of eight battalions. These reorganized troops became known as the "Maryland Line."

From this time on to the close of the war it is impossible to distinguish the military service of the men of the various counties. We find no evidence of the recruits of each county being in one company. It seems most probable that they were distributed as needed and old officers retained as far as possible.

William Richardson remained colonel of what became known as the 5th Regiment of the Maryland Line, and was actively engaged in suppressing tory rebellions in the lower part of the Eastern Shore. These increasing disturbances were partly caused by George III granting pardon to any of his subjects who would join his forces and also by an organization known as The Association of Loyalists of America. This association was authorized to employ "his majesty's faithful subjects for the purpose of annoying the sea coasts of the revolted provinces, and distressing their trade." Large numbers of tories were enrolled on the Eastern Shore who robbed and murdered the residents especially of Somerset, Worcester and Sussex county in Delaware.

The families of men killed in the Continental Service were pensioned through the county court. One example is given here:

The court orders that Susannah C......, widow of William C......, who sometime since died in the Continental Service, be allowed for the support of her two children this year (1779) 30£ current money.

A complete list of Caroline's Revolutionary soldiers has never been found. We give here the company that served under Captain Richardson in the flying camp. Although no enlistments of Captain Philip Fiddeman's company can be found, his company was raised and marched to Philadelphia.

First Caroline Company of the Eastern Shore Battalion.

Captain ....Joseph Richardson
1st. Lieutenant ....Thomas Wyer Lockerman
2nd. Lieutenant ....Levin Handy
Ensign ....Philip Casson (resigned)
Surgeon's Mate ....Zabdiel Potter

PRIVATES.

Andrew Price	William Walker
Thomas Comerford	John Hobbs
Massy Fountain	Ellis Thomas
John Webb	John Diragin (Duregin)
William Brown	Zadock Harvey
John Kanahan	Jarirs (or Jervis) Willis
Edward Hardin	Robert Waddle
Perry Gannon	James McQuallity
John Needles	Thomas Scoudrick
William Hobbs	William Allcock
John McKinney	John Ritchee (Richee)
Silas Parrott	William Sharp
Michael Walker	William Clark
John Hughs	Joseph Thomas
Robert Thomas	William Foster
Zebdial Billiton	John Froume
Alex Robbs	William Willin
Cornelius Morris	George aHndy
Hughlett Conner	Thomas Merrill

Isaac Duncan
Thomas Vaine
John Ford
James Tanner
Benj. Caulk
William Cook
John Carter
John Turner
John Cohee
John Vaine
William Cooper
Samuel Hopkins
Elijah Taylor (Tyler)
Elijah Clark
Henry Willis

John Thomas
Andrew Willis
John Ryan
John Selby Martin
John Reed
James Haven
William Dorman
John Benston
Charles Roach
Fredrick Barnicassle
William Hosier
George Martin
Jesse Parker
Charles Richardson
Isaac Broughten

COLONEL WILLIAM RICHARDSON.
(1735-1825).

Of the many famous men in Caroline's early days none stand out more prominently than William Richardson, for, besides his military activity during the Revolution, to him more than anyone else Caroline owes her existence as a county.

DAIRY AT GILPIN'S POINT.

(Richardson's home place.)

William Richardson, born 1735, was the son of William and Ann Webb Richardson, Quakers of Talbot county, but in early manhood moved to Dorchester, where he owned large tracts of land. It was while he was a member of the General Assembly from that county in 1773 that he presented a bill which provided for forming Caroline from Dorchester and Queen Anne's counties. The bill was passed and in March 1774 Caroline county was organized with Richardson as one of its original commissioners.

He became a member of the Maryland Convention of Delegates from Caroline at the January session of 1776, which position he resigned in August of the same year upon being commissioned Colonel of the Eastern Shore Battalion of the Maryland Flying Camp. In this position Colonel Richardson became a man of Continental importance, serving his country in this way for over three years. His regiment first saw active service at Harlem Heights, and so well did they acquit themselves that General Washington commended their bravery.

When the men of the flying camp were discharged (Dec. 1776) Richardson continued as colonel in a battalion of re-enlisted men known as the "Fifth Regiment of the Maryland Line." From that time until the close of the war, much of his activity seems to have been confined to the lower section of the Eastern Shore and Delaware. One example of this service is given here. During the month of February 1777, Colonel Richardson was sent with such of the militia and his own regulars as he thought necessary to assist in suppressing the tories in Somerset and Worcester counties. Something of the success of his expedition may be gathered from the following letter from the Council of Safety to Colonel Richardson:

Annapolis, Feb. 19, 1777.

Sir,

We have the honor of transmiting to you the thanks of the General Assembly of this state for your spirited conduct in marching your Battalion of Militia in order to assist General Hooper in quelling the insurrection in Somerset and Worcester Counties.

With the greatest respect and regards,

Sir, your most Obedient Servant,

The Council of Safety.

The same year he was appointed clerk of the county court, but soon found his other duties so pressing that he deputized John Baker to act for him. When the British made their attack upon Philadelphia in December of 1777, Colonel Richardson was commissioned to remove the Continental Treasury to Baltimore. This consisted of such notes and specie as the Continental Congress had on hand for supplying the needs of the provinces.

In '78 he was a member of the convention to ratify the Constitution of the United States. From 1789-1793 he was Presidential elector in the college that elected Washington president. Another prominent position in his later life was the treasurer-ship of the Eastern

Shore, an office which he held at the time of his death in July 1825.

Although not a man of great wealth Richardson lived in such luxury as was the custom in his generation. Upon his plantation, known as Gilpin Point, situated on the Choptank river, stood his family mansion, store house, granary, blacksmith and carpenter shops, and other outbuildings. Like all such estates at that time Gilpin Point resembled a little village in itself. In times of peace gay crowds assembled there, for Richardson was famous for his hospitality; in times of war, supplies were sent there from Annapolis and Baltimore to be distributed among the various companies of the Colonel's regiment.

While a young man, William Richardson married Elizabeth Green. Their family consisted of six children, namely William, Thomas, Daniel Peter, Joseph, Mary, and Ann Webb. Mrs. Richardson, Thomas and Mary, who had married James Price of Easton, died before the Colonel. The other daughter, Ann Webb, became the wife of William Potter of Potter's Landing.

In the days before the Revolution, Richardson owned part interest in a sloop, "The Omega," which is said to have carried cargoes of parched corn to the West Indies. On return trips quantities of coral stone were brought as ballast and from these stones his slaves built a wall surrounding his home.

Along with considerable evidence as to Col. Richardson's being interested in ocean shipping and trading, the following story taken from the life of Commodore Joshua Barney may be of interest here:

Capt. Barney noted for his privateering during the Revolutionary War had been captured, taken to England and lodged in Mill Prison at Plymouth in the year 1781. Upon escaping, he managed to get to the home of a friend, a minister, in the town and there met two farmer friends, Col. Wm. Richardson and Dr. Hindman of hte Eastern Shore of Maryland. These men had gone over on a merchant vessel and upon its being captured, were waiting for an opportunity to return to America. Richardson and Hindman engaged a fishing smack and Barney agreed to carry them to France where they could easily find a way home. Changing his uniform for a fisherman's suit, Barney placed his two friends in the cabin of the boat and set sail across the English Channel. After being out a few hours, the boat was overhauled by an English guard and taken back to Plymouth over a boisterous sea which for several hours had kept our Col. Richardson a prisoner in the hull of the boat and suffering from seasickness. Upon reaching Plymouth, however, Richardson and Hindman who had committed no wrong were released while Barney was again put in prison.

Parts of the old coral wall, a brick dairy, and the fast crumbling tomb of Caroline's most illustrious soldier are all that now remain at Gilpin Point to remind present Carolineans of her original sponsor.

TOMB OF WILLIAM RICHARDSON.
Gilpin Point.

COLONEL WILLIAM WHITELY.

The time of William Whitely's leaving Delaware and coming to Maryland is not definitely known but we do know that when the first gun of the Revolution was fired, April 19, 1775 he was a citizen of Caroline County, well established, of some note and ready to take up arms in defense of his country.

He at once became active in the military organization for the defense of his country and the subjugation of tories; and entered the Eastern Shore militia where he was immediately made Lieutenant.

That he was probably in active service with the Maryland Line is shown by a report (1776) of Col. Wm. Richardson who says,—"Col. Whitely will set off on Monday next and I hope will head the first Division of our Batallion at Philadelphia."

His most important military position, however, was that of Commander-in-chief of the Militia of Caroline County. As Commander-in-chief it was his business to see that all male citizens between the ages of sixteen and fifty were enrolled in the militia and drilled for service. This position was much more important than would seem to us at the present day, and for a youth in his early twenties it was certainly a responsible one. His Revolutionary work continued in some capacity throughout the war and was productive of much good both for his state and nation.

After the close of the war he left the military field and soon became prominent in politics, taking part in the many meetings called at Hillsboro and Denton prior to the War of 1812. Among these was the remonstrance meeting held at Denton relative to the Chesapeake-Leopard trouble at which Whitely acted as chairman, and was voted a member of the Committee of Correspondence which was "Empowered by the meeting to represent Caroline in any subsequent measures taken by her sister counties in vindication of the national honor." Later he became (1811) senator from this district and was a co-worker with Culbreth, signing the remonstrance against the compensation Bill of 1816.

Always a staunch Democrat, he continued for some time after this in local politics, acting as a member of Democratic Caucuses and chairman of important committees, etc.; but when a comparatively young man he withdrew entirely from public life.

While speaking of William Whitely as a military man and a prominent citizen we must not forget to land him as a member of his immediate vicinity.

His wealth made him a prominent figure of his day. His holdings included 1500 acres immediately surrounding Whitelysburg, $30,000 in stocks as well as a number of minor possessions while the ownership of 30 pieces of solid silver table service indicates his mode of living.

Yet he was a liberal supporter of all religious work, giving freely to such causes and with his family was a regular attendant of the Presbyterian Church then organized in Greensboro. Of this church he was one of the founders as well as a member of the first Board of Trustees.

His religion was practical as was evidenced by the readiness and generosity with which he extended a helping hand to his friends.

Col. Whitely retiring entirely from public life at a comparatively early age, returned to Delaware from whence the family came, and there he died, Aug. 15, 1816 aged 63 years.

He has gone! Death took him. The Whitely mansion is gone, fire destroyed it many years ago. His tomb alone remains, a colonial structure in the Whitely burying ground which marks his last resting place. The tomb is covered by a marble slab inscribed with his name and a beautiful tribute.

WILLOW GROVE—HOME OF

MATTHEW DRIVER.

Probably the best preserved example of Colonial architecture to be found in Caroline County is ''The Willows,'' onetime home of Matthew Driver, situated in the Greensboro district and now owned by T. C. Horsey. One can scarcely enter its massive doorways or look at its colonial architecture without visioning the days when ''neighbors dropped in to spend a week or two.''

No definite date is given of the entrance of the Drivers into this territory, but in 1774 when the initial Court of our county was held, Matthew Driver had achieved enough prominence to be appointed Justice of this Court, then held at Melvill's warehouse.

This position he retained during the years of the Revolution and in 1776, in pursuance of the order of the Council of Safety he acted as president of a Court-Martial held at Melvill's Warehouse.

June 24, 1777 he received his commission as Lieutenant-Colonel of Stafford's Company 14th Battalion of Militia in Caroline County, and later we find him corresponding with the Council of Safety relative to appointment of officers for a new Company of Militia in Caroline and signing himself as Matthew Driver, Commander of the 14th Battalion of Militia.

That he was a man of means is shown by the fact of his ownership at the time of his death of six large tracts of land including Willow Grove, his home estate, over £2000 stirling in money, 24 slaves, stock and other valuable holdings.

Little else is definitely known of him but as his record shows he was a typical gentleman of his day and left an unspotted name.

POTTER MANSION.

THE POTTERS OF POTTERS LANDING.

If you should visit Williston, the large brick mansion there would undoubtedly attract your attention. If you asked the history of the house and its owners, this is the story you would be told.

About the middle of the eighteenth century Zabdiel Potter, a sea captain from Rhode Island, settled at this place, building for his home a small brick house. Being an enterprising man, he soon made the place a point of commercial importance on the upper Choptank. In his honor the settlement became known as "Potter's Landing." Boats bound for Baltimore left the Landing laden with cargoes of tobacco and on return trips brought such supplies as the colonists had to import. While on a sea voyage in 1761, Captain Potter died leaving a widow and two sons.

Nathaniel, the elder of the sons, inherited the home place known as Philips Range. During the Revolution he became a prominent figure in the country. From 1774 to 1776 he served in the Maryland Conventions, was Justice of the Orphans' Court and first major in Staffords Company of Militia. In December '76, Isaac McHard, who was appointed to collect food supplies in the province, engaged Maj. Potter to collect, salt, and barrel all the pork he could procure for use in the army. So successful was Maj. Potter in this, that in '78 he was appointed Caroline agent for purchasing provisions for the army. Two years after the close of the war he died leaving a widow but no children. The home at Potter's Landing he willed to his only brother.

This brother, Zabdiel Potter 2nd, was a practicing physician in the county at the outbreak of the Revolution. He was commissioned captain of the first Caroline company of the flying camp, but resigned to become surgeon's mate that he might utilize his medical skill where it was so greatly needed.

Dr. Potter died in 1739 and, like his father, left two sons of whom Caroline is justly proud. In his will he expressed a desire that these sons should engage in trade together, but Nathaniel, the elder, preferred to follow his father's profession. He graduated in medicine at the University of Pennsylvania, and later became a member of the faculty of the University of Maryland, which position he held until his death in 1843.

William, the younger son, became a merchant in Denton. He married Ann Webb, daughter of Colonel William Richardson. For four years (1797, '98, '99 and 1804) he represented Caroline in the lower House of the Assembly. In 1806 he became director for our county of the newly established branch of the Farmer's Bank at Annapolis in Easton.

In 1809 he retired from business and returned to Potter's Landing, where he had the year previous completed the main building of the present mansion. Here he probably expected to spend the rest of his life in farming, which seems to have been his chief delight, but the War of 1812 changed these plans. During this conflict he became Brigadier-General of the Maryland Militia. General Potter three times served on the Governor's Council and in the years 1816 and 1831, being the first named, was next to the governor in state administration.

In the rear of the mansion two marble slabs bear these inscriptions:

"Sacred to the memory of Ann W. Potter who departed this life 12th of Sept. 1836, Aged 64 years."

"General William Potter who departed this life Nov. 25, 1847 in the 76th year of his age."

A few years after the death of General Potter, his sons having died and his daughters married, the property at Potter's Landing was purchased by Colonel John Arthur Willis. During the Civil War four companies of the First Eastern Shore Regiment of Maryland Volunteers were raised at Potter's Landing, it having been Colonel Willis who initiated the formation of this regiment. In later years the name of Potter Town was changed to Williston in memory of the Colonel and his family.

Potter's Landing was for over a century the leading shipping port of Caroline county. During the lives of General Potter and Colonel Willis lines of sailing vessels plied between this wharf and Baltimore, and until the close of the last century, travel between that city and the central part of Caroline was entirely by boats, all of which stopped at this landing. The wharf is still used by the farmers of the neighborhood as a shipping point for their freight.

Flax-hatchel, or Adams'[?]

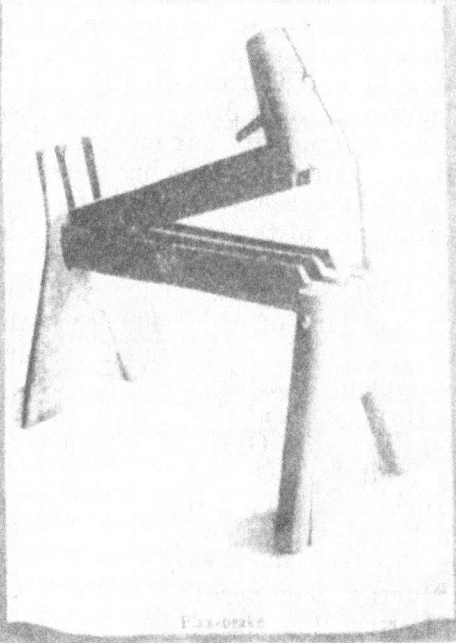

Flax-brake

LIFE IN CAROLINE FOLLOWING THE REVOLUTION.

Some idea of the general condition of Caroline county following the Revolutionary War may be obtained from a survey of the Tax Record for the year 1783. At this time about one-third of the county was reported as being in a state of cultivation besides 66 acres of meadow land and the balance uncleared. The population was about two-fifths as large as at present, hence there was quite as much cleared land in proportion to the inhabitants then as now.

Cleared farm land, on the average, was assessed at about $5 per acre, the wooded land about half as much. At this time there were recorded 290 slaves between the ages of 8 and 14 years. These were assessed at £25 (about $100 each). The 334 male slaves between the ages of 14 and 45 years were given a valuation of £70 ($300) each, while the 266 female slaves between 14 and 36 years of age were assessed at £60 ($250) each.

In addition to slaves, the personal property assessed consisted of silver plate, horses, oxen, and black cattle. There were returned as assessed 3750 horses in the county and 7946 black cattle, besides considerable silverware. The total assessment of real and personal property amounted to £247,000 or slightly over $1,000,000. It is clear, however, that property was assessed very low then in comparison with our modern idea of values.

Without any intention of being personal a few of the largest individual assessments will, perhaps, give the reader a clearer idea of the larger land holdings at that time.

Thomas Goldsborough, at Old Town, was assessed with 1148 acres of land of which 400 acres were cleared. In addition a grist mill and personal property brought the total assessment to £2630, about $12,000.

Thomas Hardcastle, at Castle Hall, about 1800 acres.
Benjamin Silvester, Oakland, 1200 acres.
William Whitely, 1500 acres.
Henry Dickinson, 1800 acres.
William Ennals, 2500 acres.
William Frazier, 1400 acres.
James Murray, 2800 acres.
Zabdiel Potter, 1012 acres.

William Richardson, 795 acres.

It will be understood, of course, that the above named persons were among the most prominent and wealthy in the county at that time. The rate of taxation was about one eightieth (1/80) of the assessed value or $1.25 per hundred dollars.

Before the Revolution there were in the county only about six or eight brick buildings. In the twenty years following the war, this number increased to approximately thirty. The reason for this increase may be explained in the following way.

The early settlers in this section had been thrifty folk, working hard and living simply. Their labors had been rewarded by flourishing crops of tobacco which brought a splendid price in England. With the organization of the county there was a natural impetus to use this acquired wealth for the erection of more comfortable and permanent dwellings, but the close-following war delayed these plans. With the close of the war, however, these people as citizens of a republic felt new power within themselves. The hard, thrifty lives, no longer necessary, men at once started to make such changes in their mode of living as their financial conditions warranted.

The houses built during this period were substantially constructed and of similar design. The main buildings, three stories high with gabled roofs, had a lower wing built at the side which was sometimes of frame rather than brick. The walls were about eighteen inches thick, the massive doors of diagonal timber. So substantially constructed were these mansions, they might have been used as forts in time of seige. Many of them have nobly withstood their worst enemy, Father Time, but others have been forced to yield to other enemies— fire and neglect. To better preserve these worthy structures, some of them have been covered with cement.

Mr. Tubbs, in his chapter on Caroline County in Colonial Eastern Shore, speaking of Cedarhurst and Daffin House, says what is true of all these dwellings:

"The doors, mantles and interior woodwork of these houses speak eloquently of the consummate art of the olden-time carpenters and joiners."

The broad winding stairways found in many of these houses are no less tributes to their makers' art.

With the completion of these fine homes a gay social life sprang up in the county. Such houses were well adapted to the house parties, dances, and quilting parties popular in the early 1800's. In winter the social and political life at Annapolis attracted many of the well-to-do people of the county, while in milder seasons fox-hunting, horse racing, and other outdoor sports were indulged in at home.

But life was not all merry making. The planters, though they usually employed overseers, daily rode over their plantations to superintend the work of slaves in the fields, shops, and stables. On some of the plantations we find records of stores having been kept. The women, beside managing the household affairs, directed the spinning, weaving, knitting, and making of slaves' clothes. The actual work was sometimes done by the slaves, but oftener by women living in the neighboring villages and on small farms. An old account book from a plantation store credits a certain widow with knitting 3 pairs of men's and 2 pairs of women's stockings and weaving 30 yards of toe linen. The same widow is further credited "By making Billy's breeches."

In the absence of public schools, children were taught

WEAVING.

at home by their mothers or in small private schools on the plantations. When the boys were old enough they were sent away to school; the girls stayed at home, for folks in those days thought it better for them to be good housewives than scholars.

The people during these years lived well. The smoke houses were filled with home-cured meats, while fertile fields supplied wheat, corn, and other necessary foodstuffs. The neighboring woods and rivers offered a supply of wild game, fish, crabs and oysters in season. From peaches and apples, pressed in copper stills, brandy was made.

Wheat bread was not commonly used. Except in the wealthiest families, corn bread was the custom. Johnny cake, made of corn meal, and plate cake of wheat flour baked on wooden boards set upon the hearth, seem to have been the favorite breads of the time. Tradition has it that so weary did the people become of corn bread that gradually the wheat acreage increased.

It is interesting to note the clothing worn by people of means at this time. The men wore tight fitting coats, cut to display their fancy waistcoats, knee breeches fastened with silver buckles, long light-colored silk hose, and low black shoes with silver buckles. For riding heavy boots replaced these shoes. Their soft linen shirts had pleated frills and were fastened at the wrist with silver buttons.

The women, not to be outdone by the men, wore gay colored silks with narrow low-neck bodies and long full skirts. Their shoes were dainty, low cut pumps which sometimes boasted high red heels. Of such splendid material were the clothes of that time made and so lasting the styles, we often find single pieces or entire outfits willed from one generation to another.

A simpler form of life was lived in the small frame houses dotting the villages and countryside. In these houses the kitchens with their broad fireplaces were the family living rooms. Over these fires the meals were cooked, near their warmth the spinning done, and by their cherry light during the long winter evenings the tired family rested after the labors of the day.

These houses were meagerly furnished. Except for an odd piece or two, the furniture was made by the men of the family. Wooden or pewter plates, spoons and bowls were used upon the tables. The iron pots, kettles, hominy mortars, and candle molds were so highly prized as to be mentioned in the wills of their owners. Even upon the large plantations, china was rarely used until in later years.

CANDLE MAKING.

The clothing of these folk was coarse, especially in comparison with the silks and linens used by the prosperous planters' families. With the organization of Methodist societies, many of the women adopted the plain full dress and broad brimmed bonnets of that sect.

It is from these sturdy people that Caroline is largely populated now. Many of the prominent old families have no lineal descendants living within her borders. Their former mansions are left to an uncertain fate, their family burying grounds unkept, their very names almost unknown.

(An account of the political conditions about this period may be found under the Life of Thomas Culbreth, given elsewhere in this book.)

OAK LAWN.

EARLY BRICK DWELLINGS IN CAROLINE.

During the early period of Caroline county's history there were a number of pretentious brick dwellings erected within her borders. Indeed some even antedate the formation of the county, having been built previous to the Revolutionary War. Nearly all of these houses were designed alike—a large main building with a low wing extending at the side or rear. Tradition has it that the bricks used in their construction were brought here from England, but there is strong evidence against this being altogether true. In the first place, English bricks of that period were glazed and those used throughout the county were not; second, splendid bricks were made here, so it seems unlikely that with the feeling then existing between England and the colonies that the people of this province would engage in any unnecessary trade with the Mother Country. Near many of these houses, wide but shallow pits can still be seen from which large quantities of clay have been taken, undoubtedly for the purpose of making bricks. For the sake of preserving the bricks many of these houses were later covered with cement.

One of the oldest brick dwellings in Caroline county is the Frazier Flats house, the home of Captain William Frazier, located several miles below Preston on a tract of land known as Fraizer's Neck. The house, built previous to the Revolution, antedates even the county in which it stands. It is a spacious building of red brick, bearing fine examples of workmanship in its colonial doorway, staircase and cornices. Until within the past generation much of the original furniture remained in the mansion, bearing the name of a cabinet maker of Drury Lane, London.

The Frazier house was one of eight similar houses built about that same period on the Eastern Shore. Poplar Grove, on the lower side of Skillington's Creek, not far from Frazier Flats, was one of the eight. It, like nearly all of the others of the group, has been completely destroyed by fire.

Willow Grove, the former home of Matthew Driver, is perhaps better known as the Brick House Farm, long in the possession of the Horsey family at Greensboro. The house, which is one of the most pretentious of the early homes in the county, is kept in splendid condition by both the owners and tenants. The interior is noted for its paneled stairway winding to the third floor, a masterpiece of workmanship. To visit this house as it stands today, more than a century after the death of its builder, gives one an insight into the character of the man whose name figures so prominently in the records of early Caroline. While no carved stone marks his resting place, the house at Willow Grove remains a monument to the memory of Matthew Driver.

INTERIOR OF WILLOW GROVE HOME.

Robert Hardcastle, who came to this county from England in 1748, settled in what was at that time Queen Anne's county. Later with the organization of Caroline, his lands were included within her borders. At the Hardcastle Landing (later Brick Mill), on the west side of the Choptank nearly opposite Melvill's Landing he erected a brick mill and dwelling. The mill was torn down about 1900 but the house is still standing.

Castle Hall, just above Goldsboro, was built by Thomas Hardcastle, a son of Robert Hardcastle of Brick Mill Landing. Mr. Hardcastle, who was a master builder in his day, was delayed in the construction of the house by the outbreak of the Revolution. From its completion until within the present generation the house and farm remained in the Hardcastle family.

An unusual type of house of a much later date may be found on the road leading from Brick Mill Landing to Boonsboro. It is a brick house covered with brown cement, with a tower-like design in one end. (Norman type). The house was built by a Mrs. Weatherby of Pennsylvania. It probably stands on or near the site of a former Hardcastle house, as in the rear of the dwelling is a burying ground with stones bearing the names of Edward and Mary Ann Hardcastle, both of whom died about 1840.

Francis Sellers, largely responsible for the establishment of Hillsboro Academy, was the original owner of the light sand-colored brick house still standing at Hillsboro. It was in this house that Jesse Lee, the famous Methodist itinerant, died while visiting the Sellers family.

The house at Plain Dealing, about a half mile below Denton on the state road, was built in 1789 for a county alms house. Later it was purchased by Mr. Dukes, who remodeled it for a private dwelling. It is one of the two old Caroline houses which has been continuously occupied by descendants of their early owners.

The second such house belonging to the Wright family is located between Federalsburg and Reliance. The land, granted to the Wrights by the English king for valuable services to his Majesty, lies in what is now Caroline, Dorchester and Sussex counties. The house having undergone changes by way of additions and repairs since its early days, is one of the best preserved of the old homes in the county.

The Captain Joseph Richardson house built in 1835 on the Denton hill was one of the finest of the older homes in the county. Its interior woodwork was of mahogany and walnut, while sills at its windows and door were of marble. Sometime during its existence it was used as a hotel, but in 1851 while occupied as a private dwelling, was totally wrecked by fire.

Daffin House in Tuckahoe Neck, built by Thomas Daffin in 1783, was the scene of many social gatherings in its early days. It is said that Andrew Jackson while visiting there met Charles Dickinson, a brother of his hostess, whom he later killed in a duel in Kentucky. A

DAFFIN HOUSE.

dungeon under the house is shown visitors as having been the place where offending slaves were confined. In later years the property passed into the hands of William H. Thawley and is commonly called at present "Thawley House." At some time during its existence it has been covered with a coat of cement, much of which has fallen off. While this gives the exterior rather a dilapidated look, the structure remains in splendid condition.

Oak Lawn, in the Oakland district, was built by Benjamin Silvester in 1783 and bears his initials with that date upon one of its gables. The main building resembles the Frazier Flats house, but Oak Lawn has a long wing extending to the rear, evidently built for kitchens and servants quarters. Some time after the death of its owner it became the possession of Mrs. Mary Bourne, his granddaughter, but has now passed out of the Silvester family.

Colonel William Whitely's home near Whitelysburg was burned about 1840. A well-marked family burying ground may still be seen on the farm.

Colonel William Richardson's home at Gilpin's Point was burned many years ago. There seems to be a diversity of opinion as to whether or not it was a brick building. In 1840, a large frame house was built upon the same sight by John Nichols but suffered a like fate as the Richardson house.

Previous to 1760, a small brick house was built at Potter's Landing. Forty years later, William Potter, a grandson of the first owner, added a three story building to it. Double porches and a cupola which overlooked the Choptank were the distinguishing features of what from its completion has been known as the Potter Mansion.

Marblehead and Cedarhurst, two brick houses near Oak Lawn, in their early days belonged to John Boon, the great grandfather of Charles G. Dukes of Plain Dealing.

CEDARHURST.

THE HUGHLETTS.

The Hughletts have figured largely both politically and financially in Caroline County ever since the first William Hughlett, in 1759, arrived from Northumberland County, Virginia, and settled near Greensboro (then in Queen Anne County).

Thomas Hughlett, eldest son of this family, came into political prominence at the time of the organization of our present county by receiving the appointment as our first sheriff. Later he became coroner, then a member of the legislature.

When the Revolutionary War broke out he entered Military service and was appointed a Captain of the Caroline County Militia and as such was active in the defense of his country, continuing in this service until the close of the war. In later years he was judge of the County Courts which position he held at the time of his death.

His tomb bears the following inscription telling of his merit and worth:

"In memory of
Thomas Hughlett Esquire
Son of William Hughlett and
Mary, his wife,
who departed this life on the 26 day of March 1805, in the 65th year of his age. He was an affectionate husband, and tender parent, a kind master, a social and agreeable friend and an active industrious and enterprising citizen. He was honored by the free suffrage of his fellow citizens with the office of Sheriff of Caroline County then a delegate to the General Assembly of Maryland for many years. A justice of the Peace, and was at the time of his death one of the Associate Judges of the County Court. His integrity, justice and moderation has endeared his memory to the citizens of Caroline. Let his virtues be a stimulus to the descendants to preserve. The slothful will be covered with shame and none but those who persevere will reap the fruit of their labor."

Thos. Hughlett's eldest son, William Hughlett 2nd, was born Sept. 9, 1769. While he held some positions of political preferment, having been in 1816 elected to the Maryland senate and acted as president pro-tem of that body he had few aspirations in that direction.

Because of his extensive land holdings, amounting to several thousand acres, he was better known in the agricultural world and was at one time a member of the "Board of Trustees of the Maryland Agricultural Society of the Eastern Shore."

As landmarks showing the holdings of the second Wm. Hughlett we have the well known line of square stone markers each having the initials W. H. cut thereon while on a few are such inscriptions as "Last grant," "Skin Ridge," "Last bit," etc. The line of markers extends from near Milford, Delaware to Whitelysburg thence through Hughes Corner above Whitelysburg and on through the Maryland line to Greensboro, while in Talbot County almost the entire neck of Bolingbroke is spanned by these markers.

On leaving Caroline this William Hughlett removed to "Warwick Manor" in Dorchester County near Secretary Creek. Later his home was at "Pleasant Valley" near Easton, where he died in 1845.

His eldest son, Col. William R. Hughlett of "Chancellors Point," was well known and highly esteemed. His daughter and grand-children are present residents of Greensboro, Caroline County, and of Talbot County, and end the long line of a well known and honorable family, whose residence in this section covers a period of more than a century and a half.

FRAZIER FLATS HOUSE.

WILLIAM FRAZIER—METHODIST ORGANIZER:

In the year 1767, Sarah Frazier of Dorchester deeded to her eleven year old son a tract of land in that county known as Willenborough. Three years before, upon the death of his father, Alexander Frazier, the boy had inherited the home plantation with other tracts of land lying between Skillington's and Edmondson's creeks, fronting on the Choptank river. With the formation of Caroline this land (about 1400 acres in all) was included in the new county and became known as Frazier's Neck.

The house upon the home plantation is still standing and its splendid structure carries out the tradition that it is one of eight similar dwellings built on the Eastern Shore about seventeen hundred and fifty. Its splendid furniture was made in London and until a generation ago many of the original pieces remained in the house.

Of William Frazier's life we know but little until in March, 1776 when he was commissioned 3rd Lieutenant of the 4th Independent Company of Maryland. In December of the same year he became 1st Lieutenant in Captain Dean's company of the 5th Regiment of the Maryland Flying Camp. Later he was promoted to a captaincy in the militia. In March 1783 he became a Justice of the Caroline County Court, but William Frazier's prominence in Caroline's affairs came neither thru his military or judicial career. He was a devoted follower of John Wesley and as such was largely responsible for the organization of Methodist societies in the lower part of the county. In his home at Frazier's Flats, the front room on the upper floor was used as a meeting place and is known to-day as the "Church Room." An outgrowth of this was Frazier's Chapel, supposedly located on the present sits of Preston, which later became Bethesda congregation and is now Preston Methodist Episcopal Church.

To Frazier's hospitable home came Jesse Lee, the Methodist circuit rider, and later Francis Asbury on his annual trips from Massachusetts to Georgia rejoiced in the rest and companionship found there. In the latter's journal we find repeatedly such notes as these:

May, 1801—We had a long ride (from Cambridge) to William Frazier's through dust and excessive heat. It was hard to leave loving souls, so we tarried until morning.

April 1805. We came to brother Frazier's. The fierceness of the wind made the Choptank impassable; we had to rest awhile, and need had I, being sore with hard service.

In the family burying ground at Frazier Flats two stone slabs may be seen bearing these inscriptions:

Captain William Frazier. Born 1756. Died 1807.

Henrietta Maria Frazier. Died 1846, in the 84th year of her age.

A nobler monument is erected to their memory in the form of Methodist churches scattered throughout lower Caroline which are the result of the patient labors of this good man and his wife.

EARLY CHURCHES AND SOCIETIES.

The Episcopal Church and the Quaker Societies seem to have been the two religious sects that were earliest represented in what is now Caroline county territory. For more than fifty years before the county was organized official accounts of the activities of these denominations have been recorded.

THE EPISCOPAL CHURCH.

A large majority of the early settlers on the Eastern Shore came from England and as a natural consequence the Episcopal Church, being the Established Church of England, seems to have been at one time the strongest denomination along the shore. Parishes were laid out, chapels erected, and clergy brought from England. Upon the outbreak of the Revolution, however, these men who were bound by oath "to be loyal and bear allegiance to the government of England," were forced to take the oath required by loyal colonists of Maryland or return to England. As most of them preferred the latter course, the churches and parishes were abandoned. Feeling ran so high in those days that the English church suffered neglect even at the hands of their vestries.

Another reason for the decline of power was the opposition to the "forty pound tax." This was a poll tax of 40 pounds of tobacco for the support of the clergy, in addition to such general taxes as were necessary for building and repairs of chapels. It was levied, irrespective of creed, for the Established Church. The Declaration of Rights, adopted 1776, forbade all further assessments for the support of the minister, but gave the legislature power to impose a common tax for the support of Christian religion in general. Everyone paying this tax was given the right to designate the denomination to which his tax should be credited. So bitter had the people become in regard to the idea of a church tax that they greatly favored the Methodist societies who made no mention of a tax and whose minister received the very humble salary of sixty dollars a year.

The Act of Assembly establishing St. John's Parish was passed in 1748. After outliving the territory taken in Queen Anne's and Talbot Counties and originally held by St. Paul's and St. Luke's Parishes the line extended into what is now Caroline County and apparently included about all of the county west of the Choptank River.

At this time the parish church was standing in Queen Anne's County near Tuckahoe Bridge (now Hillsboro). This church was evidently built considerably earlier, as a record in 1717 stated that 1100 lbs. of tobacco was paid to Thos. Fisher for repairing the said church. In 1737 the edifice seems to have been again repaired and at this time enlarged. Rev. Mr. Cox, who appears to have been the first rector of St. John's Parish, remained until 1753.

Shortly before the Revolution the three settlements at Tuckahoe Bridge (Hillsboro), Choptank Bridge (Greensboro) and Nine Bridges (Bridgetown) seem to have been quite thriving and apparently contended for the honor and advantage of having the main church and vestry house in which the rector was to live. The Vestry decided in 1767, as a compromise apparently, that the parish church should be built on the road from Tuckahoe Bridge to Choptank Bridge, and that a chapel should be built at Nine Bridges. Two acres of land for a church site were purchased from Edward Barwick for £10 ($50) at or near the present site of Ridgely. This site, however, was not used and the land was subsequently offered for sale.

The Assembly of 1768 authorized the erection of the main church at Tuckahoe Bridge and the chapel at Nine Bridges. Thomas Hardcastle, of Castle Hall, probably built the church at Bridgetown, as he received several payments from the vestry at various times. The bricks used in the building of this church were brought up the river to Choptank Bridge as well as 1600 bushels of oyster shells used in furnishing lime and mortar. John McConigal agreed to build the brick chapel and parish house at Tuckahoe Bridge for £1075. At this time Rev. Thomas Aiken was rector òf both churches.

About 1820 a visiting clergyman reported that the church both at Tuckahoe Bridge and Nine Bridges had fallen into bad repair and the congregations greatly lessened owing to the influence of Methodism.

Rev. Robert Goldsborough in 1844 settled in Hillsboro and held services in the Academy there as well as at Bridgetown. Six years later he was elected permanent rector and in 1853 the corner stone of the present church in Hillsboro was laid by Bishop Whitehead of Illinois. The building was blown down in December following, but work was soon re-commenced and the church consecrated in 1858.

Rev. G. F. Beaven took charge of the parish in 1857, succeeding Rev. Mr. Goldsborough. At this time the rector reported that the church at Greensboro had a good sized congregation. From a bequest of about $1000 by Mary Reed, the present church at Greensboro was completed in 1875.

St. Mary's White Chapel Parish.

The population of Dorchester County having increased and expanded, it became necessary in 1725 to divide the Great Choptank Parish which included territory now belonging to Caroline. A new parish was formed, known as St. Mary's White Chapel Parish. It included, beside a small part of Dorchester, all of what is now Caroline County, east of the Choptank.

Thirty years later the Assembly authorized the erection of a chapel in the parish. In the meanwhile, no doubt, services had been held within the parish, but this was the first consecrated building. The site selected was on the county road that now leads from Federalsburg to Hunting Creek, about two miles from Linchester.

The chapel was used for church services until 1776 when it, like other such chapels was abandoned by clergy and vestry. Unused for many years, about 1812 the building was torn down and the material divided among people of the community. Benjamin and Henry Nichols, who assisted in razing the building, took as their share some of the bricks which may still be seen in a chimney of the house owned by the late Jasper Nichols, near Hynson. Part of the lot where the chapel stood was used as a burying ground and has been known for the last century as "Church Old-Field." A broken marble slab, bearing the name of Sarah Haskins, is all that remains on this once sacred land.

NECK MEETING HOUSE.

QUAKER SOCIETIES.

A religious society known as Quakers, or Friends, was established in England in 1647. Later, because of persecution, many of their followers, forced to seek new homes, came to America. Maryland had been settled in the meanwhile to provide a refuge for the religiously oppressed of the Old World, and naturally received a large share of these wanderers. They were a quiet but substantial people avoiding all forms of display and living simple, peaceful lives.

The Friends did not claim to be a church but rather a "religious society." They employed no ministers but allowed members the privilege of speaking in their meetings when moved by the Spirit to do so. There were leaders in the Society who traveled about on horseback visiting the various meetings, but there was no salary attached to such services. The government of the Society of Friends consisted of a center meeting to which preparatory meetings reported monthly. The center meeting was required to report to the quarterly meeting who in turn made its reports to a yearly meeting. These reports, which consist of marriage records, settlement of the estates of minors, accounts of monies collected, and other such matters, have been preserved and contain much interesting and valuable information.

Caroline county, in its early days, sent reports from its preparatory meetings to Third Haven Monthly Meeting at Easton. As the societies grew in strength, however, a monthly meeting was established at North West Fork, with preparatory meetings at Marsh Creek and Greensboro.

In 1797 the Nicholite Friends (so called because they were followers of Joseph Nichols) located in Caroline County, Maryland. After existing as a separate society for twenty years, finding that the vital and fundamental principles of their society were similar to that of the Friends, concluded that a union might prove of mutual advantage, therefore applied, and were accepted as members of Third Haven Meeting.

Their rigid rules of discipline, especially in dress, being very objectionable to their young people, made them anxious for a little more liberty,—one of their points of self-denial being in regard to wearing dyed garments, and cultivating bright-colored flowers. Prior to the dissolution of their society, they generously transferred to this meeting (Third Haven) their three meeting-houses in Caroline County, namely: Centre (near Preston), Tuckahoe Neck (near Denton) and Northwest Fork (now Pine Grove). About four hundred persons became incorporated with the society, though some afterwards emigrated to Canada and the Western States. Among those who remained here were Elisha Dawson, Elizabeth Twiford, and James Harris, all ministers in much esteem. Dennis Kelley and family, Levin Pool and family, John Wright and family, Preston Godwin and family, Samuel Emerson and family, Wm. Maloney and family, Willis Charles and family, Jonathan Shannahan and family, and Anthony Whitely, were some of the most prominent members who connected themselves with this meeting.

FRIENDS.

The Quakers of Talbot county established in 1676 the Third Haven Monthly Meeting at Easton. This was the center to which preparatory meetings throughout Talbot and Dorchester later made reports at regular intervals. One of the earliest of these meetings was held at Marshy Creek previous to the formation of Caroline county. Later the meetings at Greensboro and North West Fork were established under Third Haven, but in 1799, North West Fork becoming a monthly meeting, both Marshy Creek and Greensboro reported there.

MARSHY CREEK MEETING.

Among the records of the Third Haven Monthly Meeting in Easton we find in 1727 an account of Marshy Creek Meetings beings held regularly, but we do not find the date of their organization. Thirty years later Third Haven ordered "the several weekly meetings to proceed to a collection to raise money to assist friends at Marshy Creek Meeting in the building of a new meeting house and to make a return of their subscriptions to next monthly meeting." This indicates that there had been a meeting house there previous to that time, but we find no other record of its existence. The house, built with the money thus collected, was a small frame building, plainly furnished, with a sliding partition which separated the men and women during business meetings. It was erected on a half acre lot deeded in 1764 by William Haskins to William Edmonson near the present site of Preston and used by the Friends until 1849.

At that time James Dixon deeded to the Trustees of the Society of Friends a piece of land located in what is now Preston for the small sum of $5. The meeting house built on this site is still standing and was used until the erection recently of a more modern brick structure adjoining it. When the land was purchased at Preston we find records of the old building and land at Marshy Creek being sold to the colored people for $100. The building was used by them as a Methodist Church until a few years ago when a new church was erected on the old site.

OLD FRIENDS MEETING HOUSE, PRESTON.

NORTH WEST FORK MEETING.

Levin Wright and Mark Noble of North West Fork asked permission in 1794 to hold Quaker meetings in their homes. This resulted in the organization of a preparatory meeting which in 1799 occupied the building previously used by the Nicholites at Federalsburg. In the same year a monthly meeting was established there with preparatory meetings at Marsh Creek and Greensboro. In later years the meeting house was moved to Piney Grove, about two miles west of Federalsburg and enlarged to accommodate the increased attendance.

GREENSBORO FRIENDS.

In 1795 the second Friends' Meeting House in Caroline County was completed at Greensboro. The house stood on a half acre of land deeded by Batcheldor Chance to Thomas Hopkins and Edward Needles for £5. Part of the land was to be used as a Quaker burying ground and a few of the old stones may still be seen on the west side of Main Street between the homes of Dr. Malone and Mr. Fred P. Roe.

A VOICE FROM NECK MEETING HOUSE.

Long have I stood and am now very old,
  Some of my tales I never have told,
But here are some that you shall hear,
  Since you are so anxious, my dear, my dear.

On long past Sundays, Friends here would meet,
  And each sit solomnly in his seat,
Then during the war soldiers came here to stay,
  Once I was school, and my grounds used for play.

Wonderful changes-have I seen,
  Sometimes I wonder what they can mean,
One day I was startled most sadly, Ah me!
  By what men call a train on the M. D. & V.

Now the horseless carriage goes riding by,
  And only last Sunday I saw one in the sky,
No wonder you children come here to see me
  And write me down as history.

THE NECK MEETING HOUSE.

About a mile from Denton, on the Hillsboro road stands the Neck Meeting House, a quaint old wooden structure of a century ago. A dense growth of underbrush almost obscures the building from public view and a substantial wire fence protects it from curious prowlers. The building, long ago robbed of its benches, librarry and other simple furnishings is slowly crumbling to decay.

In the year 1801, Quakers living near Denton who had formerly belonged to the Nicholite Friends, asked Third Haven Meeting for the privilege of holding preparatory meetings and building a meeting house. This request was granted and in the next year, the situation having been selected and plans for the building completed it was found that $60 was needed beyond what could be supplied by the Neck Meeting. This amount was raised by other Friends and on September 26, 1802 the first service was held in the new building. The land (1½ acres) was deeded by William Wilson to Tristram Needles, and other trustees, for the use of the Society of Friends in consideration of £4, 10s.

Besides being used as a meeting house, Eliza Heacock of Philadelphia held private school there about 1856. Her splendid teaching ability and sterling character built up a strong private school. Another well-known teacher of the school was Miss Rachel B. Satterthwaite, of Denton.

Previous to the Civil War abolitionist meetings with speakers of national fame are said to have been held in the meeting house. During the war, Northern troops used the grounds for a camping place and the house for barracks. The blue coats, worn and tired, would politely withdraw on Sunday morning in order that the Friends might hold their meetings unmolested and some are said to have returned at times to attend the services.

About 1890, for lack of funds, Neck Meeting House was abandoned as a place of worship. To protect the spot where his parents lie buried, Edward Tylor, a half brother of Miss Satterthwaite, secured legislative enactment to purchase the land about the meeting house and further protected the grounds by the erection of a substantial iron grating.

In a poem of Miss Sattherthwaite's she thus pays a final tribute to the meeting house:

"And a sheltering place for the birds of the air
May this house become, where once echoed prayer,
But the Spirit of God is above heat and frost
And the echoes of prayer can never be lost.
The life of a Christian for ages may gleam,
Though his sect cannot wear Christ's coat without seam."

(Written from material collected by Denton School.)

THE NICHOLITES.

A very pious religious sect known as the Nicholite Friends had in the latter part of the eighteenth century quite a stronghold in that section of our county bordering on the upper Northwest Fork river and Marshy Hope creek. The Nicholites first permanent place of public worship was in a meeting house erected on the banks of what is still known as Quaker Meeting House Branch, near the site of the old colored school at Federalsburg. About 1817, the Nicholites were accepted as members of the Third Haven Meeting and generously transferred to this meeting their three meeting houses in Caroline, namely: Center (near Preston), Tuckahoe Neck (near Denton), and North West Fork (now Pine Grove).

THE METHODIST CHURCH.

As early as 1771 we find evidence of the teachings of John Wesley having penetrated to the Eastern Shore of Maryland. Freeborn Garretson, of Kent Circuit, seems to have been the first organizer of Methodist societies in Caroline, having visited here about 1776. Later, Jesse Lee and James Moore rode this circuit in tireless efforts preaching and organizing new societies. Francis Asbury, the greatest Methodist itinerant, in his trips from Massachusetts to Georgia, frequently stopped at the homes of Captain Frazier, Major Mitchell and Henry Downes, all of this county.

Referring to Asbury and other Methodist circuit riders, Scharf says:

"The people, used to ill-read services and dull written sermons flocked to hear these marvelous preachers who prayed without book and preached without manuscript; who went on horse-

—114—

back to the people instead of waiting for these to come to them; who lived on $60 a year, and never said a word about advowsons and forty per poll, about personal livings and fat glebes."

Extracts from Asbury's journal (1789-1813) prove his enthusiasm and tireless energy. A few which mention his visits to Caroline are given here:

Nov. 23, 1789. Came through rain from Wye to Tuckahoe.
Nov. 27, 1789. There was a good attendance at Choptank Bridge. I ordained 5 persons to the office of deacons.
Dec. 1790. The next day being rainy we had but 100 hearers at Tuckahoe, whereas we expected that had it heen a clear day we should have 500 or 600. I preached in the evening at Choptank Bridge to a few people.
Dec. 1791. Attended Quarterly meeting at Greensboro, commonly called Choptank Bridge. We had a strict and living lovefeast and powerful testimonies.
Oct. 1792. Thence we rode to Choptank, now Greensboro.
.... 1795. Crossed Choptank River at Ennall's Ferry—9 men, 3 horses and a carriage on board.
July 1796. I rode to Greensboro through excessive heat.
.... 1799. Preached at Tuckahoe. Held meeting in Wm. Frazier's dwelling house.
1803. James Moore exhorted at Easton. Asbury preached. Never was preacher more respected in Talbot than our brother Moore.
May 1803. I came from Dorchester along to Major Mitchell's in Caroline. The wind was east, the evening cold and I unwell. At Denton I took to bed awhile. We continued on, however, and reached Choptank.
1813. A rapid ride brought us to Abraham Collins (near Concord) in Caroline. I preached at 3 o'clock and went home to dine with Peter T. Causey (near Smithville).

For three years after having ridden Caroline circuit Jesse Lee traveled with Asbury. While stationed in Annapolis he attended camp meeting at Tuckahoe (near Hillsboro) and there contracting a fatal fever died at Henry Sellers' home in Hillsboro, September 12, 1816.

The first Methodist church in Denton was named for James Moore, of whom Asbury writes in his journal, and was known for many years as Moore's Chapel.

The first Methodist chapels in the county were the outgrowth of meetings held in private homes. They were located at Tuckahoe Bridge (Hillsboro), Choptank Bridge (Greensboro) and near the present site of Preston. These buildings, simple in design were rudely but substantially constructed by members of the various societies. The present Methodist Episcopal Churches at these places are results of these chapel meetings.

An interesting story is told of the origin of the Methodist Episcopal Church in Denton, but how authentic it may be we cannot say. A traveling minister nearing the town on horseback decided to pass through the place singing and if invited to stop would take it as a sign that he should organize a meeting there. He carried out his plan and soon after entering the village was asked to alight. This he did, and true to his purpose, organized the first Methodist society in Denton.

Moore's Chapel, previously referred to, was the first church ever built in Denton. It stood on the site of the Methodist burying ground behind the present M. E. church. In this building on March 24, 1816, James Moore, for whom the chapel was named, preached the first Methodist sermon ever preached in the town.

MOORE'S CHAPEL.

The entrance to the chapel was through a vestibule, from which a stairway led to the gallery. This gallery was for the use of slaves, for at that time the colored people had no church of their own, but attended the same services as their master when permitted. After

—116—

service they would sometimes sing as the white congregation passed out. The interior of this church, as all others of that time, was quite different from those of the present. Carpet was not used except on the floor of the pulpit and a runner up each aisle. The desk was narrow and so tall as to reach almost to the preacher's chin. The pews, narrow and straight, were uncomfortable enough to keep even the sleepiest listener awake.

In 1867 Moore's Chapel was moved and the present brick church built. The old chapel may still be seen, almost in ruins, on North Third Street, where for a long while it was used by the colored people as a church and later as their hall.

(Material contributed by Denton School.)

CONCORD CHURCH.

In 1804 John Mitchell, Isaac Collins, Sr., Horatio Short, Francis and James Sullivan were trustees of the society then meeting at the home of Abraham Collins. These men, with the approval of the minister in charge, purchased from Mr. Collins 1 1/20 acres of land for a meeting house site. The chapel was to be known as "Concord" and from that time on the cross roads, too, have been called by the same name, apparently the only one ever given it. Twenty-five years later a permanent building was erected and the old chapel passed out of existence as such, so far as is known.

LEE'S CHAPEL.

A barn on the farm of Mr. Freeborn Elwanger near Whitelysburg has an interesting history. In the latter part of the 18th century people living in that section by the name of Lee were instrumental in building a chapel on their land. The chapel was a small wooden building with hewn framework put together by means of wooden pegs. The few nails used were made by the village blacksmith. The chapel was named for the Lee family and sometime during its existence as a church a member of that family served as its minister. With the growth of the neighborhood, Shepherd's Chapel succeeded the original one which was moved to its present site and converted into a barn.

(From material contributed by Lowe's School.

St. Elizabeth's Catholic Church. (Denton.)

Incomplete records show that previous to the organization of Caroline as a county, a Catholic mission existed in the vicinity of Denton. In the absence of a regular church building it is probable that services were held in private homes. From Bohemia Manor in Cecil and St. Joseph's Chapel in Talbot, Jesuit fathers came to serve the mission. Probably one of the earliest of these priests was Rev. Joseph Mosley, who served Old St. Joseph in 1787.

In 1824 Benjamin Denny deeded to Ambrose Marshall, then Bishop of Maryland, an acre of land which was part of the tract known as Mt. Andrew. It was on this lot that the first Catholic church was erected, a little to the north of the present building. The date of the erection of the church is not known. In Captain William Richardson's will, dated 1831, four prints and the bust of Arch Bishop Carroll were ordered removed to the Catholic Church at Denton, there to be disposed of by the priest. This clearly indicates the erection of the building some time previous to that date. Residents of Denton remember the building as being a rather pretentious one containing various pieces of imagery, busts and pictures, but bearing marks of old age. In 1890 when the present church was erected, the old building was torn down and some of its splendid white pine probably used in the new building.

In 1845 Anastatia Rhodes of this county very generously willed to Samuel Eccleston, the Archbishop of Baltimore, her splendid farm situated on the road between Denton and Williston. He was to dispose of the land "as best to promote the cause of the Holy Catholic religion in Caroline county especially for the support and good of the Catholic church in Denton." The place, which is still known as the "Catholic Farm," was not sold until 1867 when its sale brought the sum of $2500.

PLAIN DEALING.

CAROLINE COUNTY ALMS HOUSES.

For fourteen years after Caroline's organization we find the Court records filled with such items as these:

> Ordered by the court that Nancy P...... be allowed in next year's levy at the rate of 6 shillings for her support.

> Ordered that there be levied in the next levy the sum of 20£ to James J........ for burying Rebecca S........, finding coffin, sheet etc.

> Ordered by the court that 64 Lbs. tobacco a month be paid Mary B...... for support of Levi T...... now 3 years old, orphan son of Sarah T...... now deceased.

In spite of large sums thus granted for this use the poor in the county were not properly cared for. To remedy this, in November 1788 the General Assembly passed a law requiring that there be an alms and work house built at the general expense of the county. The justices were to assess and levy the sum of £300 current money in each year from 1789 to 1790 to meet this expense. An annual levy was to be made for the running expense of the institution.

William Whitely, Joseph Douglass, Thomas Hardcastle, Joshua Wallace and Henry Downes were appointed trustees to purchase land and erect thereon suitable buildings for the institution. The land selected consisted of six acres of a tract known as Lloyd's Regulation about one half mile from Denton on the road which led to Potter's Landing (Williston). It was purchased from John Cooper and Michael Lucas for £18 current money. Of the original buildings we know little except that the main one was a splendidly built brick house surrounded by numerous smaller ones of frame. While the buildings were being erected, the trustees were authorized to rent a house near the county seat for the reception of the poor and such vagrants as should be committed to their charge.

The trustees were responsible for the good government of the alms and work houses. The poor were kept in the alms house and such as were able were compelled to work, while the work house lodged the vagrants, beggars, vagabonds and disorderly people of the county. They, too, were compelled to work and in case of misbehavior were at one time subjected to ten lashes of the whip. Later, however, this punishment was changed to an extension of time in the institution.

An overseer was appointed with a salary of £75 annually beside food, fuel, and house room for himself and family. He kept a record of all persons committed to his care, all expenses for their support, and such monies as he receiped from their labor. He was also responsible for the general management of the place in the absence of the trustees.

When a man or woman was committed to either house he was forced to wear upon the shoulder of the right sleeve of his top garment a badge bearing the Roman letters P. C. cut into red or blue cloth. There was a punishment for refusal to wear the badge and a fine for the overseer allowing any one to omit it.

It was found necessary to make some provision for out-pensioners. These were people who could be cared for more conveniently in private homes than in a public institution. An allowance of not more than $30 annually was to be paid each of them and at no time was the number of out-pensioners to exceed ten. Such orphans as were committed to the poor house were, upon opportunity, bound out to tradesmen or mechanics who promised

PRESENT ALMS HOUSE.

to feed, clothe, and lodge them as well as instruct them in their trade.

In 1823 there was a general feeling in the county that there was not land enough at the Alms-house farm and that a larger tract, properly tilled, would be more satisfactory. Accordingly, the old property was sold at public auction for $505 to Mr. James Dukes and remodeled by him for private use. The brick building, which is in excellent condition, is still owned by the heirs of the original purchaser. The land purchased for the new farm contained 325 acres, known as the George Garey Farm, the price paid being $2197.58½. Since that time some of the wooded land has been cleared, the timber sold and additional land purchased.

WHEN TOBACCO WAS KING.

Tobacco played an important part in the early business transactions of our state. During the Colonial period no other crop is so often mentioned in Maryland history. Scharf says, "The processes of government, society, and domestic life began and ended with tobacco. Laws were made more or less with reference to this staple—to protect it, maintain its value in price, and to enhance its each exchangeableness."

In our county, as elsewhere, tobacco came to be used in place of money. Salaries and wages of every kind were paid in this currency, and if it were refused in payment of any obligation, the debt was absolved. It is interesting to know that one pound of tobacco would buy three pounds of beef, two pounds a fat pullet, and a hogshead, when shipped to England, would provide a family with luxuries for a year.

The culture of this crop was largely responsible for Maryland becoming a slave state. As the wealth of a man was estimated in his annual acreage of tobacco, it naturally became advantageous for the planters to have plenty of cheap labor. One slave could till with ease 6000 hills of tobacco and five acres of corn. Under pressure this amount was sometimes doubled, but it is generally recognized that the Maryland planters were not hard task-masters and usually owned sufficient slaves to prevent the necessity for extreme overwork.

The early settlers were extravagant in everything they did and in nothing more so than in their abuse of the soil for the cultivation of tobacco. New lands proved to be best adapted for this crop and each season virgin soil was broken for its culture. Upon the used land other crops were planted but with no thought for the increase of its fertility. Gradually the land "wore out" and cereals took the place of the "weed" in the field, but never in commercial importance.

During this period tobacco warehouses naturally became places of considerable importance in the county. The one belonging to David Melvill became the most prominent because of its use as a temporary court house. Others were Hughlett's at Bridgetown (Greensboro); Richardson's at Gilpin Point; North West Fork at Federalsburg; and Hunting Creek, near Linchester. The act authorizing the erection of the Bridgetown Warehouse is typical of those which provided for the others in the county. It is interesting to note the articles necessary for inspecting the tobacco:

"BE IT ENACTED by the General Assembly of Maryland, That William Hughlett, of Caroline County, be and he is hereby authorized to build at Bridgetown a warehouse, for containing and securing tobacco offered for inspection, if in the judgment of the levy court of Caroline county, the erecting of such warehouse would promote the public interest and convenience, and he, the said William Hughlett, or those claiming to hold under him, shall provide and keep constantly in repair, beams, screws, scales, weights, brands and marking irons, and all other things necessary for inspecting tobacco brought into the said warehouse for inspection; and the said warehouse, when erected and finished, shall be deemed a public warehouse, and the proprietor or proprietors thereof may demand, and shall be entitled to receive, one dollar for each hogshead of tobacco inspected at the said warehouse, before such hogshead shall be removed, as a full compensation for the expense of erecting the said warehouse, and keeping the same in repair, and for the providing of proper scales, weights, brands and marking irons, and all other things necessary for inspecting tobacco and for the payment of the salary or salaries to the inspector or inspectors of the said warehouse, as the proprietor or proprietors of the said warehouse shall agree to pay; and if any tobacco shall remain in the said warehouse above one year after inspection, the proprietor or proprietors of the said warehouse may demand, and shall be entitled to receive for each hogshead the further sum of twelve and one-half cents for every month thereafter."

Of such value were the contents of these warehouses that persons convicted of setting fire to one of them were condemned to suffer the penalty of death without benefit of clergy.

The vestrymen and church wardens of each parish were required to meet at their respective churches between the first and tenth of September each year to nominate and recommend to the Governor two or four able and efficient planters well skilled in tobacco to act as inspectors for the warehouses within their parish. The certificates of recommendation thus made were forwarded to the Governor who then made the appointments. The salaries for inspectors ranged from four to ten thousand pounds of tobacco annually. Each year these men filed with the court their accounts. The following is a copy of one from Hughlett's Warehouse at Bridgetown:

Filed November Term of Court, 1774. The account of James Ginn inspector at Bridgetown, 1774, Caroline County, Bridgetown, Warehouse, Dr.
To inspectors salary in tobacco ....4800 lbs.
To 6 lb. Lead at 6p. 3s. To 2 lb. rope 9p. 1/6.......... 36

To a new scale gallows and post, 5 lbs. To 2 new prises
at 15 fartherings 302
To 2 new sweeps, 2 crutches, 2 new tongues and putting
in, 15 fartherings 120
To cutting 7 letters in the Warehouse, Brading Iron 7/6.. 60
                                                         ————
                                                         5318
1774 Caroline County
                               Cr.

By 145 crop Hogshead of Tobacco at 20 lbs. per hogshead. 4060
By 15 Transfer Hogshead at 56 lbs. per 840
By 43 lb. gained by P. C. P. shrinkage at 16 per hundred. 56
                                                         ————
Errors Excepted James Ginn 4956
By balance due me, 362 lbs. tobacco 362
                                                         ————
                                                         5318
     December 14, 1774, then came James Ginn before me, one of
his lordship justices of the peace, for the said county, and made
oath on the Holy Evangels of Almighty God that this account is
just and true as it stand. Stated Sworn before me.
                                             Nath. Potter.

———————————

STRANGE MONEY OF LONG AGO.

———

Tobacco money! How strange it seems! Still for
many years colonial people of our own county used tobacco almost entirely as money. A man used tobacco to
pay his taxes, to pay his doctor's bill, to buy his marriage license, to buy his lumber, to pay his workers, to
purchase his slaves, to pay the governor of the province
and even to pay the preacher's salary. Just a little
above Denton stood a tobacco warehouse belonging to
David Melvill. The inspector's salary paid in tobacco
equalled about $265, as tobacco was valued at 3 or 4
cents a pound. English ships called at Melvill's Landing, where the warehouse stood and exchanged their
goods for tobacco. No doubt many hogsheads of tobacco have been rolled down our streets to the Great
Choptank in colonial days.
                                    ARTHUR LEE RAIRIGH.

THE DUEL BETWEEN DICKINSON AND JACKSON.

The circumstances connected with the famous duel between Andrew Jackson of Tennessee and Charles Dickinson of Caroline county, Maryland, are herewith given as gleaned from several apparently reliable sources.

Jackson who had been retired from public life was then (1806) living on a farm along the Cumberland River in Tennessee, about ten miles from Nashville. He had a passion for fine horses and it became a principal branch of his farming business, to raise them from the best stock imported from Virginia and North Carolina. More for the purpose of exhibiting his stock and recommending it to purchasers, than to indulge in the practices common at such places, he brought out his favorite horses upon the race-courses of the day and lost and won in many a well-contested field.

Jackson owned a favorite horse, named Truxton, which he was challenged to run against a horse owned by a Mr. Erwin and his son-in-law, Charles Dickinson. The stakes were to be two thousand dollars on a side, in cash notes, with a forfeiture of eight hundred dollars. The bet was accepted, and a list of notes made out; but when the time for running arrived, Erwin and Dickinson chose to pay the forfeit. Erwin offered sundry notes not due, withholding the list which was in the hands of Dickinson. Jackson refused to receive them, and demanded the list, claiming the right to select from the notes described upon it. The list was produced, a selection made, and the affair satisfactorily adjusted. Afterwards a rumor reached Dickinson, that General Jackson charged Erwin with producing a list of notes different from the true ones. In an interview between Jackson and Dickinson, the former denied the statement, and the latter gave his author. Jackson instantly proposed to call him in; but Dickinson declined. Meeting with the author shortly after, Jackson had an altercation with him, which ended in blows. Here the affair ought to have ended. But there were those who desired to produce a duel between Jackson and Dickinson. The latter was brave and reckless, a trader in blacks and blooded horses, and reputed to be the best shot in the country. Exasperation was produced; publication followed publication; insults were given and retorted; until, at length,

General Jackson was informed that a paper, more severe than its predecessors, was in the hands of the printer, and that Dickinson was about to leave the state. He flew to Nashville, and demanded a sight of it in the printer's hands. It was insulting in the highest degree, contained a direct imputation of cowardice, and concluded with a notice that the author would leave for Maryland, within the coming week. A stern challenge, demanding immediate satisfaction, was the consequence. The challenge was given on the 23d of May, and Dickinson's publication appeared the next morning. Jackson pressed for an instant meeting; but it was postponed, at the request of the other party, until the 30th, at which time it was to take piace, at Harrison's Mills, on Red River, within the limits of Kentucky. Dickinson occupied the intermediate time in practicing. Jackson went upon the ground firmly impressed with the conviction that his life was eagerly sought, and in the expectation of losing it, but with a determination which such a conviction naturally inspired in a bosom that never knew fear. As Dickinson rode out to the place with a party of friends, he fired at a string supporting an apple and cut the cord in two. It had been agreed that the two men should use pistols and stand eight paces apart facing the same direction and that at the word they should turn towards each other and fire as they chose.

Later, however Jackson and his second Dr. Overton decided it best and agreed that Dickinson shoot first. When all was ready and Overton gave the word, Dickinson fired and Jackson was seen to press his hand lightly over his chest while the dust flew from his clothes.

Dickinson at first thought he had missed his man and was seized with terror. Jackson now had his adversary at his mercy and slowly pulled the trigger. There was no explosion; the pistol stopped at half cock which by the rules was not considered a shot. Again Jackson took deliberate aim and fired; the ball severed an artery and Dickinson fell. Jackson with his friend and surgeon, left the ground, and had travelled about twenty miles towards home, when his attendant first discovered that the general was wounded, by seeing the blood oozing through his clothes. On examination, it was found that Dickinson's ball had buried itself in his breast, and shattered two of his ribs near their articulation with the breastbone. It was some weeks before he was able to attend to business. Dickinson was taken to a neighboring house, where he survived but a few hours.

The friends of Dickinson, and the enemies of Jackson, circulated charges of unfairness in the fight, but these were soon put down, in the estimation of candid and impartial judges, by the certificates of the seconds, that all·had been done according to the previous understanding between the parties, and proof that Dickinson himself, though able, to converse, never uttered a single word of complaint before his death.

The Secretary of the Tennessee Historical Society furnishes the following:

"In regard to his (Charles Dickinson) latter end will say that his remains were buried on the farm of his father-in-law, Mr. Joseph Erwin, then some distance west of Nashville. But the city has so grown in the last fifty years that the grave is now within the bounds of the western district of the city. Until a few years ago it was marked by an old fashioned box tomb, although it had no inscription whatever. Since the farm has become a part of the city, this tomb has been removed and there is no mark of the grave except that we know exactly its position and are trying to have it permanently marked.

In regard to Mr. Dickinson will say that it is now generally admitted that the difficulty with General Jackson grew out of the sporting life of both of them and is attributed largely to differences growing out of a horse race.

I think the verdict of history is that Mr. Dickinson was a young man of promising abilities, but in keeping with the life of the day was high strung, impetuous, and probably imprudent. There is nothing, however, justified with reference to immoral character, no more than was characteristic of life in the South at that time."

WAR OF 1812.

The War of the Revolution had passed and "political independence" was an assured fact. Now scarcely more than a quarter of a century had elapsed, when, because of Great Britain's interference with our trade came the demand from our nation for Commercial Independence.

The following is the voice of our government.

"AN ACT Declaring War between the United Kingdom of Great. Britain and Ireland and the dependencies thereof and the United States of America and their territories.

BE IT ENACTED by the Senate and House of Representatives of the United States of American in Congress assembled, That War be and the same is hereby declared to exist between the U. Kingdom of G. Britain and Ireland and the dependencies thereof and the United States of America and their territories, and that the President of the U. States be and he is hereby authorized to use the whole land and naval forces of the U. States to carry the same into effect and to issue to private armed vessels of the U. States commissions or letters of marque and general reprisal, in such form as he may think proper, and effects of the government of the said U. Kingdom of Great Britain and Ireland and of the subjects thereof, June 18, 1812.

Approved,   James Madison.

The military records from the State of Maryland of the War of 1812 were removed from the Adjutant General's office in Annapolis to the War Department at Washington during the Civil War and are not now accessible for private citizens to collect historical data therefrom, therefore the war history of local interest relating to Caroline County cannot be fully obtained.

While six thousand soldiers were Maryland's quota, twelve thousand volunteered. Without records, however, for examination, the volunteers from Caroline County cannot be fully named.

Caroline County, true to the spirit of Revolutionary days, took up the cause and called a citizens meeting which was held at Denton. Col. William Whitely, state senator, was made chairman, and Sheriff Robert Orrell secretary; while William Potter, a Federal leader, headed the committee on resolutions. The committee of eight appointed to draft the resolutions was also made "A Committee of Correspondence and empowered by the meeting to represent Caroline in any subsequent measures taken by her sister counties in vindication of the national honor."

Resolutions condemning the attack of the "Leopard" were also adopted.

Again when the nominating committee from this electoral district met in Denton, July 21, 1812, they passed resolutions which the following gives in part:

"That an important and awful crisis has now arrived.
"That it is no longer a contest between Federalists and Democrats but a contest of much more serious nature.
"That the time has now arrived for a line to be drawn between the friends of their country and those who stand up bodly and condemn the measures of government and advocate or palliate the conduct of our implacable enemies."

Then came the call for militia and Caroline responded to the call by contributing to the 12th Brigade, commanded by Brigadier-general Perry Benson, captain of the Fifth Regiment, Maryland line during the Revolution. Her contribution was the 19th Regiment, also an extra Battlion.

The Regiment and extra Battalions were officered as follows:

Governor Wright appointed Robert Orrell, Lieutenant Colonel and commander of the Regiment.

INFANTRY

Name	Rank	Name	Rank
William Potter	Major & Lieut. Col.	John Morgan	Lieut.
Nehemiah Townsend	Major	William Turner	"
Solomon Richardson	"	George H. Smith	"
John Boone	Adjutant	Thomas Manship	"
Andrew Baggs	Captain	Henry Willis	"
Selby Bell	"	Jesse Collins	"
Levin Charles	"	Richard Cheezum	"
James Colson	"	John Jump	Ensign
Frederick Holbrook	"	Nathan Russell	"
Purnell Fisher	"	James Shaw	"
Elijah Satterfield	"	Thomas Andrew Jr.	"
Hugh Taylor	"	George Andrew Jr.	"
Thomas Styll	"	Thomas Silvester	"
Joseph Talbot	"	Jacob Covey	"
Thomas Carter	"	Daniel Cheezum	"
Peter Willis	"	William Bell	"
William Chaffinch	"	Peregrine Rouse	"
Garretson Blades	"	Marcellus Keene	Surgeon
Henry Harris	"	Sharles Tilden	"
Thomas H. Douglass	"	Timothy Caldwell	Surgeon's Mate
Emory Bailey	Lieut.	Nathan Whitby	Quartermaster
Henry Jump	"	Alemby Jump	Paymaster
William Coursey	"	James Sangston	"
James Richardson	"		

CAVALRY

Name	Rank	Name	Rank
Richard Hughlett	Major	Wm. Hardcastle	1st Lieut.
Mitchell Russum	"	Daniel Leverton	"
William Boone	"	Henry Nichols	2nd Lieut.
Wm. Hughlett	Captain	John Stevens	"
Samuel Slaughter	"	Wm. Orrell	"
Thomas Goldsborough	"	Peter Hardcastle	"
Thomas Saulsbury	"	John Stewart	Paymaster
Jemfer Taylor	1st Lieut.	Stephen Fisher	Coronet

Of the extra Battalion only two officers are named indicating, probably, that it was as yet incomplete. These officers were Captain Alemby Jump and Lieutenant Samuel Culbreth.

While the British were ravaging the Eastern Shore as a whole, wanton outrages were committed at many points along the Bay, and later we will see that Caroline was probably saved by the stern resistance of the Militia along the bay coast.

Among the places suffering from British depredation were:

1   Capture of Mail packet on Bay.
2   Attack on Fredericktown, Cecil Co.
3   Attack on Georgetown, Kent Co.
4   Occupation of Kent Is. by British.
5   Attack on Queenstown.
6   Attack on St. Michaels.
7   Fleet at Castle Haven.

Caroline County was indirectly connected with some of the above. In the capture of the Mail boat this county lost a quantity of mail.

When the British fleet set sail from Kent Island and landed at Castle Haven near the mouth of the Choptank River informants said the British were coming north to the Dover Bridge vicinity, from there proceed to ravage the town of Easton and probably all the surrounding territory. A letter written at Chestertown during that period said, "This day their (British) whole fleet got under way, and stood down the bay, so that we have a little more respite but how long God knows. Report from Kent Island says they intend going up the Choptank River at or about Dover ferry."

Why they went no further than Fairhave will never be positively known but remembering the strong ressistance of the Militia at St. Michael where a British soldier was overheard to say that one officer had been killed who was more valuable than the whole town, we may give the bravery of the militia as a probable reason.

Caroline lent her aid to the unfortunate citizens in the bay section by permiting them to drive their cattle inland to the Choptank marshes where they could feed safe from the marauding British.

The war closed. We won in our second bout with the English in spite of blunders, and strange to say when the treaty was made no mention was made of the cause, i. e., Free Trade and Sailor's Rights.

Of the war, Hart says,

"The United States was like a turtle which draws its feet and tail beneath a protecting shell, yet reaches out its hooked jaws to catch its adversary in the most vulnerable part";

while of the Treaty, Tubbs says:

"The best that could be said of the treaty of Ghent was that it was an honorable one."

An Interesting Document.

Mr. William A. Stewart holds the Commission issued by Gov. Thomas G. Pratt in July 1846 whereby his father, Alexander Stewart, Esq. was appointed captain of a uniform Volunteer Corps attached to the 17th Regiment Md. Militia. This Caroline County Corps was known as the "Caroline Stars." The Commission says, "That reposing especial trust and confidence in your Fidelity, Courage, Good conduct, and attachment to the State of Md. and the U. S. you are constituted and appointed captain." Captain Stewart never saw active service, as the Mexican situation was soon well in hand.

CAPTAIN JOSEPH RICHARDSON.

Impressed Dentonian.

Captain Joseph Richardson, descendant of Colonel William Richardson of Revolutionary fame, has the distinction of being one of the American Seamen who were impressed by the British Navy, the continuance of which acts led to the War of 1812. An interesting story is told of his release later in London. He was approached by a man who offered for a certain amount of money to secure for him a passport to America. Richardson produced the money although he believed the paper a forgery, and was fortunate enough to effect an escape from further service owing to it.

Apparently his experiences as an impressed sailor cured his love for the sea as from 1817 to 1844 continuously he was clerk of the court in Caroline county. Proof of this service may be found in the court record Folio J R, Pages 1 and 317.

In 1835 Richardson built a magnificent home on what was known as the Mt. Andrew tract of land just east of Denton Bridge (site of the present residence of Dr. P. R. Fisher). It was a three story structure of pressed bricks and is said to have contained twenty rooms.

Richardson's family consisted of a wife, three sons and a daughter. That part of the family were staunch Catholics. Upon his death in 1848 he was buried in St. Elizabeth's churchyard at Denton.

In his will he mentions a library which for that time seems to have been an excellent one. After the captain's death his family moved to Cecil county and seem never to have returned to Caroline for any length of time. His wife, Elizabeth W. Richardson, was buried next him in Denton, but there seems to be no proof of the remainder of the family having been brought to their native county for burial.

THOMAS CULBRETH.

"Alert, tall, thin of visage, black hair and eyes, with courteous, dignified, serious, impressive, convincing manners, all tending to suggest strength, confidence and inspiration," so has one of his kinsman described Thomas Culbreth, the sometime Congressman from Caroline.

The time of arrival in America of the original Culbreth is contemporary with the running of the Mason and Dixon line, one of them having assisted in the survey. Later three brothers, John, James, and William Culbreth, settled near that line where it separates Maryland from Delaware, and from this John Culbreth, Thomas was a lineal descendant, a great grandson.

Culbreth was born April 13, 1786, at River Bridges (Henderson), near the Delaware border. There he spent his early youth living with his uncle on the Brick House farm, now owned by Robert Jarrell, where his educational opportunities were limited to the local schools.

Although he was heir prospective to landed estates his inclination was toward a business career, in which he felt he could become most influential, and with this in view he went to Denton where he secured a mercantile clerkship with Potter and Ross, and later entered a partnership with one, Solomon Brown.

In 1810 he married Ann Hardcastle, daughter of John Hardcastle, and by this alliance his local influence may have been increased, the Hardcastles being a family of good standing socially and politically.

When the war for Commercial Independence broke out in 1812, he entered the military field, but must have enrolled in the ranks, as his name does not appear in the appointments, and there his service although inconspicuous was no less credible.

The political trend of the Culbreths had been toward the Federal principles but when in 1807 Thomas Culbreth attained his majority he became a staunch Democrat and had gained some influence in his party.

In politics as elsewhere "There is a tide in the affairs of men, which taken at its flood leads on to fortune" and that tide came to Culbreth, following the ebb of the fortunes of the 14th Congress, after the passing of the "Compensation Bill" or "Salary Grab Bill" as it was called.

The Anti-salary men were quick to seize opportunity, and Culbreth, then 30 years old, as an anti-salary man by his "Political fervor and principles, mental acumen and force, as well as personal characteristics" was recommended, June 13, 1816, to the people as a suitable nominee for the House of Representatives, and at the election following became the chosen representative of the people. That he as a legislator met with public favor is shown by the following quoted from an appeal issued by his Caroline County constituents.

THOMAS CULBRETH

"He is a gentleman who stands high in the estimation of the people of his county. They are generally acquainted with him and they have entire confidence in him." It is further shown by the fact that after a long term of service the people, in 1822, once more urged his candidacy but ill health caused his refusal.

During his active service in Congress his position on important questions of the day was as follows:

1. He advocated:

   1. Freedom of the press.
   2. Abolition of the slave trade.
   3. Reduction of departmental expenses.

2. He favored:

   1. Appropriations for West Point.
   2. Sympathy for Spain's rebellious colonies.
   3. The position of the North in the Fugitive Slave Law.

3. Opposed:

   1. Reduction of standing army.
   2. Admission of Missouri as a slave state.
   3. Free trade.

His failing health and inability to endure the strain of Congressional activity did not retire him from public service, for records show that he was Judge of Caroline County Courts in 1822 and following that became Clerk of the Executive Council of Maryland, a position much like that of the present Secretary of State. This he retained under five Governors (1825-1835) ending his 30 years of public service, 1835, when he retired to the Orrell farm, near Boonsboro, where he spent his latter days, his death occurring in 1843.

The rank and file of to-day's citizens know nothing of this unique character nor of the political prominence he attained. The name of Thomas Culbreth was a century ago a factor on the Eastern Shore of Maryland, but is now known only by the local historians and revered only by his kinsmen, who have learned of his strong character together with his pictured personality, "Dignified, impressive, with the black hair and eyes of the Moorish Celt."

EARLY POSTAL SERVICE.

Years before the Colonial Mail Service which was established about 1790, the Legislature of Maryland established a law providing for the more speedy passage of public letters and packets and the payment thereof. This measure provided that the Sheriff of Anne Arundel county would deliver all such mail for the Eastern Shore to the Sheriff of Queen Anne County at Kent Island, thence to the Sheriff of Caroline County from Queen Anne etc. For this service our sheriff received about $25 per year. Doubtless as the quantity of mail increased the compensation increased accordingly until the Federal Government about 1789 took charge of the mail service thereby releasing the states.

As to postmasters and postal routes the following is taken from the official records at Washington: The earliest record shows Charles Sevins as postmaster at Denton in 1801, followed by Thomas Culbreth in 1810; Montgomery Denny in 1811; George A. Smith in 1814; William Mulliken in 1815; Gove Saulsbury in 1822, John R. Wright in 1825; George Martin in 1825, and Oscar Jones in 1831.

The postmasters at Hillsboro were: John Tillottson in 1807; Francis Sellers in 1811; James G. Seth in 1812, and David Casson in 1816, and Wm. B. Tillotson in 1831.

At Greensboro the records show postmasters William Crawford in 1801; Warner Busteed in 1807; Robert Fountain in 1812; John Matthews in 1813 and William Turner in 1831.

The earliest record of a postmaster at Upper Hunting Creek that could be found was that of John L. Mills in 1831.

One record was found showing the amounts of postage accruing for the year ending March 31, 1827, at Denton $97.22; Greensboro $63.31; Hillsboro $25.48, and Hunting Creek $2.24.

The earliest record noted of post routes was in 1824. Route No. 41 apparently began at Easton, running through Hillsboro, Denton, Greensboro, Whitelysburg, and ending at Frederica.

In connection with the bid for carrying the mails on Route No. 1403, Easton, Maryland to Laurel, Delaware, Roades Hazzard in his bid of October 2, 1835, states:

"I will also carry the mail on Route No. 1403 from Easton to Laurel, Del., once a week part of the route say from Easton to Seaford in two horse stage or other passage carriage the balance of the route on horseback or in sulky for two hundred and forty dollars per annum."

The route started at Easton, Md., Talbot County, touching Upper Hunting Creek, Caroline County; Federalsburg, then in Dorchester County, Maryland, and Cannon's Ferry, Seaford, Middleford, Concord and Laurel, Delaware. The contract on Route 1403 was dated 3d December, 1835. Other bidders were P. Robinson and William Heather.

THE PLANTATION.

Looking backward to the days when forests stretched for miles over an acreage now covered by fertile farms, we see about five miles N. E. of Greensboro, some distance from the Eastern bank of the Choptank River, a small clearing appear. Soon arose a small unpretentious building typical of its day. Tall pines overshadowed it. At dawn the song of the woodland bird awakened the sleeper, while during the hush of eventide the call of prowling wild animals sent a thrill of fear through the listener. Such in the 17th century was the beginning of the Baynard plantation—the largest in the Greensboro section—extending over an area of more than six hundred acres.

Time was in the. early slave days when tobacco flourished there, and negroes, singing their wierd, melancholy songs "toted" the tobacco to their storeroom. From thence it was carried over the woodland road and delivered at the warehouse of William Hughlett for even in the 17 hundreds the dense green of Maryland pines had given way to the paler green of cultivated fields. First the Baynards planted tobacco, but later cereals formed the base of income; while in the last days of the plantation, to these were added the returns from tanbark and railroad ties.

In 1812 "Old Massa Baynard" died and Mistress Betty, then sixteen years old, became—under her mother—the Autocrat of the Plantation.

The home with its rambling negro quarters had been enlarged and, while never ostentatious, held old china, colonial furniture, a grandfather's clock and other antiques such as delight the eye.

There after her mother's death Betsy Baynard lived alone save for her house servant, Myna, and two powerful dogs who stood guard day and night. Completing this plantation community were her slaves who filled their huts to overflowing, at times numbering more than two hundred.

Although not given to slave dealing, at the time of enlarging her house to obtain the needed money Betsy sold a servant "South into Georgia."

"They say" the cartwhip was daily used as a ruling power among her colored people but the blows must have fallen lightly for many of her slaves remained contentedly on her plantation until old and infirm, and when she died ten years after Emancipation some half dozen of her slaves were yet with her.

An amusing anecdote of the Baynard slaves relates that a young negro, returning from a dance, in the cold, gray dawn went to the well for a drink of water. As his eye followed the bucket on its descent he saw something white. True to race superstition he believed it a spirit and ran to tell Miss Betsy of "De hant in de well." She returned with him and found a sheep had fallen in and all but drowned.

A tragedy of the plantation was the death of Miss Mary Reid, a cousin of Miss Betsy's, who at times made her home there. A slave girl, on being reprimanded for some delinquency, took offense and attempted revenge on Betsy by way of Paris green. The poison miscarried, resulting in Miss Reid's death almost immediately.

As a memorial to the Baynard generosity stands Irving Chapel. While the name is that of the first minister, the plat of land on which Irving Chapel stands was donated from the Baynard plantation, and the lumber for the building was added on condition that the church members cut it from the forest. Miss Baynard also gave a sum of money, large in those days and sufficient for church erection.

Betsy Baynard died without direct lineal descendant. The land was sold in small sections, and is owned principally by Rosanna Richards, G. W. Richards, A. K. Brown and J. A. Meredith.

All that remains to recall the story of other days is a portion of the old home which is yet in use by J. A. Meredith, and a small family burying ground with three markers—

William Baynard born 1769, died 1812.
Litia Baynard born 1773, died 1843.
Elizabeth Baynard born 1796, died 1873.

Written from material collected by
PAUL MEREDITH.

SLAVERY.

I. Origin.

The period at which slavery was introduced into Maryland is somewhat indefinite but some historians claim Claiborne had negro servants at the time of the settlement of Kent Island.

The Royal African Company, chartered in 1618, whose chief profits came from the importation of negroes into the American Colonies was the first organization for slave trade. The traffic of this company was greatly encouraged by the King.

The first record we find of Maryland slaves is that of 1708 when the London Board of Trade wrote to Gov. Seymour concerning slave importation by this company (Royal African). The Governor in reply stated that Maryland trade was not through the above company but through independent traders or "interlopers," who were licensed.

II. Growth of Slavery.

From 1700 to 1750 slavery was rapidly on the increase. Governor Seymour in a letter of 1708 said, "At present the trade seems to run high, there having been between six and seven hundred negroes imported hither this year." This increase then changed to a decline which soon became rapid.

III. Decline of Slavery in Maryland.

Scharf says.—

"In no state of the Union had emancipation so rapidly progressed as in Maryland; and while several of the counties had now (1833) a larger number of slaves than of white inhabitants, yet there were in the state at this time, not only the largest proportion, but actually much the largest number of free colored people of any state in the Union."

By comparing the census reports we see as follows:

Years	Whites	Slaves	Free Colored.
1755	107,108	46,356	
1800	216,356	105,635	19,587
1860	516,128	87,188	83,718

Approximately the change was as follows: 1755 all colored people in Maryland were slaves; in 1800 about one-fifth were free; in 1860 one-half were free.

Then, too, free negro property holders were allowed to vote in Maryland until 1851, when it was constitutionally restricted.

An American Colonization Society was formed in Washington during December 1816, for the purpose of colonizing in Africa free people of color from America.

In January 1831 Maryland organized an auxiliary for the same purpose. McSherry says, "It was therefore determined to establish an independent organization in the state and plant a separate colony under the name of 'Maryland in Liberia.' "

Proving the activity of this body we find that in October 1831 colored immigrants numbering 31 were sent to this colony. Also the December session of Legislature made an appropriation of $10,000 each year for 26 years, to be used for benefit and transportation to Africa of negroes. In 1852 when this act expired the Assembly reenacted the law to be enforced for six years. Then again, at its expiration in 1858 for four more years.

To again quote from McSherry,

"We are, therefore, justified in maintaining that no State did as much as Maryland toward emancipation and improvements of the condition of the African race within her borders. Her early statutes protected them from cruel treatment and authorized their manumission. She looked to their gradual and voluntary removal as the only means of solving the difficult problem which their presence involved."

IV. Slavery in Caroline.

Caroline County was active in these matters and her rapidly decreasing slave population shows her attitude. Even in the days when this section belonged to Dorchester and Queen Anne the slave population was small as compared with other counties.

In 1712 Queen Anne and Dorchester, which at that time included Caroline County held comparatively few slaves. Queen Anne with an entire white population of over 3,000 had only 550 while Dorchester with practically the same number of whites held only 387 slaves.

By the census of 1790 we find the highest number of slaves held by any one man in Caroline County was 57. The holdings of the majority of the people owning slaves at all varied from one to five negroes, while of those with larger holdings less than fifty families owned more than ten slaves.

The following table shows the gradual decrease of slaves and the increase of free colored people in Caroline from 1790 to 1840 as well as their number in proportion to the whites.

1790—Population of Caroline County—1840.

Year	Slaves	Free Colored	White	Total
1790	2,057	421	7,023	9,506
1800	1,865	602	6,579	9,226
1810	1,520	1,001	6,932	9,453
1820	1,574	1,390	7,144	10,108
1830	1,171	1,652	6,247	9,070
1840	768	1,727	5,373	7,868

Slave trade was never carried on to any extent in Caroline County; Marcy Fountain and Patty Cannon being probably the best known two who "traded"—that is sold South into Georgia.

Then as Maryland, and with her Caroline County, was rapidly transporting or manumitting her slaves came the year 1861 and Maryland true to her principles stayed in the Union and her spirit is expressed in a quotation from a prominent Baltimore newspaper of that day—"God forbid that a time should come when our people shall be unwilling to let the flag of the Union float over them."

OLD SLAVE KITCHEN.

V. *Miscellaneous Court Orders.*

An account of the sale of a negress and her child is
here given.

Know all men by these presents that I Jeremiah ....
of Caroline County, planter, have and in the commission of the
summon of sixty pounds of current money to me in hand and before the sealing and delivery of these presents by Isaac ....,
the receipt whereof I do hereby acknowledge, having bargained and
sold by these present, do bargin and sell unto the said Isaac .....,
one negro woman lately the property of Samuel ...., deceased, called Fann; also her child called Rachel to have and to
hold the said negroes and each of whom by these presents we bar-
gined and sold unto the said Isaac ...., his executors, administrators, and assigns for ever, and the said Jeremiah ....,
for myself by executors and administrators or any other person or
persons whosoever shall and will forever warrant and defend the
same as witness of my hand and seal this sixteenth day of May
1774.

The following is an account of an unknown master giving freedom to four of his slaves.

I am in possession of four negroes named, Sarah, Lucy, Eve, and Pompey and being desirous to give them all their liberty in a legal manner therefore do discharge the said Sarah, from my service from the day and date thereof, and Lucy and Eve and Pompey shall be free when they arrive unto the age of twenty and one years of age and doth covenant and agree both for myself and for my heirs executors and administrators. Lucy was born on the fifteenth of August in the year 1768; the said Eve was born on the 27 day of November 1768 and Pompey was born on the 4th day of September in the year of 1772.

Given under my hand and seal this nineteenth day of March in the year 1774.

Signed, sealed and delivered in the presence of Jacob Boone.

(Seal)

Various items in regard to slaves which were brought up at court are here given.

March 1776.

On petition of Nathaniel Potter's negro Pompey, slave of the said Nathaniel Potter, is by the Court set levy-free for the future.

November 1776.

On petition of Christopher Driver ordered that he be exempt from the payment of any public tax or levy for his old negro man Joseph, for the future.

It was necessary for every colored person even though free to make known to the clerk of the court his or her intention to leave the province for a stated time.

To
Joseph Richardson, Esq.,
Clerk of Caroline County Court.

I the undersigned, a free negro of Caroline County, wish to visit the city of Philadelphia for the purpose of seeing my brother. By an Act of the Assembly, of this State, it is necessary my intention of leaving this State should be known to you. It is my intention to return here again within three days from this date.

Given under my hand this 12th day of October 1841.

Joseph Bell.

Test:
Joshua Jump.

The Clerk would then issue a certificate like the following.

State of Maryland, Caroline County, to wit:

Whereas application has been made to me by a colored woman named Mahala Scott for a certificate of her freedom agreeably to the Act of Assembly in such case made and provided by which said

Act, free negroes and mulattoes are permitted to travel out of this state, upon the obtaining of a certificate of being free born, And whereas also upon the oath of Sarah Williams, of Caroline County, that the said colored woman named Mahala Scott, for whom this certificate is made, was free born. I do therefore grant her said application and hereby certify that she is seventeen years of age, or thereabout, about five feet high, of a complexion nearly black, was born and raised in Caroline County, and has a large scar of a burn across her right wrist, and a scar of a cut on the inside of her right wrist-joint, another scar on her left cheek directly under the eye and no other notable mark or scar that I have discovered. In testimony whereof I hereunto subscribe my name and affix the public seal of my office this 14th day of March in the year of our Lord eighteen hundred and twenty six.

Richardson,

Clerk of Caroline County Court.

VI. Acts of Assembly.

In 1822 laws regarding slaves were enacted as follows:

"BE IT ENACTED By the General Assembly of Maryland, That from and after the first day of October, in the year one thousand eight hundred and twenty two, it shall be the duty of the constables in Worcester and Caroline counties, to arrest and bring before a justice of the peace, any slave or slaves that may be going at large and bring him, her or themselves within their respective hundreds, or who may not have a fixed home in the family or on the estate of his, her or their owner, or be hired with his, her or their owner."

"AND BE IT ENACTED, That in all cases where a slave or slaves shall or may be brought before a justice of the peace under the provision of the first section of this act, if it appear to the satisfaction of the said justice of the peace, that said slave or slaves so arrested and brought before him, were going at large in violation of an Act of Assembly passed in April session seventeen hundred and eighty seven entitled, An Act to prevent the inconveniences arising from slaves being permitted to act as free, and the supplements thereto, or of this Act, he shall forthwith issue an order to the constable who shall or may have brought the said slave or slaves before him, to hire such slave or slaves for the entire balance of the year in which they may have been arrested; and for each examination of slaves had before him under this act, a justice of the peace shall be entitled to twenty-five cents, to be levied on the county as part of the county expenses for the ensuing year."

"BE IT ENACTED, by the General Assembly of Maryland, That all such parts of the act of Assembly passed at September session, seventeen hundred and twenty three, chapter fifteen, which directs punishment of negro or other slaves by cropping their ear, be and the same is hereby repealed."

"AND be it enacted, That for the offense specified in the act thus repealed, punishment by whipping not exceeding thirty-nine stripes, shall be and is hereby substituted."

The following may serve to show conditions in part:

In 1858 James Wheeler, a free colored man, living near Denton had acquired some real estate through his industrious efforts and being desirous of leaving same to his children at his death, had to have the Legislature authorize him to bequeath his property to his children at his death as in the case of white people. Without this law his children would not have secured his property by will.

A few interesting extracts from wills probated in Caroline County are given as examples of the provision for slaves by their masters:

Two old negroes named Bacchus and Silvey are to be taken good care of and well treated by my children. I direct that they shall never be sold or disposed of.

I give and devise to all my negro slaves freedom, liberty and freedom.

I give unto my negro man Essex, two acres of land during his life.

I desire that my son shall receive but one shilling from my estate if he refuse to free all his slaves upon his becoming sixteen years of age.

I give and bequeath to my negro woman, named Esther, her youngest child named Judy, to her forever.

I give unto my negro man Will a donation of five pounds current money per year.

I give unto my son William, old Bet, whose life is to be made comfortable.

CARL—*The Last Slave.*

"Gone are the days, when my heart was young and gay,
Gone are my friends from the cotton fields away;
Gone from the earth, to a better land I know,
I hear their gentle voices calling Old Black Joe."

We found him sitting in the twilight, his eyes clear and bright for all his ninety years, yet filled with dreams of the past. We had met his grand children at the door, hastening to some entertainment and the room was filled with the happy confusion of their outgoing.

Cheerily he greeted us. Then by degrees we led him to talk of bygone days,—his days of bondage. Happily he spoke of them, of his home life, of his master, of tobacco days in Maryland. Once when questioned he told of the fear of being sold to the cotton plantations in Georgia. Then his eyes blazed with the fire of youth and his voice took on a different tone.

Once more his mind turned to the happier vein of thought and told of driving old Massa to church in Greensboro, sitting outside under the rustling green trees, listening to the birds and bees until the service had ended. "Ah!" he said, "He was a good master."

Quietly his voice wandered on telling of plantation life in Caroline and as the light in the room dimmed slowly, his gray head sank forward and he sat silent, with his hands resting on his cane, dreaming of the past. We rose and passed out into the darkening night, leaving him there—the last representative of slavery days.

> "I'm coming, coming, For my head is bending low,
> I hear those gentle voices calling Old Black Joe."

Feb. 21, 1919.   LAURA COCHRANE,

After a visit to last slave in Greensboro.

TAVERN OF JOE JOHNSON.
The Son-in-Law of Patty Cannon.

SLAVE DEALERS.

Altho Maryland was a slave state, it is generally
known that previous to the Civil War half of her people
were opposed to slavery and public sentiment strong
against the slave traffic, which, nevertheless, was carried on to some extent along the Maryland and Delaware
peninsula.   Chief among the dealers were Patty Cannon, Joe Johnson and Massy Fountain.

Patty Cannon and Joe Johnson, her son-in-law, kept
a tavern at Johnson's Cross Roads, now Reliance. The
location was ideal for their nefarious purpose, for the
house was on the border of Sussex, Dorchester and Caroline counties, twenty miles from a court house and ten
from a town of any size.   Under the strangely sloping
roof of this hostelry was a concealed garret which served

as a pen for captive slaves and free negroes who had been kidnapped to sell. Scattered about the counties, Patty Cannon had secret places where her agents collected victims. The poor negroes who were luckless enough to fall into her hands were sent to one of these hiding places until taken in charge by a southern trader, who to prevent any trouble arising during their detention and journey handcuffed them together in what was known as a "coffle."

A force of men was employed to kidnap free negroes and indeed stories are told of the like disappearance of white people whose complexion resembled that of mulattoes. "Aunt Patty," as she was commonly called, often assisted in this work and is credited with capturing men single handed, so great was her physical strength. She is still remembered by a few old people in the county as a short, thick-set woman with black hair and eyes, vivid coloring, and rather handsome in her cold, bold way.

Joe Johnson was a staunch ally in all Patty's schemes. After having been captured in Delaware and flogged at the whipping post for some unlawful business, he confined his activities to Maryland.

Not only were Patty Cannon and Joe Johnson accused of illegal transactions in connection with the slave traffic, but other accusations such as robbing the mails, and killing travelers who stopped at the tavern and were suspected of having considerable money with them. After years of terrorizing the neighborhood, Patty Cannon was delivered by the Maryland authorities to Delaware officials. Before the time for her trial, however, she died in Georgetown Jail. This was supposed to be a great relief to many prominent people throughout the state, as in the course of a court trial they would undoubtedly have been exposed as accomplices in some of her questionable transactions. Joe Johnson made his escape and no definite information was ever found as to his whereabouts.

Massy Fountain, one of the prominent men in the Bridgetown community about 1820, was also a slave dealer. Tradition has it that he was one of Patty Cannon's crowd of kidnappers, but we find no proof of this and he was never accused of the other crimes of which she was instigator. Certain it is, however, that he bought and sold slaves. Maryland slave owners, feeling it a disgrace to deal openly for negroes, would secretly bring them to Fountain, who in turn would sell them to southern dealers. The cellar of the Fountain home was used as quarters for the darkies until convenient for the dealers to move them south. This being "sold south into Georgia," as the slaves termed it, was the greatest terror of their lives.

Fountain was a man of considerable means and owned large tracts of land in the county. He was one of the most influential men in upper Caroline, and greatly feared in political affairs, until his death in 1864. His grave may still be seen in the Bridgetown church yard, just over the boundary line in Queen Anne's county.

EARLY CORN SHELLER.

AN OLD TIME MARYLAND SCHOOL (1838).

(The Original 'Possum Hollow School).

The school was but a quarter of a mile distant from home; but to our childish fancies it was so far that mother gratified us by putting up our dinners in a little basket. Only big Sister Retta could be entrusted with that presious basket, and Emma and I cast many interested glances towards it as, hand in hand, and bearing the books, slates, and inkstand, with goose quills to make pens, we proudly marched along the winding highway, under the leafless branches of the great white oaks which bordered the farther side.

At last with a gathering group of expectant children, and youth of from five to twenty-one years of age, we stood before the open door of the new school-house. Not that the word new describes the house; very far from it; but the school was new. The school-master was a new arrival in the neighborhood, and the house was newly and for the first time used for so noble a purpose. Will the reader believe it? The house was really a deserted negro cabin, that stood by the highway side, near

Townsend's Cross Roads, three miles from Denton, the county town. For an area of twenty-five square miles between that town and the Delaware line, this was the only school, and this was started by a private subscription managed by my father. The Maryland law, at that time, liberally provided that if the people of a neighborhood would subscribe for the tuition of twelve scholars at five dollars each, then the State would furnish a like amount for the education of the same number of "charity sccholars." There were no public provisions for school houses, and whether there was house or school, depended altogether upon the character of the population that, amid rural mutations, might happen to gather in any given neighborhood.

This new school and every school in that region for several years, was in a rented house. This particular house was built of logs, the interstices being filled with clay to keep out wind and rain. It was eighteen or twenty feet square, and about eight feet to the eaves; with a door front and back, each opening outwards. Midway between the doors and the north end where stood the chimney, at a convenient height, part of the log was sawed out, the aperture being filled with a three-light hanging window, which, as occasion required, could be propped up for ventilation.

Where the chimney stood was an aperture six feet wide and four feet high, into which the stone and mud walls of the fire-place were built to a height above where the blaze of the great log fire would usually reach; and above that point the flue was made of logs and sticks, liberally daubed within of clay. At the south end of the house, in order to adapt it to its use as a literary institution, almost an entire log had been removed. This aperture was covered by a wide board, fastened by hinges to the log above, and secured to that below by staple and hook. Like the sash before mentioned, this board was propped up to admit needed light and fresh air. Just below this aperture was the writing desk, extending across the room against the wall. Here, alternately, the girls and boys made pot hooks and hangers with their goose quill pens, after the pattern set by the teacher; and finally graduated to the distinguished accomplishment of being able to draw a note of hand or receipt for ten dollars, good and lawful money of the United States of America, and to affix thereto their own real, written signatures. The teacher "set the copies" during the noon hour; but made and mended pens at all hours, when they happened to be presented for that purpose. Hence the name still so commonly applied to the pocketknife. It was not unusual to see the teacher dividing his time and attention between a page of Comly's spelling-book, where some sweating pupil was painfully struggling with the problems of orthography, and the quill he was slitting and whittling, meanwhile stealing an occasional moment for a furtive glance about the schoolroom, to see that there was no pinching, or pin-sticking, or snickering behind books or slates going on among the unruly urchins.

In addition to the so-called writing-desk, the furniture of this schoolroom consisted of a desk and chair for the teacher, and three or four slab benches across the end of the room, next the writing-desk. In cold weather a bench was set near the great fire-place, and was occupied by alternate platoons of the shivering scholars to thaw themselves out. Three formidable hickory rods, of varying size and length, adapted to the sex and size of the culprits; and a pretty, little, red maple switch, suited to the esthetic tastes and tender sensibilities of the smaller urchins, completed the outfit. The entire curriculum of our school was covered by the three cabalistic letters, R., R., R., understood to represent the three great sciences, Readin', Ritin' and 'Rithmetic. The three G's, Grammer, Geography and Geometry, had then scarcely been dreamed of as ever possible to be taught in a country school. It was not until several years after—not indeed until the renowned Chinquapin schoolhouse had been built, over a mile away, on the road to Punch Hall, that we ever heard of such a study as English Grammar or Geography. The primer, or rather a primer—for it mattered not what it was, so long as there were A, B, C's in it—was the text-book most in demand at Mr. Marshall's log cabin school.

Rev. Robert W. Todd, D. D.

CAROLINE HIGH SCHOOL COUNTY ATHLETIC DAY.

THE PUBLIC SCHOOLS.

I. Introduction.

An event that we can always recall as contemporaneous with the war for Commercial Independence is the establishment of our system of Free Education. Previous to this time the various counties as well as the state had given much attention to the education of the young, the expense being provided by state appropriation plus private subscriptions. By this means learning had been disseminated extensively but the money was not sufficient nor the system efficient.

II. Free Schools.

The growing sentiment in every portion of the state favoring public education expressed itself through the General Assembly in 1812 by a feeble effort to raise enough money to establish at least one Free School in each county. The money for the support of these schools was to be raised by requiring the banks of the state to bind themselves to pay the sum of $20,000 on or before January 1, 1815. This sum to be paid annually was to be apportioned according to the capital stock actually paid in at the various banks. Other financial matters were involved in this act and the banks made a vigorous and temporarily successful fight against the whole measure.

In 1813 the school matter again came to the front, By the enactment of this year the state required, not the payment of a specified sum per annum for schools, but instead, an annual tax of 20 cents on every $100 of capital stock actually paid in. Connected with this were some other conditions relative to the Cumberland Turnpike. Any bank refusing to subscribe to the Act within six months forfeited their charter while those accepting guaranteed the renewal of their charter for a term of fifteen years. Denton promptly accepted and her Bank Charter was extended to 1835.

This means of raising money was so successful that by December, 1816 at the meeting of the Assembly the sum was found sufficient for distribution to counties, and nine sensible and discreet men called Commissioners of the School Fund were appointed in each county. These men were to apply the apportionments in their respective counties as their judgment deemed best. Caroline's commissioners were Col. Wm. Potter, Richard Hughlett, Elisha Dawson, Thomas Goldsborough, William Hardcastle, Elijah Satterfield, Willis Charles, Levi Dukes and Peter Willis.

The same session of Assembly also made provision to turn over to the counties their respective shares of school money—said money to be paid to authorized representatives of the commissioners. To increase the school fund it was decided to arrange if practicable to draw a lottery for $50,000 each year for five years.

When this commission of five had organized they were to give notice of an election to determine upon a site for a school-house and to decide whether it should be erected by voluntary contributions, or by a proportionate tax upon the assessable property of the section.

As soon as a suitable school was built in any section, the justices of the levy court were apprised, and they in return gave a certificate of its establishment, which certificate entitled them to their share of the school fund, pledged by the Act of Assembly, 1813.

Notice was to be given of the opening of school, and all white children, especially orphans, were to be taught gratis in their respective districts, but not beyond the "Double Rule of Three" unless with the consent of the trustees. After the first year the trustees were to be elected annually by voters of the respective districts, at an election held the first Monday in May.

In 1821, five years after the opening of free schools. the Assembly took away all power and authority given to the Commissioners of School Fund by the Act of 1816, and vested it in the Justices of Orphans Court, ordering that all monies in the hands of Commissioners be turned over to the Justices. The Orphans Court was also empowered to appoint five Commissioners in each election District, who pointed out to the Court which schools in their respective districts were entitled to a part of that school fund which was to be annually apportioned. One-third of the school money in each district was at the disposition of the commissioners to be used directly for the education of orphans, or any children whose parents were unable to pay. In truth the prime idea in the establishing of a state Free School Fund was to provide for this class of children and from this it later became known as the Charity or Free School Fund.

HOME ECONOMICS EXHIBIT.

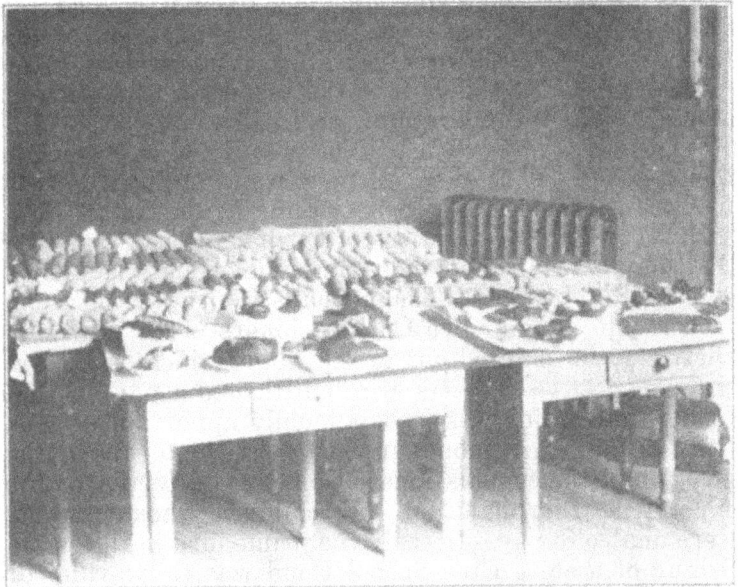

AGRICULTURAL DISPLAY.

To still further aid such children the legislature in 1823 made it obligatory on every college, academy, etc., receiving "state aid" to give tuition to one charity scholar for each $100 received—giving both teaching and text books.

We might here make mention of one Act which never became active in Caroline County. In 1825 the Assembly made an enactment providing a State Superintendent of Public Instruction, who had almost unlimited powers. This law became effective only in the counties which adopted it. But six counties, including Caroline, rejected it.

III. Growth in Caroline.

For the first thirty years of their existence free schools did not progress very rapidly, neither was the increase in numbers great in this county. However about 1830 a "boom" came, which was somewhat at the expense of Academies. Previous to this the Academies at Hillsboro and Denton had been receiving largely from the state but this fund was now withdrawn and placed in the hands of the Orphan's Court to be distributed among located free schools. "At this time," it is said, "local interest in elementary education was at its zenith," and exemplifying this we find a number of free schools built from private means of large land owners. Again, in 1831 the Act relative to state donations to academies increased that fund in Caroline Co. to $800, the distribution giving $250 to the Upper District, $300 to the Middle District and $250 to the Lower District to be used entirely for Free Schools. At the same time a Commission was appointed to locate schools, particularly in sections without them. This Act was followed in 1832 by one providing that a sum not exceeding $100 be appropriated from the surplus in the hands of Orphan's Court for the erection of a comfortable school-house on each site certified by Commission appointed in 1831 to locate new schools.

The Constitutional Convention of 1851 might be described as a vigorous war of words, at the close of which the school question remained practically the same as at the beginning. However in 1852 the Legislature made progress and provided for the payment of several sums of money appropriated previously for the benefit of Free Schools.

The adoption of the State School Law of 1865 did away with many troubles of the Caroline Legislators and seemed for a time to solve the problem of Education, by centralizing the administration. It gave a State Superintendent of Public Instruction and Dr. Libertus Van Boklen was appointed to that office. Acting with him was a State Board of Education who jointly appointed one Commissioner for each of the four school districts of this County. Each Commissioner had entire control of the eight or nine schools in his district. He hired and discharged teachers at will, distributed the text books for which pupils must pay in advance, etc. In this school control the taxpayers were mere onlookers, though through no fault of our officials who were very intelligent and earnest men. To this Board, Mr. William Stevens, of Denton, recently deceased was Clerk and Treasurer.

The law of 1868 wrought another radical change in the management of the schools. The power was taken from the state and once more put in the hands of the people, the office of State Superintendent being abolished. At the General Election, voters of each District voted for one School Commissioner for that District. They also elected two School-House District Trustees. The Commissioner of the District made the third member of the Board of Trustees. This election was held annually on the first Saturday of May. The elective features of this law were repealed after one election had been held, and the appointment of School Commissioners made one of the duties of the Judges of the Circuit Court. Afterwards, as at present, the Governor of the State was given the appointing power. For several years minority party representation was made compulsory but the School Law of 1916 tended to eliminate politics entirely and dared not even suggest any term connected therewith.

The personnel of the County School Board in 1867 was as follows: Rev. Chas. B. Boynton, Dr. M. A. Booth, Mr. William S. Ridgely and Col. James E. Douglass. The new school law went into effect in 1868 and Col. James E. Douglass, Samuel I. Jarman and Robert H. Wilson became the new Board which in turn elected Rev. Geo. F. Beaven, Secretary and Examiner of the schools of the county, the first really provided by law. For several years Rev. Mr. Beaven, who was also rector of the Episcopal church at Hillsboro, faithfully and well discharged his duties until he retired in 1882 and was succeeded by Prof. James Swann of Ridgely. The Board at this time consisted of John F. Dawson, E. E. Goslin, and Dr. Enoch George. Prof. Swann continued as Examiner until 1886 when he was succeeded by M. Bates Stephens, who remained in office till 1900, when he became State Superintendent of Public Schools, and was succeeded in the county position by Prof. W. S. Crouse, who had been principal of the Denton High School.

Until Dr. M. Bates Stephens became State Superintendent in 1900, there had been no real head of the State School system since 1867. For a part of this time the principal of the State Normal School exercised some functions, though his authority was only nominal. At another time, S. E. Forman, State Institute Conductor, had some directing power.

Realizing the inadequacy of the various school enactments prior to 1916 to meet the needs of the times, a well organized school law was that year passed, based upon a very careful and critical survey of our public school system by representative men from our state and experienced educators without.

Caroline's early schools were of two classes, namely, small free schools promoted by private citizens of means, and Secondary schools or Academies which received State aid. Of the first class we will mention three: 1st—The Bloomery School—In 1798 James Wright, who was probably one of the Wright brothers elsewhere mentioned, sold to several persons an acre of land and provided a house thereon to be used for a school, reserving unto himself and his heirs, one-twentieth of the rights of the school thereon established. The site of this school was near the present Bloomery Church. 2nd—Liden's School—From the tract of land along the road from Andersontown to Smithville a building site was given by Deed in 1827 by Shadrach Liden. Thereon was erected a building to serve as a house of worship and a school for the community.

3rd—Chinquapin School—This building stood on the road between Denton and Burrsville, and was probably erected about 1840, as in the records of that time we find the deed of a site given by Gove Saulsbury.

4th—Whiteley's School—This school had been started before 1825 by two men, Dr. William Whiteley and

Edward Carter, who built it for the needs of the neighborhood. This school was afterwards discontinued, then reopened later by Benjamin Whitely as will be explained more fully elsewhere.

Of the second class or Academies we have two, both so noted in their day as to be yet well known.

1st: The Old Hillsboro Academy. John Hardcastle, Jr. donated the land for a section called in the deed Hackett's Garding. The building was begun in 1797 and was originally intended only for a local school but with the passing of the School Act of 1798 it was incorporated as a Secondary School.

The erection seems to have been entirely from local subscription and much generosity in the matter of money is credited Francis Sellers. Later aid was received from the state. The curriculum first included the elementary studies but later the classics were included, until 1844, when it was made a "Primary District."

2nd: Denton Academy. By Act of General Assembly, 1804, which supplemented Denton's Charter, one-fourth acre of land in the N. W. corner of the public square was set apart as a school site. Not until 1808 was there a centralized effort to build a school but at this time they were not successful in so doing. Legislative annals show the frequent recurrence of Denton Academy legislation followed by a "donation." Finally some time between 1840 and 1845 the building was completed largely from accumulated state donations.

IV. In Conclusion.

Quoting directly from Steele we might add,—Caroline was among the foremost of the counties to establish a Secondary School a century ago; she was among the foremost in the effort to establish Free Primary Schools on a practical basis, anterior to the adoption of the State school system; she has been for years, and is now, among the foremost in school enrollment according to population. She stands not very far from the top in per cent. of pupils in and above sixth grade and she may be relied on to be in the vanguard of educational procession, and bearing her little part bravely if the time ever comes and it seems to be coming when all the States will be banded into an educational system or union with national supervision.

It seems that public schools for colored children in our county began to be organized shortly after 1866 by virtue of a School Board resolution of that date which reads as follows: Resolved—that our Board appropriate the sum of one hundred dollars to each school for colored children that may be started in our county at such time as the Commissioner of the district where such school is to be located, shall report that the colored people of said locality are ready and willing and able to raise such other sum or sums as shall be necessary for building a school house after such model as shall be furnished by our Board. The first payment of public school tax to colored schools was made in 1869.

A more complete description of the county's early schools may be seen in the sections assigned to the various localities.

MURRAY'S MILL.

EARLY FACTORIES.

As soon as a community was formed in early Maryland, a grist mill made its appearance, and these were the first manufacturing plants of the Colony. The early settlers could make or import their clothing and furniture, prepare their food locally, but a necessary part to every establishment was an old grist mill, on the bank of a stream which furnished power to turn its wheels.

Of these early mills, Caroline county had its share and most of them are standing today, so well constructed were they, being chiefly of brick.

Murray's Mill at Linchester is probably one of the first built and best known. Before the Revolutionary War this mill which had been established, perhaps, as early as 1670, belonged to Col. Jas. Murray and during the Revolutionary War ground flour for the soldiers. Though rebuilt at various times, a portion of the original structure still stands.

Records show a lease of the Mill at Potter's Landing (Williston) in 1778 made between Nathaniel Potter and James White, both of this county. A part of the lease is here given:

Nathaniel Potter "Doth grant and let .... that Mill, on the head of Cokiases Creek, together with four acres of land, lying convenient to said Mill, with liberty of timber for use of said Mill, and dwelling house now built on said land, to have and to hold the said Mill and four acres of land, for and during the term of twelve years and every year therefore shall pay the full and just sum of 7£ 10s common circulating currency, and to grind the said Potter's grain, toll and hopper free, and boult (sift) the same for the use of his family; the aforesaid to be paid yearly on the first day of January and the said Mill and appurtenances thereon to be left in sufficient grinding repair."

This mill seems to have been rebuilt by General Wm. Potter on a large scale which included the building of a heavy dam (now the state road) and the providing of a ship channel up to the mill. This mill still operates and is owned by W. C. Todd.

The Brick Mill along the Choptank about three miles north of Denton was probably built by either Thomas Hardcastle or John, his son, both of these men being great builders. The landing at this place was also well known in the early times, as it marked the turning point of boats in the river and served as a shipping centre for a large territory roundabout. This mill was destroyed some years ago but the old brick house nearby still remains.

Mills, some of them brick and still standing, were early established as follows: Bloomery Mill near Smithville; Fowling Creek (lower down the stream than the present site); Hog Creek, Anthony's Mill, Driver's Mill (now the water power plant of the Electric Lighting Co.), Nichols Mill (Knott's Mill near Hillsboro), Bradley's (now known as Crouse's), a mill at Old Town Branch which in 1782 was owned by Thomas Goldsborough.

Only a few years later appeared the up-and-down saw mill, several of which were located in the county on small water courses. These held sway for many years until supplanted a generation or two ago by steam saw mills.

Tanneries were also quite numerous in the rural sections before 1830. The art of tanning had been introduced into America as early as 1630, the old process of using bark and lime being, of course, in general use.

There were several reasons for the early growth of this industry—the great cost of imported leather, large quantity of cattle and hides, and cheapness of labor.

While the process of tanning was very slow, the quality of the leather produced was much superior for endurance than is the product of our modern manufactures where hides may be changed into so-called leather within 24 hours.

As is to be expected, there was a tannery located in nearly every trading centre of the county at that time as at Greensboro, Hillsboro, Potter's Landing, near Hunting Creek, and the North West Fork.

Some iron ore had been found in the county as early as 1780 and this together with the State law which encouraged the establishing of iron foundaries, led to the starting of at least one or two plants in Caroline County.

The Douglass brothers, who came from England about 1780 and located near Smithville, constructed the first foundry, perhaps. One of these men had learned the trade of iron master in his home country, which largely accounts for his undertaking here, no doubt. It seems likely that this plant was not continued very long on account of the poor quality of any ore that may have been found.

Very early, too, in the county some plow factories were erected—the more important ones, perhaps, being the one in Denton as described elsewhere and one near Beartown an early settlement located in the vicinity of Mt. Zion.

Crude as must have been the products of these early enterprises when the metal parts of plows were probably moulded as one single piece of cast iron, this implement was much superior to the earlier plows and paved the way for the modern forms of plow machinery.

Carding of wool for spinning, all of which had been heretofore done by hand in the home was given a fresh impetus when a machine for such a purpose was constructed at Anthony's Mill near Denton, the same to be operated by water power.

SOAP MAKING.

THE CIVIL WAR.

Late in the year 1860, the people of Caroline County were naturally much disturbed at the threatened Civil War and disunion by the secession of some of the Southern States. Public sentiment divided the people into two classes, the larger, perhaps, being in favor of maintaining the Federal Union; the other class in favor of secession.

Many people who had heretofore been friends were bitterly opposed to each other—some for the North—others for the South. This was the condition in Caroline County when four companies of Union soldiers were enrolled in the four centres of the county.

For some time our people felt the restrictions and great inconvenience of army regulations, though not much of the time under a military guard. Persons could not go to Baltimore, could not return home by boat without a pass from the Provost-marshal. As the war continued, many men were deprived from voting at the general elections, unless they took the oath of "allegiance," which some refused to do.

During this period also, a new Constitution was adopted by our state for the purpose of disfranchising those who in any way were in sympathy with, aided or abetted the southern cause. How could such a measure be passed when a majority of sentiment was against it is explained by Scharf's quotation from the *Denton Journal* of that time: "In counting out the ballots in this district (Denton), but forty-seven votes appeared against the Constitution; whereas eighty-nine voters whose names appear upon the poll-books, have certified and propose to swear, that they voted against the Constitution. Five others likewise signified." Fortunately this obnoxious document was set aside at the close of the War and a new one made. It is likely, too, that some of our citizens were imprisoned for a semblance of not being strictly loyal to the Federal Union. Doubtless there was much needless inconvenience and annoyance arising from arbitrary acts of soldiers who exceeded their authority when suspicions were aroused, but such seem to be the outcome of civil strife and nearly always the accompanying agents.

The person, perhaps, most directly responsible for the unnecessary and unlawful acts of soldiers and guards during the Civil War was not Lincoln, as many have supposed, but rather his Secretary of State—Wm. H. Seward, whose bigotry and un-democracy may be readily observed from his boastful remark to Lord Lyons: "My Lord, I can touch a bell on my right hand, and order the arrest of a citizen of Ohio; I can touch it again, and order the arrest of a citizen of New York; and no power on earth except that of the President can release them. Can the Queen of England do as much?"

Perhaps, several young men from our county with courage and strong feelings for "Southern Rights" went South and entered the Southern Army at the risk or sacrifice of their lives in defense of the principles they conscientiously entertained. Unfortunately we have been unable to secure the names of but two such young men—Messrs Alexander and Frank Gadd—brothers of our former Countian and well known citizen, Col. Luther H. Gadd. It was with much difficulty that these and other men from Maryland entered the Southern Army. The Potomac River and Chesapeake Bay were well guarded to prevent just such happenings.

The story is told of some men from Queen Anne county who had planned to drive down to the bay shore in Dorchester county and then take a boat to the Virginia Shore. To prevent suspicion while on their way through Caroline and Dorchester counties, they carried along some hunting dogs and whenever they found themselves watched, did not hesitate to climb out of the wagon with their dogs and spend some time in rounding up the birds and rabbits in that section before proceeding on their way.

On the 4th of August 1862 President Lincoln ordered a draft of three hundred thousand militia for nine months, unless sooner discharged, and directed that if any state did not furnish its quota of these men, the deficiency of volunteers in that state would be made up by special or individual draft. Of this number, Maryland was to furnish 19,000 men and Caroline County 304. As 231 county men had already volunteered into service, only 56 were required to be drafted after allowance was made for excess apportionment. The long-expected draft took place throughout the state on the 15th of October 1862, after the enrollment had been completed. Those drawn for service were notified to present themselves at the place of rendezvous within five days. Substitutes were accepted in place of those unwilling to serve in person; and a lively business was done in that traffic, prices ranging from $200 to $600. Some of these substitutes, escaping from the camp of instruction, sold their services over again.

In 1864 another draft of 2000 men from the state was made and Caroline County likely furnished about thirty.

Unfortunately we have been unable to obtain a list of the drafted men from our county, though a complete list of volunteers is given below.

First Regiment, Eastern Shore Infantry.

The First Eastern Shore Regiment of Infantry, Maryland Volunteers, was organized at Cambridge, Maryland, in September, 1861, to serve three years.

On the expiration of the term of service of the regiment the original members (except veterans) were mustered out, and the organization, composed of veterans and recruits, retained in service until February 23, 1865, when it was consolidated with the 11th Regiment of Infantry.

Companies A, B, and C were recruited in Dorchester County, Companies D, E, F, and G in Caroline County, Company H in Talbot County, Company I at Baltimore City, and Company K in Somerset County.

The 1st Eastern Shore Regiment of Infantry, immediately after its organization, was assigned to special duty on the Eastern Shore of Maryland.

In November, 1861, it formed a part of General Lockwood's Brigade in its expedition into and pacification of the Counties of Accomac and Northampton, the eastern shore counties of Virginia.

Upon the invasion of Maryland and Pennsylvania by General Robert E. Lee's Confederate Army in June 1863, the 1st Eastern Shore Regiment of Infantry asked to be sent to the Army of the Potomac at the front, and, with General Lockwood's Brigade, the regiment was transported to Baltimore, and thence marched to the battlefield of Gettysburg, which it reached on the morning of July 3, 1863, and immediately went into action with the 12th Army Corps on Culp's Hill, where it did good service.

After the battle of Gettysburg the 1st Regiment, Eastern Shore Infantry, continued with the Army of the Potomac until Lee's Confederate Army was driven out of Maryland, when, after a brief duty on the upper Potomac, the regiment again returned to the Eastern Shores of Maryland and Virginia, where it continued in the performance of special duty until its consolidation with the 11th Regiment of Infantry, Maryland Volunteers.

During its term of service the 1st Regiment Eastern Shore Infantry, marched seven hundred and sixty (760) miles, was transported by rail two hundred and eighty-three (283) miles and by water one thousand three hundred and twenty-three (1323) miles.

The death list of the 1st Regiment, Eastern Shore Infantry, during its term of service was as follows: Killed in battle, nine (9) enlisted men; died of disease, wounds, etc., fifty-two (52) enlisted men; or an aggregate loss by death of sixty-one (61).

Roster of Soldiers From Caroline County.

Company D. (Greensboro Section).

Name	Rank
Wm. H. Comegys	Captain
afterward Lieut. Col.	
Jas. L. Clendening	Captain
Richard H. Comegys	1st Lieut.
Marcellus Jones	2nd Lieut.
Anderson, John	Private
Anderson, Wm.	"
Anderson, Leven	"
Adams, Wm. K.	"
Baggs, Joseph	Sergeant
Baynard, John W.	Private
Baggs, Andrew M.	"
Boone, John W.	"
Bickling, John S.	"
Bickling, Wm. H.	"
Bennett, John C.	"
Baker, Wm. H.	"
Cooper, James	"
Carter, Wm.	"
Connor, Wm. T.	"
Commegys, John T.	"
Commegys, Wm. J.	"
Cooper, Isaac	"
Cooper, John K.	"
Colgan, Wm. B. C.	"
Chance, Clement	"
Carter, Jas. H.	"
Cannon, John P.	"
Cleaves, Thos. A.	"
Carroll, Chas. E.	"
Clendening, Robert N.	"
Carter, Wm.	"
Draper, John W.	Private
Dukes, Geo. W.	"
Davis, Wm. F.	"
Donovan, Henry J.	"
Downs, Samuel Y.	"
Earickson, Thomas B.	"
Evans, Richard	"
Ford, Wm. H.	"
Faulkner, Thos.	"
Gibson, Chas. W.	"
Harper, Shadrach	"
Harrington, Thos. E.	Musician
Hubbard, N.	Private
Harper, James S.	"
Harper, Wm.	"
Heather, Theo.	"
Honey, James H.	"
Hobbs, Amos H.	"
Hall, James H.	"
Jones, Richard C.	Corporal
Jones, Samuel T.	Private
Jester, John H.	"
Kemp, John B.	Sergeant
Kirk, George W.	Corporal
Lecompt, John C.	Sergeant
Legar, George F.	Corporal
Lang, John	Private
Lucas, Edward M.	"
McKnett, John R.	Corporal
McClain, Wm.	Private
Mounticue, Robert H.	"
Mounticue, Wm.	"
Mounticue, John	"

Name	Rank	Name	Rank
Mounticue, Jas.	Private	Patrick, Wm. J.	Private
McGee, Levi	"	Rawlings, Wm. P.	"
McCullough, Thomas	"	Roberts, Chas. H.	"
McClerkin, Jas.	"	Rawlings, Henry C.	Corporal
Melson, Daniel H.	"	Shaw, James H.	Teamster
Melvin, Jacob	"	Shubrooks, Wm. J.	Private
Miller, Augustus	"	Spry, Wm. G.	"
McCann, Michael	"	Sloan, William C.	"
Murry, James	"	Shaw, William	"
Noblett, Isaac	"	Turner, Samuel	Corporal
Outen, Warren	"	Truitt, John	Private
Parker, Geo. W.	1st Sergt.	West, William M.	Musician
Poor, Wm. E.	Sergeant	Wyatt, Elias	Private
Pippin, Robert H.	Private	Whitby, Nathaniel	"
Porter, Robert W.	"	Wooters, John W.	"
Porter, Wm. E.	"	Williams, Benj.	"
Patrick, Noah	"		

Company E. (Preston Section).

Name	Rank	Name	Rank
Andrew Stafford	Captain	Hutchinson, Wm. A.	Sergeant
Jas. R. Hooper	"	Hollis, Wm. H.	Corporal
Jesse W. Blades	2nd Lieut.	Hammond, James R.	Musician
Andrew, Tilghman A.	Private	Hutchinson, Chas. F.	Private
Andrew, John W.	"	Holloway, Robt. J.	"
Arvey, John W.	"	Hollis, James M.	1st Sergt.
Andrew, George	"	Knox, Samuel F.	Private
Blades, Eli K.	Sergeant	Luer, Samuel	"
Butler, Peter W.	Private	Lecompt, Benj. F.	"
Blades, Thos. L.	Corporal	Legates, Wm. T.	"
Bland, Geo. T.	Private	Lane, William	"
Brennan, Michael	"	Moore, Edward T.	1st Sergt.
Beachamp, Batchelor	"	McNeese, John	Corporal
Brumbly, Wm. T.	"	Mason, William	Private
Briddle, James	"	Nichols, Luke H.	Musician
Baker, Peter	"	Nichols, Simon P.	Private
Butler, Wm. E.	"	Patton, Wm. I.	Sergeant
Corkran, Sol. R.	Sergeant	Perry, William E.	Private
Comaskey, Daniel	Corporal	Perry, Chas. W.	"
Cannon, Jas. H.	Teamster	Pool, Levin	"
Cicil, George F.	Private	Patton, Joseph	"
Cheezum, Wm.	"	Potts, William	"
Covey, Joshua	"	Ross, Wm. H.	Corporal
Cheezum, Charles H.	"	Ross, Josiah B.	Private
Covey, Richard	"	Richardson, John T.	"
Carlisle, Alex.	"	Rose, Joseph	"
Christopher, Silas	"	Stewart, Wm. G.	Corporal
Carey, George T.	"	Towers, Wesley	"
Charles, Simon P.	"	Turner, Robt. H.	Private
Conaway, William H. H.	"	Towers, Thos. P.	"
Carroll, Saulsbury	"	Townsend, Alfred	"
Dukes, Geo. T.	"	Townsend, Joshua	"
Dukes, Isaac P.	"	Turner, Jas. H.	"
Dean, Robert H.	"	Turner, John R.	"
Dillon, James B.	Corporal	Trice, John W.	"
Dillon, Lewis J.	Private	Trice, Andrew M.	"
Dean, Bennett A.	"	Terrington, Geo.	"
Eaton, Wm. H.	"	Windsor, Wesley W.	"
Frampton, Wm. E.	"	Walker, Robt. F.	"
Frampton, Chas.	"	Wilson, Jas. V.	"
Fluharty, Daniel R.	"	Watson, William	"
Goetchious, John	"	Waterman, Geo.	"
Gootee, Kelly	"	Williamson, Warner	"
		Walker, Thomas	"

Company F. (Denton Section).

Name	Rank
Thos. Numbers	Captain
Jas. B. Austin	1st Lieut.
Robt. J. W. Garey	2nd Lieut.
Anderson, Wm.	Private
Andrew, Petter	"
Andrew, Matthew M.	1st Sergt.
Andrewson, Geo.	Corporal
Atkinson, William W.	"
Atkinson, Wm.	Private
Alberger, Nathan F.	"
Andrew, Jas. E.	"
Ayers, John H.	"
Busteed, Richard M.	Sergeant
Barkley, Andrew	Private
Barwick, John	"
Beck, Josiah	"
Brannock, Sam. C.	Sergeant
Barnick, Jas. A.	Corporal
Butler, James H.	Private
Baker, Thos. P.	"
Cooper, Nathaniel G.	"
Cooper, Wm. W.	"
Collison, Jos. A.	"
Christopher, John E.	"
Cooper, Sam'l. J.	"
Cooper, John	"
Conoway, Francis	"
Dean, William T.	Corporal
Dickerson, Philip S.	Private
Eaton, John F.	"
Flanagan, John	"
Farley, John	"
Gordon, Chas. L.	"
Griffith, John H.	"
Hammon, Thos. L.	"
Harvey, Charles	"
Hickson, Andrew	"
Joiner, Robt. H. B.	"
Kirkman, Isaac A.	Corporal
Lecompte, Alex.	Private
Long, Alex R.	"
Love, Thomas	"
McNutt, Wm.	Private
Moore, John D.	"
McCaslin, Russell Y.	Corporal
Morgan, Wm. F.	Private
Morgan, George	"
McQuay, Chas. E.	"
Maloney, John	"
Pinkine, Francis E.	"
Pierce, Wm. M.	"
Porter, Joseph	"
Pool, Daniel	"
Parker, Thos. H.	"
Philips, Geo. W.	"
Philips, Wm.	"
Philips, Peter D.	"
Porter, Francis A.	"
Roe, Thomas	"
Robinson, Wm. E.	Teamster
Roe, Alex.	Private
See, James	Sergeant
Sorden, Robt. H.	Private
See, Dallas M.	Corporal
Sorden, Wm. T.	Sergeant
Sherwood, Geo. C.	Corporal
Scott, Hezekiah	Private
Stafford, Wm. P.	"
Spence, James H.	"
Syphers, Francis	"
Scott, Aaron	"
Tharp, Phineas	"
Thomas, Samuel	"
Thomas, John R.	"
Thomas, Sam'l E.	"
Voss, Holiday	"
Willis, Chas. H.	"
Wothers, Jas. W.	"
Wilson, James A.	"
Webber, Wm. T.	"
Webber, Jas. T.	"
Wothers, Daniel	"
Webber, Wm. S.	"
Williams, Geo. W.	"

Company G. (Federalsburg Section).

Name	Rank
Alburger, Wm. H.	Corporal
Andrew, Isaac W.	"
Andrew, Zach.	Private
Andrew, Wm. E.	"
Bannnig, Asbury	"
Banning, Wm. H.	"
Bending, Alex. E.	"
Burke, Jas. T.	"
Cohee, Levin W.	Corporal
Cohee, Mitchel H.	Private
Corkran, Wm. E.	"
Carroll, John W.	"
Collison, Levin R.	"
Charles, Ezekiel A.	Private
Corkran, Sydnaham	"
Corkran, Wm. J.	"
Collins, James C.	"
Camper, Wm. H.	"
Davis, James W.	Corporal
Davis, Chas. M.	"
Davis, Solomon C.	Private
Dixon, George S.	"
Emmerich, John W.	"
Flowers, Alcaid N.	"
Flowers, Wesley	"
Flettwood, William W.	"
Gray, Wm. L.	"

Griffith, John S.	Private	McColister, Benj.	Private
Hirt, Wm. T.	"	Marine, Matthew F.	"
Hill, Jeremiah	"	Neal, Cyrus	"
Hemmons, Wm. J.	"	Payne, Covey	Sergeant
Hines, James W.	"	Payne, John W.	Musician
Insley, Elijah	"	Pattison, John	Private
Jester, John F.	"	Payne, Wm. J.	"
Jester, James A.	"	Poundon, Robert	"
Jester, Mark A.	"	Randolph, Jno. W.	"
Jennings, John J.	"	Stokes, John H.	Teamster
Jones, Chas. W.	"	Stokes, Geo. W.	Private
Kenney, Jos. T.	Sergeant	Smith, Chas. F.	"
Keys, Wm. W.	"	Smith, Levin	"
Lloyd, Jacob W.	Private	Smith, Benj. S.	"
Lloyd, Edward	"	Sutheralnd, John W.	"
Lloyd, Thos. F.	"	Trice, John H.	"
Lowe, Wm. T.	"	Truitt, Benj.	"
Lowe, Marvel R.	"	Tull, John W.	"
Lankford, David E.	"	Thomas, Tilghman H.	"
Lewis, Noah F.	"	Wheatley, Wm. T.	Sergeant
Moore, Daniel W.	1st Sergt.	Williams, Jas. H.	Private
Mowbray, Jacob T.	Musician	Williams, Wm. H.	"
Malloy, John W.	Private	Williams, Thos. F.	"
Moore, Chas. F.	"	White, Henry	"
Milligan, Jas. H.	"	Wright, Twiford N.	"
Milman, Elijah S.	"	Wright, Sam'l J.	"
McCullough, John	"	Wheatley, Edward H.	"

MARYDEL VICINITY.

MARYDEL (HALLTOWN).

About 1850, William Hall purchased a large tract of land. This tract covered part of two counties, Caroline County, Maryland, and Kent County, Delaware. It was covered by a forest.

In a short time a small clearing was made by means of axes. On this clearing William McKnett built a sawmill, where trees were made into lumber for building purposes.

The first house built and owned by William Hall was just across the Delaware line. Part of the house was a shoe shop, where the owner made and sold shoes. This house is still standing, but is used as an outbuilding.

Halltown, as it was then called, consisted of three houses. This name was kept three years. It was then changed to Marydel, taking its name from the two states in which it was located.

Erection of Hotels and Store.

Shortly after the founding of this little village, John Walters erected a building which served as a hotel and bar. In a short time two others were erected. One of these was built by George Jones, who not being able to secure a license for a bar, sold the building, which was afterwards used as a dwelling.

The first store was owned and kept by James Smith. The building is still standing and is occupied by Thomas McGinnis, as a dwelling.

Industries.

In those early days the inhabitants provided food for the winter days. This was partly done by means of evaporting fruit. So litle of this kind of work could be done by hand that it was found necessary to build a factory for this purpose. The first enterprise of this kind was carried on by Joseph T. George. It is said that this one was the largest of its kind on the Eastern Shore of Maryland.

The First School.

Perhaps you are wondering where the children first went to school. A room in the "Evaporator" was used, and the school master was William Jarman.

Later a school house was bulit about a mile from the village, on the Maryland side. The children attended this school until it closed for vacation, which was early in the spring. Theye were then allowed to attend the school on the Delaware side by paying the small tuition of one dollar per month for each child.

First School on Delaware Side.

This school was a two-story building, which served as a school house and church. The first floor was used for school purposes and on the second service was held each Sunday provided a minister could be secured.

Boys and girls in those days were compelled to attend Sunday School twice each Sunday, morning and afternoon.

The First Church.

The first building which was erected and used for religious service was the M. E. Church, South. This building was about one-quarter of a mile due north of the village, on the right hand side of the railroad, just across the Delaware line. The land surrounding the church was used for a cemetery.

In 1871, the first M. E. Church was built, having as its minister A. S. Mowbray.

Another church was added to our number in 1918. This one was the Roman Catholic.

Our Railroad.

If I were to ask you how people travel today you would say first of all by automobiles, motor-cyles, the auto-bus, and then horses, buggies, carriages, and farm wagons. But if I were to ask your grandfather how he traveled when he was a boy I would have a different story.

In those days there were no automobiles and very few railroads in our country, and the railroad which we see from our windows was not there.

The railroad which passes through our town (a branch of the P. B. & W. road) began at Clayton and was laid to a point then known as Jack's Bridge, between Kenton and Hartly. In a short time another strip connected this point with Marydel. The third strip reached to Greensboro, and thence to Oxford, which was the terminus.

The first station-agent (Joseph T. George) occupied a very small building which still stands and is now used for a dwelling.

After the railroad extended as far as Oxford, excursions were frequent. This story has come to us: One day a lady was to take her first ride. She was standing on the platform when the train came in, but made no effort to get on. When the train had gone someone noticed her still standing on the platform and asked why she had not gotten on the train. She replied, "Well, I thought the train took the platform along."

A Duel.

Back in the 70's occurred an incident which served to arouse our then sleepy burg and furnished food for gossip for many days to come. It was the "Fighting of a Duel," the stage for which was set not far from the site of our present school.

The principals were of national and later of international fame; James Gordon Bennett, famous journalist of New York and Paris, and William May, noted clubman, traveler and explorer. While the encounter amounted to but little at the time, it was said to have caused Bennett to move to Paris, where he died in 1918 preceded by a few months by the death of May in Washington, D. C.

Templeville.

About two miles to the north-west of our little village is another village which was formed before our own. In the early times it is said Patty Cannon's agents were busy in that part of the county. They would buy slaves and bring them to this village and hide them. The slaves were hidden in the attic of the hotel, which was then kept by Henry Whiteley. This kind of work did not meet the approval of the proprietor, but when travelers came for lodging they were compelled to care for the slaves also.

Choptank River.

About one-fourth of a mile east of Marydel is the source of the Choptank River. It begins as a tiny stream and widens until it becomes a ditch twenty feet in width. It keeps widening as it gently flows along, until we find a large pond. The waters of this pond turn the wheels of a mill known as the Choptank Mill, now owned by John Medford. This pond furnishes good skating for the girls and boys of the surrounding country. We find this stream winding its way through beautiful groves until at last we have the grand old Choptank.

We are told in one of the groves along the west bank of the Choptank may be found a mound which was once the resting place of an Indian Chief who belonged to the tribe of Indians that made their homes in that portion of this county. This Chief's body was, in later years, removed to Baltimore and kept as a relic of the past.

MAUD HUMMER and Pupils.

The Marydel Duel.

The recent death of one of the principals, James Gordon Bennett, of Paris, formerly of New York, recalls the duel which took place here in 1876. In some way Mr. Bennett and Fred May, of Baltimore, became estranged, presumably on account of the breaking of a matrimonial engagement by Mr. May's sister. A "field of honor" was deemed necessary. A challenge was given and accepted. Pistols were selected as the weapons and the authorities of five states became vigilant to prevent the duel.

May was the first to fire. He missed, but by so slight a margin that the bullet clipped a lock of hair from Bennett's head. Then Bennett's pistol was raised slowly until it pointed directly at May's chest. There was a tense second! Calmly and deliberately Bennett then pointed the pistol upward and discharged it into the air. The dueling party and principals escaped arrest by flight.

The arrival at Marydel that cold, damp December morning of the dueling party, or rather the two parties, was unaccountable and the meaning of the visit was not known by the residents of the town and vicinity for several hours after the meeting. In the party were eight good looking young men, all dressed in fine apparel, several of them carrying blankets in their arms, it being later inferred that the blankets were to be used in case of death or wounding of the men. They left the train immediately after its arrival and walked south down the track, one man of the party remaining at Marydel. The man left behind proceeded to make arrangements for teams to take the eight men away in a short time, giving one excuse or another for the visit of the strangers and their hasty departure. He climbed on the top of a box car on the siding and with a field glass watched the party as it proceeded to a secluded spot in the distance. The farmer who lived nearest to this spot heard two pistol shots and then after a short time the duelists and the friends of each man came back to town. Bennett with his second, surgeon, and one other going to Clayton by a carriage, and May and his chosen ones to Dover, where they still eluded identification, and escaped.

This affair is said by many who were close to Bennett to have been the real cause of his self-expatriation, since it was the only way by which it gave rise. He spent nearly all his time in Europe after the event of Marydel, but he developed in New York one of the finest newspaper properties in the world.

EDINBURGH.

This school which was organized about 1892 took its name from the tract of land on which it was erected.

Meredith House, Henderson.
Old Mud Mill.

Pippin's Church.
Henderson School.

HENDERSON LOCALITY.

HENDERSON—ITS EARLY HISTORY.

Arrow heads, stones, axes, and other Indian relics have been found in the gardens and fields of our neighborhood, so we know that long ago Indians lived where we live today.

The many paths through the forests proved that rabbits, raccoons, opossums, squirrels, foxes, deer, and bears were once plentiful; but there came a time when pioneers came and made it necessary for the Indians, and the larger animals to move farther inland; and there came a time when our village began and this is the way it happened.

At the close of the eighteenth century there was a man by the name of Edward Thawley who owned the little farm now known as "The Carmine Place" or "The Carrow Place."

A widowed daughter, a Mrs. Patrick, with several children, came to live with her father, Edward Thawley. Among these grand children was one very amiable maiden named Elizabeth Patrick. About 1831 a young man from Delaware, Joshua Meredith, came a wooing this Elizabeth Patrick and in 1833 they were married in Busic's Church. Their first home was on the farm now owned by Alonzo Cohee.

When Edward Thawley died this Joshua and Elizabeth Meredith came into possession of his little farm, and in 1849 they built the house which now stands on this land.

The cross roads in our town was first called Meredith's Crossing for this family of Merediths.

Joshua Meredith died 1851. In 1880 Elizabeth Meredith married John Wesley Carmine, and they continued to reside in her old home. Mr. Carmine died in 1891. Mrs. Carmine died July 6, 1899. They were buried in the "Gibson Burying Ground," which is on Mrs. Elizabeth Dills' farm near Henderson.

The name Henderson was given to the town in 1868 for a Mr. Henderson who was a stockholder or director of the Delaware and Chesapeake Railroad.

The first two houses in our village were built in 1866 for Joseph Wilson, who for many years resided in Barclay. The store now occupied by Edgar McKnett and the house just east of this store are those two houses.

Our School.

The earliest records known to us of a school for this community show that a school known as "Cool Spring" stood on a site a few yards northeast of Harry Melvin's house. The name "Cool Spring" came from a spring which was just across the road.

The earliest trustees on record for "Cool Spring" were William Wilson, William Hynson, and Robert Culbreth. Some of the "Cool Spring" teachers were Mr. Tarr, Benny Barnes, Bee Hynson, Bob Booker, and Angie Downes Clark.

About 1873 an attempt was made to move Cool Spring schoolhouse to the site where the present schoolhouse building stands, but the old schoolhouse fell down on the way. School was then kept for a time in the house now occupied by Mrs. Blanche Pippin, or in a building near it called "Gough's Shop." In 1874 a one-room building was erected by Charlie Gibson and Thomas Jones of Henderson, on the spot just north of the intermediate room of the present building. The first teacher in that building was William Straughn. In 1891 another school room was added. The contractor was Edward Insley of Greensboro. In 1911 the original school room was sold to Carroll Johnson and moved. It is now used for a dwelling house. Two new schoolrooms were added to the one that was built in 1891. The builder was William Reed of Henderson. The first teachers to occupy the building after it was remodelled were Foster Davis, Louise Higgins, and Olivia Coffin.

Our Church.

The first meeting house remembered by our oldest residents was a Methodist Church that stood on the north-west corner of Melville's Crossroads. When it was abandoned as a place of worship in 1854, it was used for a stable. Later it burned. In 1854, on the southwest corner of Melville's Crossroads a new church was built. It was called Pippin's Church.

The next church for this vicinity stood where the present church stands. It was dedicated in May 1889. Its first pastor was Albert Chandler. Its last one was Charles D. Sharpless.

In May, 1919, this church was torn down and a new one erected on the same foundation. It was dedicated

September 14, 1919. The minister in charge of the morning service was Rev. Dr. Wise, district superintendent. The afternoon service was conducted by Rev. Mr. Leach of Greensboro Methodist Church. In the evening the late Dr. Clinton T. Wyatt, once a first district resident, and one of the Wilmington Conference's most able ministers, preached. The entire indebtedness on the church was raised that day. The pastor is Charles D. Sharpless.

OUR MILL.

It is hard for us to imagine a time when grain was crushed, by hand, at home, on farms in a stone or wooden mortar.

It is harder still for us to think of the little hand mills which served their day. There was a time in the history of our own community when farmers went to mill just as they did in any other pioneer community. Try to picture a grain sack thrown across the back of a horse, the farmer astride, and a ride through the woods to the mill by the trails worn by Indians.

You would expect to find a mill in the region of running water, for those were the days of water-power, so on the Choptank River that is about two miles east of Henderson you will find the original mill in this vicinity. This mill is locally known as "The Mud Mill." Legally it is known as "The Choptank Mill." It is now owned by John B. Medford. We have not learned what date the mill was first operated, but we have been told it was in operation 97 years ago and the appearance of the building insinuated that it was an old mill then.

OUR POST-OFFICE.

J. C. Koons, first assistant post-master general, wrote that the records show that the first post-office for the vicinity was established February 2, 1855 and John J. Fisher was appointed post-master at Melville's Crossroads.

In those days mail was driven from Easton to the head of the Sassafras River. Melville was on that route.

The name Melville came from a Thomas Melvin, the man who built the early buildings at Melville's Crossroads. The name of our post-office was changed to Henderson July 24, 1868 and William L. Clough was appointed post-master on that date.

Our Railroad.

The railroad that passes through our town is the Delaware and Chesapeake. It is said that the railroad came through Henderson in 1868.

The first depot stood in front of the house where Alda Montague lives. When it was opened a Western Union telegraph instrument was installed. The first agent was John Richardson.

When the line was first opened there was but one engine. It made two trips a day, one up and one down, carrying both freight and passengers. It burned nothing but wood. That engine was called "The Baltimore." The next engine that came into use was called "General Tilghman."

In 1891 the first depot of Henderson was moved to Chapel, Md. A building was brought here and put on the site of the present depot. In 1903 the present building was moved here from Greenspring, Delaware.

Our Telephone.

In 1904 the Diamond State Telephone line reached Henderson and a pay station was established in Clarence Hallingsworth's store.

Drama— "Stage Coach Days."

Time—After supper.
Place—Grandmother's sitting room.
Characters—Grandmother—Bertha Meredith.
Grandson—Jacob Melvin.
Spinning wheel and fireplace used in this drama.

Jacob: Grandmother, we were talking to-day at school about the early days of Henderson—the time when you were young, when the Newlees, Merediths, Patricks, Ayres, and Culbreths lived around here. Tell me about the trains those days.

Grandmother: Trains, why bless you child there were no trains here those days. No indeed, people around Henderson saw no trains, when I was a girl.

Jacob: Why grandmother how did people get from one place to another, and how did you get mail?

Grandmother: Those days people rode on horseback then, too, stage coaches jogged over the sandy roads to carry passengers and mail. The stagecoach that came nearest to us came from Easton and went to the head of the Sassafras River. It stopped at Melville, for our postoffice was there then.

Jacob: How did people know when the stagecoach was coming and where did they wait for it if they wanted to take a ride?

Grandmother: Tra—ra—ra—the postillion would blow his horn long and loud as he neared villages, crossroads, or inns. County folks all around would gather at the stopping places to see the stagecoach pass. This didn't happen every day remember, once or twice a week perhaps. (Grandmother looks over her glasses and says:)

Ah! those were merry days, and it was a jolly time when the old stagecoach drew up before the postoffice door. While the mail was taken off, if any passengers were waiting they took their seats in the coach if the day was rainy; or on the top if the day was warm and fair, travelers chatted with the country folks who had gathered to hear the news. When all was ready the postillion blew his horn the driver cracked his whip, the people cheered and amid the barking of the dogs which had come along with their masters the coach was off on its journey.

Ah! those were merry days. Will I ever forget them! (Grandmother takes off her spectacles, wipes them, puts them on again.)

Jacob: What became of the stagecoaches, grandmother? We never see them now.

Grandmother: When this Delaware and Chesapeake Railroad came through Henderson the stagecoach seemed old fashioned and slow but that is another story for another day when you want to hear more about Henderson's early history.

OLIVIA M. COFFIN.

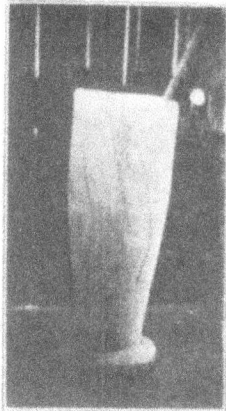

HOMINY MORTAR & PESTLE.

CASTLE HALL.
Built by Thomas Hardcastle in 1781.

GOLDSBORO.

The history of Goldsboro dates back to the completion of the D. & C. railroad in 1867. At this time there were only three houses in the village, with a population of nine persons. It was then called Oldtown, as it was situated on Oldtown Lane.

As everyone knows, a railroad is always an advantage to a section through which it runs, so the country folks around soon become interested, and one of their first desires was to give the village a more modern name. Therefore in 1870, as the land surrounding the village was owned by Dr. G. W. Goldsborough, the name was changed from Oldtown to Goldsborough.

In 1871 the road running to Sandy Island was opened, and in 1873 the road running north past the Hardcastle farm was opened. A few years later a cannery was built by Mr. Robert Jarrell. This is still in operation.

The first merchant was Thomas R. Smith, of Delaware. He was succeeded by Isaac J. Reed, who was burned out. The railroad facilities, and canning industry caused growth of the village. In 1889 Mr. T. Jarman opened a store. In 1907 Mr. J. F. Lane opened one. These were followed by Mr. A. G. Dennison, Mr. A. C. Smith, and Mr. H. L. Morris. The population increased until it now numbers about two hundred.

Castle Hall, the ancestral home of the Hardcastle family, is located a little to the north of the village.

Thomas Hardcastle, the founder of this estate and the builder of the present building at present owned and occupied by J. Spencer Lapham, purchased several hundred acres of land from Capt. John Fauntleroy about 1775.

It seems likely that shortly after Thomas Hardcastle settled at Castle Hall a school was provided, a piece of land being set apart for the purpose and a building erected. This seems to have been the original Castle Hall School.

With the growth of the community this school became semi-private and was attended by the boys and girls of the neighborhood.

Started about 1820 Castle Hall served as a site for the school for the white children until 1898 when the front of the Goldsboro school was erected and Castle Hall school given over to the colored people.

The church which belongs to the Southern Methodist denomination was built in 1871 through a committee of five men, one of whom was Robert Jarrell, father of the present Robert Jarrell, Sr. The site was granted by Thomas Jones.

Before the erection of the church, Sunday School was held in the old Dennison home on the Henderson road.

By 1909 Goldsboro had grown to be a prosperous village with considerable banking business. To meet this situation several representative men organized a state bank, rented a room in Jarman Bros. building, and began business. By 1912 business had grown so rapidly that a new building was found necessary and was built the same year.

Sandy Island bridge which spans the Choptank river a mile east of the village is a concrete structure 200 feet in length and was completed in 1919. By means of this bridge and the excellent shell road leading into Delaware, Goldsboro has become the shipping centre for a large territory extending east, and perhaps ranks next to Ridgely as a forwarding point.

BRIDGETOWN.

Nine Bridges, latterly called Bridgetown, is a small village located near the Queen Anne county line. This settlement has the distinction of being the first incorporated village in our county, as well as being a well known trading centre nearly one hundred years ago.

Located, as it is, near the headwaters of the Tuckahoe river, the causeway leading into Queen Anne county was at one time said to have nine small bridges which have been gradually reduced in number to a single concrete structure of considerable size.

When the county was young, a family by the name of Mason was so prominent in this section that the branch nearby took its name therefrom.

In this section also in Revolutionary War times a company of soldiers was assembled, some of whom perhaps entered the service.

Another indication of the early importance of the place is seen in the establishment of a church just across the line on the Queen Anne side. At this time much rivalry existed between the villages of Hillsboro, Greensboro, and Bridgetown, each of which fought for the honor of having an Episcopal church erected within its limits. Hillsboro won out, but soon after a chapel was erected at Bridgetown, bricks, shells, mortar, etc., for which were hauled from a wharf along the Choptank river.

From 1830 on until the Civil War Bridgetown was the home of a noted citizen and slave trader—Marcy Fountain, whose remains were interred in the village church yard. The house in which this man lived is still standing in the village. A cellar beneath is pointed out as the dungeon in which slaves were confined either for safekeeping or disobedience. It is supposed he was associated in the slave trade with Patty Cannon, a well known character residing near Federalsburg.

In this locality also, one of the first canneries of the Eastern Shore is supposed to have been located. This was in 1867. Peaches were the fruit canned.

Earlier than this a hotel and tavern were kept in a brick building which has ceased to exist.

Long before 1865 a public school existed in the neighborhood. Bridgetown is on the proposed line of the state highway extending from Ridgely to a point beyond Goldsboro.

With the rising energy of the present generation, who knows but that this heretofore sleepy village will outdistance its competitors?

BEE TREE.

For nearly one hundred years the neighborhood of which the present Bee Tree school is the centre has been known by the name of Bee Tree, presumably called by virtue of there being so many swarms of bees in this section.

For years this community has supported a school, public or otherwise, and history recalls that many well known persons have either studied or taught in this institution. Trustees for the school were first appointed by the School Commissioners in 1865.

In 1886 the present site was purchased from Thomas D. Merrick and a new building erected. This school is located not far from Melville's Cross Roads, a well known place during the time of the late Wm. H. Casho. Because of the inaccessibility to trade, many Tories lived in this section during the Revolutionary War and made trouble for the American cause. Later on the section was made famous by the legislative efforts put forth to drain the surrounding territory—a thing which was never fully realized.

BARCUS.

Barcus school, better known as "Dogwood College," has been for thirty years situated on the road leading from Greensboro to the Union colored settlement.

Originally named for the person who owned much land in the community and contributed the first site, it has had at least three locations and as many buildings. The present building was erected in 1895.

Owing to the school's being once nearly surrounded by dog wood trees, the term "Dogwood College" has tenaciously clung to the little institution.

MOORE'S.

In 1856, Thomas Moore came from Sussex County, Delaware, and bought a large tract of land for fifty cents an acre along the east side of the Choptank river, extending from the shell road to what is often called the Zimmerman farm. On this land he built a grist mill and a saw mill.

Mr. Moore, seeing the need of educational facilities for his neighborhood succeeded with the help of others in getting a school house built in 1857 or 8. It was erected on land given by Betsy Baynard.

The first teacher in this building was David Moore, a son of Thomas Moore. Since he was the first teacher and his people were so influential in obtaining the school, it has been called Moore's School. Robert Baggs, a northern man, was also among the first teachers.

About twenty-seven years ago some of the leading people of the district, among who was David Greenlee, were in favor of moving the schoolhouse to what seemed to them a more central location. David Greenlee had a road put through from the Greensboro-Hollandsville road to the Moore Mill Lane, as the road which the school was then on, was called. The building was finally moved to a central location on this new road and placed on land given by William Hutson. Here it stood without any change until 1912, when it could no longer accommodate the large crowd of children attending, when a large room was built in front of the old one.

Before Moore's school was built it is said an old log

schoolhouse stood on the Zimmerman farm near Betsy Baynard's land. There was also once a log schoolhouse, near what is now called "The Cool Spring," between the lands of Wilmer Draper and Thomas Bilbrough.

Betsy Baynard was a large land owner and slave holder. Her old home was about a half mile northwest from our school along the east side of the Choptank River.

Some stories: Miss Baynard was good to her slaves. After the Civil War her slaves were free, but many of them came back, finding they could not make a living. One poor ignorant woman when told she was free gathered up her husking pegs and other belongings, strung them about her body and started off in high spirits. After many days she came stumbling back, ragged and nearly starved to death.

Betsy had two sorrel horses which her servants had trained. When they wanted to ride these horses, they would hit them on the knee and say "Get down" and these horses would get down on their knees and stay there until the rider was on their back.

Betsy Baynard's slaves had their gala times. One man relates how they sometimes had a "husking bee" in the evening followed by a big dinner, music, dancing, games, and wine.

One of Betsy Baynard's slaves, Marie Hawkins, was about fifty years old when the Civil War ended. Miss Baynard did not want Marie to leave her, so gave Marie a lot close by the Choptank River and built a log house thereon.

The people of this community, (Moore's district), feeling the need of a suitable house of worship set to work to erect one in 1873.

Betsy Baynard gave the land for the church site, which is just across the road from her home, and also lumber for the building. This was about five years before her death.

Rev. John Irvin, a Methodist for whom the chapel was named, was the first preacher. David Greenlee was the class leader.

Prior to the building of this church, services were held in the old schoolhouse.

John Irvin also preached at Cedar Grove Chapel and the Kent County, Delaware, Almshouse. His remains lie in the Cedar Grove graveyard. —Contributed.

SUMMER RESIDENCE OF A. A. CHRISTIAN.

GREENSBORO (Choptank Bridge).

An act for erecting a town at the bridge near the head of Great Choptank River in Dorchester and Queen Anne's counties was passed in 1732. The act made these provisions for the laying out of the town.

1 Commissioners were to purchase twenty acres of land in each of the counties at Choptank Bridge, lying most convenient to the river, and have it surveyed and laid out in forty equal lots, allowing sufficient space for streets etc. with posts towards every street. For better distinction the lots were to be numbered from one to forty.

2 The owner of the land on each side was to have first choice of one lot, after which the remaining lots were to be taken up by others. No person could purchase more than one lot during the first four months and these were to be purchased only by inhabitants of the respective counties. Any lots not thus taken up at the expiration of six months could be bought by any one desiring them, and gave the purchaser an absolute estate in fee simple, if they complied with other requisites of the act.

3 The surveyor was to return a plat of the town to the Clerk of the court of each county, to be kept among their records.

4 To secure the ownership of a lot it was necessary within eighteen months from the date of purchase, to erect thereon a house covering 400 square feet of ground. In case this was not done any one else had the privilege of building there, by paying the original sum set and assessed upon such lots.

5 Lots not taken up within seven years after publication of this act were to revert to the original owner.

6 The name given to the village was Bridge-Town. Possessors of lots were to pay one penny current money of Maryland each year to his lordship for each lot.

A sale of one of the lots above mentioned is recorded in the following.

August 27, 1734. Nathaniel Wright of Queen-Anne's County conveys to Peter Rich, of same county, for 500 lbs. of tobacco, "A lot or parcel of ground lying or being in a town lately laid out at the head of Choptank River called Bridge-town, the said lot being numbered six, beginning at a chestnut stake marked as aforesaid and runs according to the plat of said town, together with all houses, gardens, orchards, wood-way, waters, water sources and all profits, commodities etc."

The warehouse at Bridgetown was built under the follwing act:

"BE IT ENACTED by the General Assembly of Maryland, That William Hughlett, of Caroline County, be and he is hereby authorized to build at Bridgetown a warehouse, for containing and securing tobacco offered for inspection, if in the judgment of the levy court of Caroline county, the erecting of such warehouse would promote the public interest and convenience, and he, the said William Hughlett, or those claiming to hold under him, shall provide and keep constantly in repair, beams, screws, scales, weights, brands and marking irons, and all other things necessary for nspecting tobacco brought into the said warehouse for inspection; and the said warehouse, when erected and finished, shall be deemed a public warehouse, and the proprietor or proprietors thereof may demand, and shall be entitled to receive, one dollar for each hogshead of tobacco inspected at the said warehouse, before such hogshead shall be removed, as a full compensat on for the expense of erecting the said warehouse and keeping the same in repair, and for the providing of proper scales, weights, brands and marking irons, and all other things necessary for inspecting tobacco and for the payment of the salary or salaries to the inspector or inspectors of the said warehouse, as the proprietor or proprietors of the said warehouse shall agree to pay; and if any tobacco shall remain in the said warehouse above one year after inspection, the proprietor or proprietors of the said warehouse may demand, and shall be entitled to receive for each hogshead the further sum of twelve and one-half cents for every month thereafter."

Another interesting act passed in regard to this village is given here.

"BE IT ENACTED, by the General Assembly of Maryland, That it shall and may be lawful for any person or persons residing within the limits of the said village, after the first day of March next, to seize and secure any swine or geese that he may find at large within the limits of the village aforesaid, belonging to any person residing therein, and the same retain in his, her or their possession, till the owner or owners thereof shall pay the sum of five shillings for every hog or half dozen of geese, and a proportionable sum for every goose, so taken up, one half for the use of the person or persons taking up and securing the same, the other half for the use of the poor in said county; and in case the owner or owners of swine and geese seized and secured as aforesaid shall not, within three days notice after such seizure pay the aforesaid sum of five shillings for every hog or half dozen geese, and in proportion for every goose seized as aforesaid, to the person or persons seizing the same, in such case the whole of such seizure shall be absolutely forfeited for the uses aforesaid, and it shall be lawful for the person or persons, seizing to sell the game, by public vendue, in the said village, within five days between nine and ten o'clock in the forenoon of the said day, and to apply the monies arising from such sale to the use aforesaid."

In November 1791 the General Assembly of Maryland authorized the purchase of "any quantity of land not exceeding one hundred acres contiguous to Choptank bridge."

This was to be surveyed and erected into a village to be called Greensboro and takes in what was originally known as Bridgetown.

Bridgetown was the site of the county court which was held here for four sessions—Nov., Dec., 1778, June, 1779, Oct., 1779, March, 1780.

It has long been an open question as to where the Bridgetown Court met. However we have definite knowledge that it met in an Almshouse which stood about a quarter of a mile down from the present Choptank Bridge, at some distance back from the water. Since then the river has changed its course somewhat and the site is now closer to the water. A few years since, almost a century and a half after the courts, while excavations were being made for some buildings the workmen dug up bones from what had once been the old pauper graveyard. (For the above information we are indebted to Mr. James Nichols and older citizens of Greensboro.)

A RHYME OF BYGONE YEARS.

Listen, good people, and you shall hear
The story of many a bygone year,
Reaching back to the days of yore
When Indians wandered on Eastern Shore.
Even to sixteen-hundred eight (1608)
When Smith explored the Eastern state.

Once more, five years ere Baltimore came
Claibourn exploring found again
Metapeake, Nanticoke, and Choptank,
Lurking in forests deep and dank.

Sixteen-hundred sixty-nine (1669)
This is the year in which I find
Governor Calvert—Charles by name
Granted the Indians certain claim
To lands. These they could call their own
A "Reservation". The Indians home.
Six beaver skins they yearly sent
To the Lord Proprietor for rent.

For sixteen-hundred eighty-three (1683)
An interesting chapter see.
To the home of William Troth one day
A drunken Indian chanced to stray,
He, both with tomahawk and gun,
Tried for Troth's life—Then away he run.

The trial came, Court judgment sent
The Indian far. 'Twas, "Banishment".
On the Court records e'en to-day is
The noted trial of Poh Poh Caquis.

Years passed. In seventeen-hundred-four (1704)
The rising power of the white man bore
The Red man backward through forest glade,
'Twas then the Nanticoke Treaty was made.
So civilization rose like the tide
And the Indians were scattered far and wide.

As time rolled on the traffic grew,
And so, in seventeen thirty-two (1732)
The government granted the people right
To plot a town on Greensboro's site,
A bridge across the river was thrown,
Accordingly it was called Bridgetown.

Twenty acres in Dorchester lay
Per acre twenty-four shillings they pay,
Twenty more by Queen Anne were given
Shillings per acre, twenty-seven,
And the purchasers paid for years,—oh many
The Lord Proprietor a tax of one penny.
Such is the story I tell to you
Of Greensboro,—Seventeen thirty-two.   (1732)

In fifty-six Arcadians came (1756)
The Huguenot French well known to fame,
Who knows but some fair Evangeline
At Bridgetown crossing was oftimes seen.

Then just before the birth of our Nation
Caroline County was given foundation,
Made from Queen Anne and Dorchester—
Talbot also formed part of her.
Caroline Calvert the name was for,
Wife of Lord Eden, the Governor
Who served the King on Eastern Shore
The year of our Lord, seventeen-seventy-four.   (1774)

Soon was the Revolution here
With its midnight ride of Paul Revere.
Soldiers were gathering by the score,
And Caroline added one company more.

What found we then in a soldiers pack?
What carried he in his haversack?
One half pound powder; a bag of 'ball;
Two pounds of lead, Nor was this all,
A cartridge box filled with cartouch;
A powder horn. What more could you wish
Except his flintlock with trigger set,
And barrel pointed by bayonet.
Some of the bravest no doubt were found,
Carrying guns from old Bridgetown
Then, they made the English run,
Just as yesterday they made the Hun.

Seventeen hundred ninety-one (1791)
War was over. Peace had come.
The State Assembly authorized
That Bridgetown be reorganized.
The old town stood as heretofore
But added one hundred acres more
Purchased from lands on the Western bank
Where the bridge led over the old Choptank.
There on an Indian summer day
Old Bridgetown was laid away.
The new town born was called I trow
By its present name of Greensboro.
Both records and folk-lore prove I ween
That the town was named for one Valentine Green.

You know the rest,—How Greensboro through
The following century steadily grew,
How in eighteen-eight (1808) a new bridge was thrown
Over the Choptank. The old was down,
How eighteen-sixteen (1816) Public School
And free education became the rule,
Then at a date that has not appeared
A Presbyterian Church was reared.

Later Episcopal and M. E.
Were added to Greensboro's family tree.
In eighteen-twenty-five (1825) you get
Your medicine from Dr. Rousset.
In 1880 a newspaper. Guess?
Why of course the Greensboro Free Press.
Railroad, factories, canneries came.
Now Greensboro is known to fame.

Here's a toast. May her fame spread far and wide
Then, higher rise, like a Choptank tide.
And though in distant lands we roam
May we e'er be proud to call Greensboro—Home.

Recited by BESSIE EDWARDS.

LANDMARKS.

The following are links in the chain connecting Greensboro's past and present:

THE AILANTHUS GATEWAY.

On the Main street of Greensboro adjacent to Four Corners stand two Ailanthus trees, separated by less than six feet, their sturdy trunks and towering tops telling of the passage of time.

The story goes that almost a century ago when the house was first built what is now the sidewalk formed a narrow front yard. The owner brought home his young bride and together they planted two slender trees, one on either side of the gateway.

Time passed and the slender trees grew until their massive trunks and overhanging branches formed an archway beneath which swung the gate.

As the years rolled on the hand of time rested heavily on the house, on the inmates, on all save the trees, which stand like faithful sentinels casting their shadows on the third generation who stand beneath at the Ailanthus Gateway.

THE OLD TILDEN HOUSE.

On the south-west corner of Main Street and Railroad Avenue stands a residence gray with the passing

Old Main Street, Greensboro.
Ailanthus Gateway.
Crawford House.

Saddle Bags of Dr. Roussett.
First School.

years. This is one of the oldest buildings in Greensboro. The time of its erection has not been definitely determined but we place it about 1844.

The court records give this land as part of a tract known as Ingram's Desire, and the sale of said lot, containing "One hundred and thirteen perches and seven hundredths of a perch" to Chas. M. Tilden by Henry M. Godwin on Apr. 11, 1844 for $138. No mention is made of improvements, but shortly afterward the property was sold at a much higher amount, indicating a building.

THE FRIEND'S MEETING HOUSE.

On the south side of town along Maple Avenue may be seen a plot of ground marked by two marble slabs. These are of a comparatively recent date—1862 and 1864—but they serve as a landmark and carry the mind back to the days of long ago.

Folk lore tells of the burying ground—The God's Acre of the Quakers—that lay there. Tells of many other graves, always unmarked, now levelled and become but a memory. The property at that time extended from the present property of J. C. Smith to Main street. The Friend's meeting house stood next the street where part of it is incorporated in the present home of William Kennard (colored).

THE HUGHLETT RUIN.

On the North side of Greensboro may be seen sections of the lower part of a one time substantial building in early days the property of the Hughletts, once proprietors of all Denton Valley.

Many conjectures have been made as to the time of its erection, etc. Appended are some facts that may aid in its "time" and "use":

1. The William Hughlett family came from St. Stephens Parish, County of Northumberland, Virginia in 1759.
2. William Hughlett died in 1771.
3. The purchase of the section on which the old ruin stands was in 1769 as recorded on stone post "W. H. 1769".
4. Thomas Hughlett, a son prominent in both political and military circles of Caroline Co. was born 1740.
5. On a door of the old ruin yet preserved are the initials and date "W. H. 1769" formed by brass nails.

These have been looked upon as the work of the supposed original owner (W. H., Sr.) but as he died in 1771 that theory seems incorrect. Wm. Hughlett, son of Thomas, was then 20 years old and it seems more like the work of that youth to bring into prominence the old and respected "W. H." which marks a line of stone posts that make a land line reaching over into Delaware.

The most plausible lore is this: In the early days even before Caroline County was, law breakers must need be taken as far as Cambridge or Queenstown for safe keeping. At times this was difficult so W. Hughlett to meet his own personal needs for tobacco storage etc. as well as those of the community built the brick structure before mentioned.

Pointing to this as the correct solution we have the facts that the lower section of the building was divided by brick walls into four compartments or cells. In one of these was a chimney and fireplace for heating. No other use or reason has been assigned for such division.

The second floor had, as far as the memory of the oldest inhabitant goes, groups of large spikes driven in such a manner as was customary for the hanging and drying of tobacco.

The third story seemed to be used for making baskets, packing cases, etc.

According to this the erection dates at any period from 1769 to 1775, the time of Wm. Hughlett or touching the time when his son Thomas was first sheriff of Caroline County. Later it passed from the Hughletts to other hands.

About 1825 Jonathan Nichols met Jos. M. Bernard and a partnership was formed after which a tannery was opened in the building. After the removal of the tannery John Sangston used it as a drying house for a number of years.

Since then it has fallen into disuse and most of the brickwork has been removed for other uses.

REED'S BIG STORE.

This building altho' now removed from its original location and reincarnated as Wheeler's Feed Store, is worthy of mention.

In its early days it stood on the corner now occupied by the Caroline County Bank and was looked upon by Caroline County with even more respect than we today look on Hutzler's of Baltimore. People came from far and near to see the wonderful mercantile venture, and the aisles were thronged on a Saturday by sightseers as well as buyers.

Being built somewhat over 100 years ago it really was unusual in its day for its "bigness."

George Reed, previously mentioned, was sole owner and proprietor.

THE ALMSHOUSE.

This was previously mentioned in the History of Caroline County Courts.

It stood on the Eastern Bank of the Choptank about ¼ mile down stream from the Bridge. It is believed to have been there from 1778 to 1780 and served as a meeting place for the County Court. Nothing remains of it and even as a memory it was almost gone when a few years since some men in making an excavation found a number of scattered human bones. Then J. M. Nichols recalled the lip history received from his father of the Almshouse, the Courts, etc.

OLD MAIN STREET.

"Greensborough" in 1791 was somewhat different in its plan than today. Main street at that time lay nearer the river. It joined R. R. Avenue a block below the present conjunction, then by a winding way reached the present Main street but a shore distance from Riverside Hotel.

The old street has practically fallen into disuse but one need only walk that way to see the years that mark Greensboro's growth.

The weatherbeaten Crawford and Rousset houses tell the story better than any words can.

A FEW FACTS.

The earliest remembered families of Greensboro were:

a. The Hasletts, living over the river near where the present Christian home stands.

b. The Crawfords, whose first home seems to have been the brick building on "Old Main Street." This building has been previously referred to as the first home of Dr. Rousset. Later the Crawfords built and occupied the home now that of the Lobsteins. The latter house at that time fronted on "Old Main" but has since been reversed as shown by the front hall stairs ascending from the rear end of the hall.

    c. The Tildens, whose Main St. home has previously been described.

    d. The Hughletts, previously discussed.

In the early days of Nichols and Bernard's tannery a present day citizen of Greensboro worked for 12½ cents a day (and board) driving the mule that furnished power for the tan bark mill.

In the days when a private school was held here (Miss Rich) punishment seemed even more severe than in public schools. In one case the girls were grouped close together, then a barrel hoop was put over their heads and slid down about their bodies. There they stood and any restlessnes was corrected with a switch.

Another—three girls did not know their definitions and were whipped with a "cowhide."

(By a Pupil)

HISTORY OF GREENSBORO PUBLIC SCHOOLS.

Nineteen-sixteen was the Centennial year for the Public Free Schools of Maryland. Such schools were, a little more than a century ago, unknown in our state, but in 1816 a law was passed establishing free education.

Altho' the date at which Greensboro opened her first free school is not definite, folk lore points to a period almost immediately after the passage of the law. Some time later a building for school purposes was erected on the north side of town. At the present time it is known as the Wyatt home.

At the time of erection it was a two story, two roomed structure. The upper room was at first used only as an Odd Fellows Hall but later a private school was conducted there. The lower room was the District School, where, when the master found his pupils wanting on any subject he stimulated their mental activity by the use of the rod. He thoroughly believed in the old proverb, "Spare the rod and spoil the child."

In 1845 this building was repaired and continued in use as the district school until 1873. After that it was in use time and again for a primary school.

At this time (1873) the number of pupils demanded more room. W. C. Satterfield made a deal with the

Board of Education contracting to erect a new school building near the Choptank bridge, and accept the old building in part payment. The ground on which the old (Wyatt) building stood had been originally donated for school purposes hence a clear deed of ownership could not (and cannot) be given for the property. As an evasion of law the foundation was (temporarily) removed and replaced by "props," and the house classified as movable or personal property.

The new building (Satterfield's) was located near where the Leverage home now stands. There school was conducted successfully for three years. Then in July, 1876 the new school was burned through some unknown cause.

A somewhat weird tale is told concerning the loss of this building. The ground on which it stood formed part of an old cemetery. There existed a superstition that any building placed on this consecrated ground would be destroyed by fire. The idea was based on the occurrence of a number of fires previous to this one, some very destructive.

After the unexpected destruction of the riverside building the construction of the new (Maple Avenue) building was hastened and completed before the opening of school, September, 1876. The rooms (2) of the present building which front on Maple Avenue were opened. J. E. Carroll, who later became Superintendent of Kent Co. Schools, Delaware, was principal.

Since then by a process of addition and division of rooms this Centennial Year building has been made meet the educational needs of the town. It is a low rambling structure of seven rooms.

Although from time to time a number of private schools have been organized, and at one time the dignity of a boarding school was reached by one of these yet none of them had any permanency. Our state educational system alone remains and only the Wyatt house and the primary rooms of our school remains as landmarks of the educational history of Greensboro.

Late in 1919 the people of Greensboro raised by subscription about $1800 and purchased five acres of land from the Bernard estate for a new school site.

During the 1920 session of the Maryland legislature, provision was made for a new building by an Act authorizing the sale of $60,000 worth of County bonds for said purpose. A. W. Brumbaugh was the local member of the Legislature and the following persons compose the building committee: C. B. Jarman, A. W. Brumbaugh, Burt Hobbs, W. P. Manlove and Jesse W. Porter.

HISTORIC ENTERTAINMENT.

Given by the Greensboro School, March 5, 1919.

PROGRAM.

1. Song— "March On!"
2. Recitation— Bessie Edwards
   "A Rhyme of Bygone Years."
3. Song— "Grow Greensboro!"
   ' Now as we sing this oldtime song
   Where the Choptank is washing to and fro,
   Upon its banks our Greensboro stands,
   Which was founded many, many years ago."
4. Original Play— First Primary
   ' The Red Men of Caroline County."
5. Indian Drama—
   "Poh Poh Caquis."
   Scene 1 Fifth Grade
      Attack on William Troth.
   Scene II High School
      Trial of Poh Poh Caquis.
6. Song— "Maryland, My Maryland."
7. Selected Story Play— Grade Two
   "Little Black Sambo."
8. Dramatization— Grades Three & Four
   "Greensboro's Slaves."
9. Historic Dialog— Grades Six & Seven
   "Greensboro's Ancient Days."
10. Song— "Home Again."

THE PLAYLET—GREENSBORO'S SLAVES.

During February our history work was about the slaves that lived around Greensboro before the Civil War.

We found there were quite a number. Some of them were owned by Miss Betsy Baynard, who lived a few miles from Greensboro. She was always kind to her slaves and they loved her and worked hard.

We found, too, that there was a slave dealer named M. Fountain who lived near here. He sometimes sold slaves into Georgia.

From these facts we wrote a play called "Greensboro's Slaves." It was in two acts.

The characters in the first act were: Nancy, an old black mammy with her little black baby which she is trying to get to sleep. Nine pickaninnies who were always getting into mischief. The characters in the second act were:

Betsy Baynard, a slave owner.
M. Fountain, a slave trader.
Karl White, a Virginia planter.
Liz, (colored), a little house girl.
Mick, (colored), a boy who helps around the house.
Old Mose, (colored), a slave that had been in the Baynard family for years.

ACT I.

Nancy enters the kitchen limping, carrying her sleepy baby on her arm. She sits down in a chair and says, "Dear me. How tired I is." She rocks her baby. Nine pickaninnies are playing around the kitchen.

Nancy: Sh! Sh! Sh! Everybody keep quiet while I gets ma baby to sleep.

Violin plays "Humoreske". As Nancy sits rocking her baby the nine pickaninnies begin stepping softly to the music for eight measures—eyes wide, hands lifted—making no noise to disturb Nancy, their mammy.

Nancy stands and sings the following while she sways with the music while pickaninnies still step softly: Go to Sleep Ma Dusky Baby—Tune, "Humoreske."

Sleep and dream of angels maybe,
While yo' mammy rests a little while,
Shut yo' eyes while I'se asingin,
And the honey bees am winging
Makin' honey fo' ma little baby chile.

Nancy: (To the baby) "Bless its little heart! Mos' asleep. Mammy'll put this chile to bed." She reaches behind her for the chair but a mischevious picaninny (Pete) had slipped it away while she was singing and Nancy comes near sitting on the floor. She catches Pete by the arm, shakes him well and says: "Why Pete! You pull a chair from under yo' mammy? Sposin I'd a sot down in dat flo'! I'd a most bust mysef open! Just you clean out ever las one of ye fo' I lick ye all."

Pickaninnies all scamper from the kitchen followed by Nancy.

Nancy: (as she walks out) "Pete most woke up ma baby. Mammy'll put you to bed right away. Most time I was gettin denna any how."

ACT II.

Betsy Baynard enters her parlor fanning herself with her hat. She carries her sewing bag on her left arm. "How very warm it is this morning! I think I'll sit here by the window where it is cool and sew a while."

Liz: (a little house girl enters with her broom) "Missy, want me to sweep up fo' you this mo'nin?"

Betsy Baynard: "I wish you would Liz. This room hasn't been swept to-day. Be sure to sweep well around the fire place."

Liz: "All right, Missy. I'll do my bes." (L. begins sweeping vigorously. She hums "Old Black Joe" as she sweeps. She raises such a dust that Betsy B. has a terrible spell of coughing.)

Liz: "Fo de land sake, Missy, what am de matta?"

Betsy Baynard: "Why Liz, you are making so much dust!"

Liz: (beginning sweeping again) "Dis aint no dust Missy, dis aint no dust." (A knock is heard at the door.)

Liz: (listening hand at ear) "Missy, I believe I hear a knock." (Another knock) "Sure as you's alibin dat am a knock. Shall I go to de do?"

Betsy B.: "Why yes, Liz, don't keep them waiting."

Liz: (goes to door. Bows three times) "Mornin Massy, morn-in. You want my Missy?"

Mr. White: (a stranger) "I want your Missy or your Master or somebody."

Liz: "You sot down here on the piazzy while I go tell Miss Betsy."

White sits down. Liz runs in to Miss Betsy. Liz: "Fo de land sake, Missy, you jus ought to see that good looking guy out thar."

Betsy B.: "What does he want?"

Liz: "He wants you."

Betsy B.: "Did you tell him to come in,"

Liz: "No mam shall I?"

Betsy B.: "Yes indeed. Don't keep him standing."

Liz: "Missy, he aint a standin. He's a settin." (Goes to door) "Come right in Massy, come right into the parlor. Dat's whar Miss Betsy's at." Liz listens at door.

Betsy B.: "Good morning."

Mr. White: "Good morning. My name is White."

Liz: (Aside) "He sho am white." (Runs off stage).

Miss Baynard and Mr. White sit down.

Mr. White: "As I was traveling thru this part of the country I came thru Bridgetown. Quite an interesting place is Bridge-town."

Betsy B.: "What interesting places did you see?"

Mr. W.: "I saw the old ware house that was built by Wm. Hughlett in ——"

Betsy B.: "In 1789."

White: "That was the year. I saw it on a stone at the boun-dary of his farm. You have quite a number of granaries along the river."

Betsy: "Yes, we have quite a number up and down the Chop-tank."

White: "Why, do big boats come up to Bridgetown?"

Betsy: "They come as far as the stakes and the slaves bring the grain the rest of the way in scows."

White: "Scows—what are they?"

Betsy: "They are large, flat boats which have to be poled up and down the river. My slave, Mose, was helping one day last week and his pole broke. He fell overboard of course and such a splashing time as they had!"

White: "Well, I should think so. Miss Baynard, I think I had the best supper I ever had in my life down at the tavern last night."

Betsy: "Well, you know Maryland is noted for its cooking."

White: "That certainly was a fine supper! (a knock is heard at the door. Mick, a little colored boy runs to the door) "Missy, I hear a knock." He opens the door and there stands Marcellus Fountain. "Howdy, Massa, howdy." He puts his hand to his mouth and says, "Fo de land sake it's Massa Fountain. Wonder what he's oin round here! Spec hes uine to buy some of us niggas."

Fountain: "Is Miss Betsy home?"

Mick: "Yes Massa, yes sar. Walks right into de parlor. Shes got company but that don't hurt."

Fountain: "Miss Betsy, I've come for that slave I bought last week."

Betsy: "Mr. Fountain, I'm very sorry to sell Nancy. She's —"

Nancy: "Fountain! Missy, has you sold old Nancy?"

Betsy: "Nancy, I'm so sorry but I needed the money. You know that it means a thousand dollars to me."

Nancy: "O Missy, please don't sell me! I've worked hard fo' you fo' years."

Fountain: (pushing her on) "Gon on. I'm tired of this foolishness. You're my nigger now."

Nancy: "Missy, Massa Fountain 'll sell me way down to Georgia—away from my baby."

Fountain: (flourishing whip) "Get out of here I say!"

White: "What are you going to do with that slave?"

Fountain: "Take her home. What do you suppose I'm going to do with her?"

White: "I'd like to have a woman like that for our nurse down in Virginia."

Nancy: "Buy me, Massa, buy me. You's a kind man I knows."

Fountain: "Go on out of here, I tell you!"

White: "I' give you a thousand dollars for her."

Fountain: "No sir. You can't have her, I just gave a thousand dollars for her myself."

White: "I'll give you eleven hundred."

Fountain: (pushing Nancy ahead of him) "No, sir."

White: "Twelve hundred."

Fountain: "Did you say twelve hundred?"

White: "Yes."

Fountain: "Well then, take her."

Nancy: "Thank you, Massa, thank you! You'll be good to Nancy, won't you?"

White: "Yes indeed. We'll be good to you down in Virginia."

Both leave stage.

Fountain: (counts his money, slaps his knee) "Gee but it does pay to sell slaves. Made two hundred dollars in about two minutes." Walks off stage.

Enter Mose, a poor old darky, leaning on a cane. He walks slowly across the stage. "Poor old Nancy, poor old Nancy. Missy done sold old Nancy to Massa Fountain. Speck Massa Fountain sell her way down in Georgia. Nancy was a good cook. My she was a good cook. I wonder who's gwine to cook dem possums now. Poor old Nancy! Missy done sold old Nancy! Fust thing I knows Missy'll be asellin me! Mose don't want to be sold. Mose is an old nigga."

As Mose limps back across the stage, the cihldren all sing the first verse and the chorus of "Old Black Joe." They sing softly to the accompaniment of the violin.

BAPTISMAL SERVICE AT GREENSBORO STATION—1920.

DR. HENRY ROUSSET.

One of Greensboro's Earliest Physicians.

Looking northward along Old Main Street one may see a house noticeable for the oddity of its structure. Its long low lines, its hipped roof, its dormer windows, its shadowy gray look all mark it as belonging to the days of long ago.

The property which is slowly falling into ruin and disuse was once a show place of the town,—an American type of the French Chateau, having its grounds surrounded by a close clipped boxwood hedge so that even the tallest person could no more than catch a glimpse of what lay behind it.

The enclosed grounds formed an old fashioned garden filled with pansies, mignonette, sweet Williams, and all the riotous blooms dear to our great grandparents. Through this garden, at eventide passed a dark man of medium height carrying himself in an erect and military manner, while at his side walked a petite figure with laughing eye and golden brown hair,—Dr. Henry Rousset, perhaps, Greensboro's first resident physician, and his wife, Augusta Mohlen Rousset.

Both were born "over-seas"—he in Breslau, she in Hanover; but both were loyal Americans, true to the land of their adoption.

Dr. Henry Rousset was born in Breslau, Prussia, November 1, 1785 of Franco-Prussian parentage. Little is known of his early life except that he was a lineal descendant from a noble family, and at an early age was sent to Paris where he was educated in the University and became thoroughly French in his ideas.

With true patriotism he served as a Sergeant-General under Napoleon Bonaparte and was with him at his defeat at Waterloo. In this battle he received a wound almost directly between the eyes. This wound must have troubled him somewhat for he covered it constantly with a surgical patch.

Shortly after the downfall of Napoleon in 1815, Rousset came to America and stopping in Philadelphia met, wooed, and won Augusta Mohlen, then but 14 years of age. After his marriage they returned to France where he practiced medicine for six years, but the youthful bride longing for America they arrived in Philadelphia again in the spring of 1823. Coming via Baltimore he crossed the bay and came up the Choptank with Captain Cornelius Comegys, and was met at the Greensboro landing by Thomas Hughes, who with mule and cart transferred him to the old brick Crawford house.

Soon after he purchased the frame building which became his permanent home. The interior they fitted up in a manner pleasing to themselves. Many things were brought from overseas for the decoration; among which was a large French fire-place—now transferred to another Greensboro home.

An anecdote is told of their housekeeping troubles. Both were "To the Manor born." Servants were scarce, hence, the preparation of food became a problem. A chicken was to be killed—but how? Dr. Rousset overcame the difficulty by performing a surgical operation that ended the life of the fowl.

Hospitality was the home motto—Tea and cakes always awaited the caller.

Dr. Rousset was known far and near as an eminent physician. According to the custom of the day, when visiting his patients he rode on horseback with his saddle-bag filled with medicine, strapped behind his saddle.

His work is done! He went into the beyond in 1871 and his wife followed him in 1885.

On old Main street stands the age stricken house marking where he lived. In the old Methodist cemetery a gray slab marks his final resting place, while folklore has kept alive the patience, skill and wonderful healing power of Dr. Rousset.

THE METHODIST EPISCOPAL CHURCH.

As early as 1785 the Society of Methodists was formed in Greensboro, or Choptank Bridge, as it was then called. The meetings of this Society were held in the homes of the different members, but the members increased so rapidly that it became necessary to have a building in which to worship.

The church was probably erected in 1789 and a deed for the site is now recorded in the Clerk's Office in Denton.

It was in this old building, located on the bank of the Choptank river, the site on which Greensboro then

METHODIST EPISCOPAL CHURCH.

stood, that many had the opportunity of listening to Freeborn Garrison and Francis Asbury, who were among the ministers that visited and served these people at that time.

This church served the people until 1843 when it was decided that a new building was needed, and as the population had by this time extended to the west, it was thought best to have a building near the center of the town, and the site selected was the one now occupied by the old church on North Main Street.

In 1903, sixty years later, when the town having extended still farther to the west the members of this same Society of Methodists, or as they were then called, the members of the Methodist Episcopal Church, built the new church on Railroad Avenue which is in use by them today.

THE CHURCH OF THE HOLY TRINITY.

The Church of the Holy Trinity at Greensboro is apparently the result of the work of two women: Mrs. Angeline Goldsborough, widow of Dr. George Washington Goldsborough, and grand-daughter of Thomas Hardcastle, and Miss Ella Betts, who taught a private girls' school. These two became interested in some children who belonged to no church and organized a little Sunday School of five pupils. This led to thoughts of a parish at Greensboro. The matter was brought before a Convention at Easton by Mr. Ernst and in 1870 a new parish was formed by taking a part of St. John's parish at Hillsborough. The present church building was dedicated in 1875, April 13th. It is said that Miss Mary Reed who lies buried in the old Methodist churchyard provided in her will about $1500 towards the erection of this building.

Mrs. Goldsborough was chairman of the committee which selected the name for the church. The Rev. George Beaven was in charge until Rev. Frank Adkins was installed. The congregation at present is much reduced and is served regularly by the Rector from Denton.

Mrs. Goldsborough is still living and at the age of ninety-two still takes a keen interest in the affairs of the church.

THE HELVETIA PLANT.

June, 1920 opened at Greensboro one of the largest plants on the peninsula. It is one of sixteen owned by the "Helvetia Milk Condensing Company," whose headquarters are at Highland, Illinois.

The plant proper is constructed of hollow tile and is fire proof. It is 279 ft. long and 176 ft. deep, part being one and part being two stories high, while the stack which is constructed of reinforced concrete, measures 10 ft. at the base, 6 ft. at the top, and 125 ft. high and is the largest in this section.

HELVETIA MILK CONDENSING PLANT.

Four milk storage tanks having a capacity of 70,000 lbs. each are installed, while the water tank is 18 ft. in diameter, 50 ft. high and has a capacity of 100,000 gallons. The entire capacity of the plant is between 150,000 lbs. and 200,000 lbs. of milk daily.

The boiler room has three boilers of 150 horsepower each and room for three more of equal size. The building will have its own electric plant and practically all of the machinery will be run by motors.

Employment is given to about thirty men, whose number will be increased as the milk supply increases, until it reaches the plant's present capacity—60 men.

When running at full capacity the farmers will receive $100,000 monthly for milk.

As a future prospect a tin shop, for making cans may be opened, doubling the working capacity of a plant even now, one of the largest on the Eastern Shore.

WHITELEY'S AND LOWE'S.

The history of these communities need necessarily be written in connection because of their joint activities through all the early period.

Doubtless because of the section's proximity to Greensboro, the earliest settled and developed part of our county, and the natural fertility of the soil hereabout, this community seemed to attract and hold men who became prominent not alone in county matters, but in state as well.

Of these early families, Whiteley was probably the best known. It seems that William Whiteley came to this county from Delaware and located just west of the state line, though likely owning real estate in Delaware. There is a record in our Clerk's Office that William Whiteley purchased over 1000 acres of land in a body shortly after the Revolutionary War. Elsewhere in this volume is given an account of this man.

Thomas White, another prominent man of this county, and one of our first court justices lived in this section. This family came from the section of Delaware near where White's Chapel now stands. When Bishop Asbury, who had been preaching Methodist doctrine on the peninsula was forced to suspend work for about two years during the Revolutionary War, he found refuge at the home of Mr. White on the Delaware side. Perhaps it should be explained that the Tory element, which was in considerable strength at that time in this section, naturally held to the Episcopal church, the established Church of England, and opposed any counter doctrine as advocated by the rising Methodist denomination. It has been stated elsewhere that the Carter family succeeded to the ownership and possession of the property of the Whites in this section.

Being along the main highway from Queenstown to Dover, these fertile lands peopled by prominent and active families and tilled by numerous slaves, it can readily be imagined that this entire section was very busy in these early times.

Lee's Chapel that stood on the road from Carter's Corner to Whitelysburg seems to have been the first place of worship in this neighborhood. It seems likely too, that it was once used for a school, though we have no authority for this assertion. This building was erected in the latter part of the eighteenth century. A family of Lees who lived across the road from where the Chapel was erected, used their influence in having this church built, and a member of this family, Rev. Lee, was among the preachers of the church. This Chapel is a small wooden building; the frame work is all hewn and is put together mostly by means of wooden pegs. Very few nails are used, but those which are used were made by the village blacksmith.

At that time almost everyone went to church regularly. Shoes were very scarce at that time so the boys and girls went to church bare-footed just as long as the weather permitted. The grown men and women carried their shoes in their hands until they were almost in sight of the church and then put them on. They took them off again as soon as they were coming home from church. This church was used until the Civil War when Sheppard's Chapel was erected to take its place.

When the state law as to schools was changed in 1868 and trustees were appointed by the School Commissioners, provision was made for Whitelysburg. This name of the school was continued until 1883 when Whiteleysburg was discontinued as a public school. About this time Benjamin Whiteley recognizing the great need for a school nearer than Lowe's built a school house and planned a school for the children of this section. Late in 1885, the School Board again decided to pay the teacher and thus Whiteley's was again open, remaining so until about 1906 when the very small attendance necessitated the school's being again closed.

Besides giving money towards the school, Mr. Whiteley always sent a Christmas box to the school. This box contained a gift for each pupil and for the teacher. He also wrote a long letter each year to be read to the children.

Thus did Benjamin Whiteley, the worthy son of his highly representative father, keep alive his interest in childhood though advanced in years. Mr. Whiteley died in Catonsville a few years ago at the age of nearly one hundred years.

On the road to Greensboro, William Hughlett and Dr. Rousset owned much land, acquired either by grant from the state government or by purchase. As both of these men will be treated under the Greensboro section, no further notice is necessary here.

About the year 1855 the old Rawling's school was built. This school was erected on Mrs. Rawling's farm at the end of her lane, on what is known as the Whitelysburg road.

After a time Esma Lowe bought the farm on which the school stood; then its name was changed from Rawling's to Lowe's, the name which it bears today, though the location has been changed slightly and a new building erected.

Several years ago a Seventh Day Adventist Church was built at Whitelysburg, also a small school provided for the children of this denomination in the neighborhood.

In 1919 a joint public school with Kent County, Delaware, was started in this small building.

Contributed by ETHEL EVELAND, *Teacher*,
and the Pupils of Lowe's School.

BURRSVILLE SCHOOL.

Formerly an M. P. Church. Erected About 1833.

BURRSVILLE. (Union Corner, Punch Hall).

The first name above seems to have been given the adjoining villages of Union Corner and Punch Hall about the time of the establishment of the postoffice there, years ago.

Two very different stories are in circulation in regard to the origin of the name Punch Hall. One authority tells us that the name originated from the fact that runaway slaves hid under a building called a hall standing on what is known as the F. C. Porter lot. To capture these fugitives the citizens used long poles to punch them out. Thus came the name Punch Hall. Other authorities claim that the name Punch Hall originated from a citizen by the name of Hall living in that end of the town who kept the inn and sold strong drink.

The name of Burrsville was probably selected for the postoffice without reference to any suggestions in the neighborhood. Be this as it may, we know that Union Corner was a little hamlet, long years ago, while the central group of buildings was designated as Punch Hall.

The first public school for this section seems to have been Chinquapin, provision for which was made by the Legislature about 1840. This building stood on the Saulsbury land about one mile west from the village on the Denton road and continued as the school for the neighborhood until sometime in the seventies when it was discontinued and a school building erected on the spot now occupied by the Union M. P. Church. This was Burrsville's first public school and the building thereof by private means was prompted doubtless for fear the colored people after the passage of the Fifteenth Amendment would be allowed the privilege of attending school with the whites at Chinquapin.

In eighteen hundred and eighty-four this building was moved about a mile west of the village to a corner of the county farm where it has since been used as a colored school. The old M. P. Church, erected in 1833 or 1834, was purchased by the county and is still used as the public school building for Burrsville. Thus this village has the honor of having its school housed in one of the oldest frame buildings in the county, perhaps, in the state.

At the time the church was purchased for the school, the school lot was sold or traded to the church trustees for a church site as indicated above.

WESLEY M. E. CHURCH.

The following is taken from a note book kept in eighteen hundred thirty-three by Thomas Baynard:

"A record of the proceedings of the trustees legally appointed in the year of our Lord one thousand eight hundred and thirty three for the Methodist Episcopal Church near Burrsville which church is not yet built but is in contemplation and to supply the place of the old church near the said village which is now in a condition not fit for worship."

The said church which was completed in eighteen thirty-five, was named Wesleyan Chapel and dedicated December twenty-fifth of the same year.

The site for this church was purchased from Reuben R. Richardson of Burrsville and was located between Burrsville and the present M. E. Church. This building served as a place of worship until eighteen seventy-two, when it was sold to John Cahall, a son of Archibald Cahall, who was one of the building committee of eighteen thirty-three, and is now used as a barn on the Cahall farm.

The present M. E. Church is known as Wesley's Chapel and was erected in eighteen seventy-two on a corner of the Cahall farm. It is said that Thomas Melvin, one of the founders of the Methodist Protestant Church, then living near Burrsville did about 1834 deed a piece of land to be used as a site for an M. P. Church to be erected. The church that was built about this time is in the main the same structure that has been used as the public school since 1884.

From Burrsville neighborhood have gone out some men of state and national fame. Among them are the Saulsbury brothers who attended Chinquapin school and in young manhood moved to Delaware. One of them, Gove by name, became a prominent physician of Dover, and later governor of the state. Another brother, Willard, became Chief Judge of the state and a third one, Eli, served as United States Senator from Delaware for nearly a generation. The Melvin family from which sprang several important men who have filled honored places in the Maryland Annual Conference of the M. P. Church was prominent here years ago. Among them are Walter Graham, D. D., and T. H. Lewis, D. D., President of Western Maryland College, also three Melvin brothers who served with honor in the ministerial ranks. Still later we have Dr. M. Bates Stephens, State Superintendent of Public Schools.

Contributed by MARY E. RAUGHLEY.

CENTRAL.

A sketch—An Old Time Maryland School—in this volume describes the school at Townsends' Cross-Roads which was the forerunner of the famous Chinquapin school erected on the road to Burrsville in about 1840.

After this old building (Chinquapin) had stood about fifty years there were a good many people moving in around Towson's Cross Roads. These people thought it was too far to send their children to this school, hence they wanted a new building.

John R. Wyatt gave one acre of wood lot on the North West side of his farm for their school building. The timber was cut and the building erected in 1879. After it was completed they decided to call it the Wyatts' school in honor of Mr. Wyatt.

A few years later the Methodist Church was built
by the side of the school. The people in the community
decided to name it Central it being about central of the
community and midway between Burrsville and Denton.
The school has since been known as Central.

DROWNED VALLEY, NEAR CENTRAL.

Caused by the Raising of a Mill Dam.

CAMP GROVE (Chilton's).

The first school for this section was organized many
years ago, because legislature records indicate that provision was made in 1830 to move from the present Sheppard's church site a school building, to the south end of
Carter's or White's Lane, hence the name Carter's,
which was applied to the school for many years afterwards.

One reason, of course, for this early school was the
fact that several prominent men lived in this community
in Revolutionary War times. Among them may be mentioned Col. Mathew Driver, who built and lived in what
is the Brick House on the Horsey farm. A complete description of this man and his home is given elsewhere in

this book. Thomas White, another large land owner, lived on what is now the Carter land. Between the camp-ground and Burrsville was the Fountain estate. Of this family Andrew Fountain was a captain of militia in the Revolution, while Marcy Fountain became a prominent citizen of the upper section of the country.

At this time or a little later, William Chilton possessed the land around the camp ground and former mill site and erected at the head of Chapel Branch a mill which continued for many years. Upon the schools' being located on his land, or a lot therefrom, it was given the name of Chilton's, which is used by many at present, though the official name is Camp Grove.

Two school buildings have been burned on the site of the present one which was erected in 1918 through the cooperative efforts of a few enterprising residents of the community.

Camp Grove School takes its name from being on a part of the old Chilton's camp ground. For many years this grove was annually tented, and religious services held under the auspices of the Methodist Protestant denomination. Along with improvement in travel and other changes in events, the camp, in the main, has ceased to function as in olden times, and is rapidly disappearing.

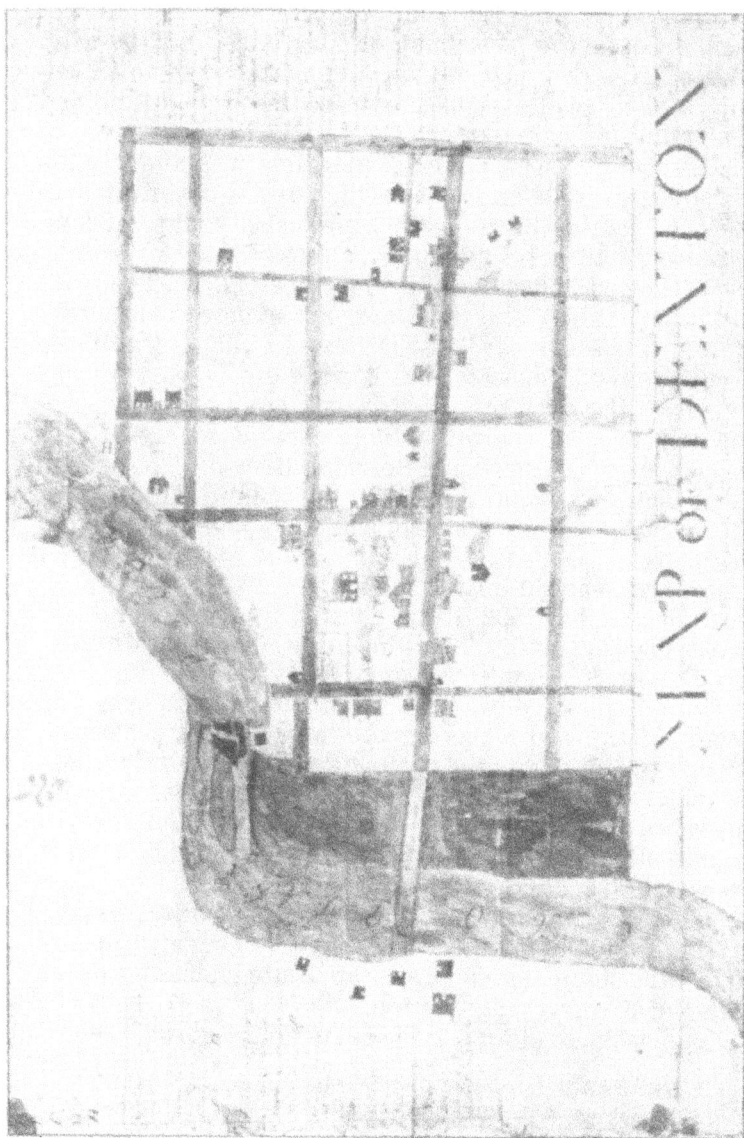

MAP OF DENTON

DENTON.

Denton, for more than a century the county seat of Caroline County, on the east border of the Choptank, was originally named, "Edenton," in honor of Sir Robert Eden, proprietary Governor of Maryland in 1769-1774. The "e" was dropped, thus changing Edenton to "Denton" a little while subsequent to the Revolution and Governor Eden's departure for England.

The county seat, which at the time was at Melvill's Warehouse, a mile and half farther up the river, was removed to Denton in the early nineties; a square of land containing four acres having been purchased for the erection of a court house and jail in October 1791. The price paid was "thirty shillings, current money, per acre." The old map on record in the office of the Clerk of the Circuit Court, an interesting showing of the work of that day, bears the signature of Robert Orrell, surveyor, and those of three of the five village commissioners—Levin Charles, Alex. Maxwell and Solomon Brown. The village as shown by the map numbered forty-nine buildings in all. It was then a village of some commercial importance as is evidenced by "shop," "store," "wharf" and "granary" marked on the map.

In November 1792 it was enacted by the General Assembly of Maryland, "That Joseph Richardson, Christopher Driver, William Robinson, Henry Downes and Robert Hardcastle have full power and authority to open and lay off a road, and make a good and sufficient causeway, through the marsh on the east side of Choptank river, opposite, or as nearly opposite the court-house of said county as they may think best or proper, and erect a wharf at the end of said causeway, if they shall think it necessary."

In 1796 William Richardson, William Potter, George Martin, Henry Downes, Christopher Driver, Joshua Driver and John Bennett were appointed commissioners to attend to surveying Denton.

The act providing for the surveying follows:

"WHEREAS it is represented to this General Assembly, that the owners of the land contiguous to Denton, in Caroline County, are desirous that a village should be surveyed and laid out, with convenient streets, lanes and alleys; therefore, BE IT ENACTED, That the said commissioners, or a majority of them, are hereby authorized and empowered, with the consent of the proprietor or proprietors aforesaid, to survey and lay out any quantity of land, not exceeding fifty acres, including the public square called Denton, in Caroline County, and the lands thereto contiguous and the same, when surveyed, to be erected into a village, and to be called and known by the name of Denton; and such village, when surveyed and laid out, to divide into lots, which lots shall be numbered and bounded by stones, at every corner of the same; and the said commissioners, or a majority of them, are hereby authorized and empowered to survey and lay out a sufficient number of streets, not exceeding fifty feet wide, as also a sufficient number of alleys, not exceeding twenty feet wide, through the said village, for the public convenience; * * *."

At the same time provision for relaying the public square was made in the following act:

"WHEREAS it is represented to this General Assembly, that the public square of Denton might be much more advantageously located, by exchanging a part of the said public square for a small quantity of land lying on the south side thereof, by means whereof a communication with the main street, leading through Denton, will be formed with the said public square; therefore, BE IT EN-ACTED, That the said commissioners, or a majority of them, are hereby authorized and empowered to survey and lay out anew the public square, which was originally laid out and condemned in pursuance of the act of assembly to which this is an additional supplement; and in case the said commissioners, or a majority of them, shall deem it most advantageous to the public, they, or a majority of them, are hereby authorized and empowered to ex-change a part of the said public square lying on the northernmost side thereof, not exceeding one acre, for the like quantity of land on the southernmost side of the said square and upon the pro-prietor or proprietors of any such land so exchanged executing a deed or deeds of bargain and sale, agreeably to the laws of this state, such land shall be forever thereafter deemed and taken to be part of the said public square, and as such to be used and en-joyed."

The Old Market Place.

Nearly a century ago, there was erected on the Southeast corner of the public square facing Market Street, where the Masonic Hall now stands, an open building about thirty feet long, which was used as a market place. Across the pillars which supported the roof extended boards for shelves. Some green produce, eggs, and meat, including beef by the quarter and whole pigs as well as smaller quantities, were brought here and either sold from these shelves or the wagons which were backed up there for that purpose. Here also slaves may have been sold.

The following comes under date of 1827:

"Whereas the commissioners of the village of Denton have erected on the public ground in said village a market house, and Whereas the members of Washington Lodge No. 59, of Free and Accepted Masons, have erected over said market house a room or rooms to be occupied as a Lodge room or rooms, Therefore

"BE IT ENACTED, by the General Assembly of Maryland, That James Sangston, John Brown, Nehemiah Fountain, Bennett

Wherrett and James Hand, the commissioners of the village of Denton, and their successors, or a majority of them, shall for ever hereafter hold, possess and enjoy, all the public ground on which said market house and Lodge house and Market-street, and also all the public ground between said market house and Lodge house and Second-street, and twenty feet of public ground immediately contiguous to the west side and north end of said market house; Provided that nothing in this act shall be construed so as to authorize the said commissioners or their successors or the officers of Washington Lodge to erect thereon any other public buildings for the use, convenience and benefit of the said village.

"AND BE IT ENACTED, That the members of Washington Lodge No. 59, and their successors, shall for ever hereafter hold, possess and enjoy, the said room or rooms erected by them over the said market house, in as full and ample a manner as if they had an actual deed for the premises on which it is erected, without any let, hindrance or molestation, of any person whatsoever; and in case at any time the said Lodge shall go down, the commissioners of the village of Denton shall have it in their power to rent the room or rooms now occupied as a lodge room or rooms, and apply the prceeds to the payment and costs of the subscribers for the erection cf the rccns now occufied as a Lodge after keeping up all necessary repairs, any thing in any law to the contrary notwithstanding."

BANKS.

In December 1813 a number of citizens of Caroline County prayed that a bank be established in Denton. The acts regarding the same are given below:

"BE IT ENACTED, by the General Assembly of Maryland. That a bank to be called and known by the name of The Bank of Caroline shall be established in the village of Denton, in Caroline County."

"AND BE IT ENACTED, That the capital stock of this bank shall consist of two hundred thousand dollars, money of the United States. divided into eight thousand shares of twenty-five dollars each."

FIRST NATIONAL BANK IN COUNTY.

COL. PHILIP W. DOWNES.

Denton is the possessor of three prosperous banks. Of these the most important as well as the oldest in Caroline County is the Denton National. This bank was organized in 1881 with Col. P. W. Downes as first president and R. T. Carter as first cashier and transacted business on the site of the present bakery. Later on the bank moved into its new brick home on the corner of Main and Fourth Streets. In 1902, the present handsome pressed brick building was erected at a cost of $18,000. The present capital stock of the bank is $100,000, with a surplus of $200,000, which gives the bank a high rating, standing as 16th in the state. There are now six persons regularly employed in this bank, with Harvey L. Cooper as president and W. I. Norris, successor to T. C. West, who served thirty-two years, as cashier.

The Peoples' Bank which became a State Bank in 1919 was organized in 1898, with a capital stock of $50,000 as a National Bank, with Joseph H. Bernard as president and George Wallace as cashier, and transacted business for a number of years in the Masonic Building. Later, the present bank was built at a cost of $20,000. Mr. Bernard procured some Indiana limestone, saved from the Baltimore Fire, as the building material. Henry T. Nuttle of Andersontown, is now president and T. F. Johnson is cashier.

The youngest bank of Denton is the Farmers' and Merchants State Bank, which was organized in 1919 with John T. Carter as first president and Sherman Hignutt as cashier. It is located on Main and Third Streets in the Carter Building. Its Capital Stock is $30,000. The Board of Directors are pleased with the business they are transacting and it promises to become a strong banking institution.

First Factory.

Perhaps the first factory built in Denton, was the old plow factory, located on the northeast corner of Main and Fourth Streets and erected about 1835. Henry Wilson, father of the late Charles Wilson, an eccentric old gentleman, but highly esteemed by Caroline Countians, was proprietor. The factory produced complete plows for many years, one of which is still owned by Mr. C. H. Stewart. After the death of the owner, the manufacture of plows was discontinued and after much wear the walls finally decayed. Many of the residents of Denton recall the happy hours of their childhood when "coming home from school they looked in at the open door" and wondered at the sights and sounds of the first factory they had ever seen.

Leading Merchants in 1820.

In 1820, according to the diary kept by the late Jefferson Pratt, Sangston and Hardcastle were the leading merchants of Denton. They bought tan-bark, wood, grain, dried fruit, feathers, wool, poultry and other country produce, which they shipped to the city by sail vessels. In this year corn sold at twenty-five cents a bushel and wheat from sixty to eighty cents.

Old Coins Used Long Ago.

During the early days of Caroline County the coins that were in general use were very different from those that we use to-day. At that time they had the twelve and one-half cent piece which was called a "levy," the six and one-fourth cent piece which was called a "fip," the three cent piece, and the two cent piece. In some sections of the county the levy was called a "bit" and even today in some localities we hear of the quarter dollar being called "two bits."

Early Travel Across the Choptank at Denton.

It has not always been as easy and convenient for the people of this community to travel across the Choptank River as it is now. In the early days their only way of getting across here was by means of small boats or ferry which perhaps landed near what is now the jail, then called Pig Point.

About 1792, probably in order to shorten the distance of the ferry across here, there was a causeway laid through the marsh on the east side of the river. This causeway was very low at first and was often covered with water. Later it was raised and travelling across it was much easier. Many of our older residents remember a few occasions when they had to be rowed to the top of the hill in boats.

DENTON IRON BRIDGE. Erected 1875.

A few years later in 1811, a number of citizens on seeing how much more convenient it would be to have a bridge here, decided to form a company to erect one, so they were incorporated by the General Assembly under the name of "The President and Directors of the Denton Bridge Company."

This first bridge was a narrow one way drawbridge with a draw twenty-six feet long and a toll bridge to all persons not residents of Caroline County. The Levy Court paid a small sum ($280) each year to allow these to go over free. Those who came here from other counties had to pay twenty-five cents for a four-wheeled vehicle; twelve and one half cents for a two wheeled vehicle; six and a fourth cents for a horse and rider; three cents for each mule or horse, and two cents for each foot passenger. In 1818 this toll was doubled.

This bridge remained a toll bridge until shortly before the Civil War, when it was sold to the county and in about 1875 replaced by the iron bridge which remained standing until 1913 when the concrete bridge was constructed.

OLD STAGE ROUTES.

The old stage coaches which ran between Denton and various points, long before the railroads were built in Caroline County, are well remembered by a few of our citizens. They were large substantial vehicles usually drawn by two horses and carried both mail and passengers.

Travelling in these old coaches was very slow and tiresome, although the rate of speed depended, to a certain extent, on the condition of the roads and the weather.

Sometime before 1860 there was a stage line started between Easton and Felton, Del. via Denton. After 1860 the stage met the Chester River boat at Queenstown. It usually left here between six and seven o'clock in the morning and was due in Queenstown anywhere between ten and twelve o'clock. If the tide happened to be low it was necessary for the passengers to be carried out in a row boat or a scow before they would get aboard the steamer which was then anchored out some distance from the shore.

OLD BRICK HOTEL.

Our First Steamboats.

The first steamboat came up the Choptank River to
Denton from Baltimore before 1850. It was named the
"Cyrus." People gathered here from miles around, or
on their own shores, to see it as it passed. There was
talk among the very small boys and also the negroes that
the waves would probably wash them away from the
shore. So when the darkies saw it coming they all ran
and hid and none could be seen anywhere.

"The Cyrus" perhaps only made one trip, but a
little later "The Dupont" with Captain Case as captain
made weekly trips between Denton and Baltimore. Instead of having wheels on the side, as "The Cyrus" had,
and as most of the boats of to-day have, it was propelled
by one wheel from the back. If there were any passengers on this boat coming down to visit a home on the
river shore, where the wharf was not deep enough for
the steamer to dock, the captain would sometimes have
the small boats lowered and send them ashore.

An Old Grave.

One of the oldest graves that can be identified in
this vicinity is that of Major John Young in the old
cemetery at the rear of the Methodist Church. In some
places the brick wall which was built around it, has fall-
en. The marble slab, though much worn and molded,
still shows the following unusual inscription:

"Dedicated
to the memory
Major James Young,
who was born the 14th day of June 1775,
and died January 1822,
aged forty eight years and seven months.

The blow, how sudden, how severe the dart,
This marble shows life's fleeting scene.
Proclaims it but a passing dream
While time rolls on, while moments fly,
This stone cries out, 'Prepare to die,'
Friends, be not careless concerning your duty to God, for time is
on the wing. Heaven is worth striving for.
Philosophy, age, and experience tell us there is no real pleas-
ure in this world, our hopes and pursuits of such end with disap-
pointments, with this a strong influence that reason is loudly pro-
claiming to the universe, there is a world 'beyond this where a
Heaven of enjoyment is awaiting the Righteous."

This Major Young was a Caroline Countian by birth
and at one time a banker of Denton. He was also a
member of the State Legislature and a Major in the War
of 1812. One of his sons, Captain Edward Young, was
for many years a commander of a boat on Maryland waters and was widely known on the Eastern Shore.

A UNION SHIP VISITS DENTON.

In the early years of the Civil War a Union cutter
came to Denton and anchored at the bridge. This ship
brought about fifty men commanded by Captain Numbers, whose purpose was to arrest and punish any Southern sympathizers that had spoken too freely of their own
opinions. Some of these were: Messrs. Thomas H.
Slaughter, Ezekiel Saulsbury, Eben Wright, Josiah
Beck, Silas Christopher, W. P. Stafford, and Frank Porter.

Number's men had been directed to the Slaughter
residence. Upon nearing it, they saw a horseman riding
rapidly toward them. As soon as the rider discovered
the presence of the officers he rode about fifty yards to
the edge of a swamp and escaped to Hickory Ridge where
Wesley Smith fed him till it was safe for him to return
and prepare to join the Confederate Army. Later on
the soldiers tried to capture David Wright, father of the
later Mr. Wright of Andersontown, also a Southern sym-
pathizer. They compelled Mr. Hobbs, then a neighbor
of Mr. Wright to lead them to the house of the suspect
but upon their arrival they found that Mr. Wright had
escaped.

The soldiers left Denton about forty-eight hours after their arrival, without a single prisoner, but they had thoroughly scared all Southern sympathizers.

An Unfortunate Celebration.

A company of Union soldiers was stationed at Denton, as guards in 1863, and in celebrating the Fourth of July brought quite a disaster upon the town they were supposed to benefit.

They had been celebrating with the use of skyrockets and other explosives used on the Fourth of July, and it was some of these that started the fire. At the back of Mr. Blackiston's store, where Mr. William Bullock has a garage, was a rum shop. While the lower part of the building was used as a rum shop, the second floor was used as a store room for flax and cotton. Some of the rockets landed on the roof which started the flax burning. This being a late hour, and the town being unprepared to fight fire, it burned about all the business part of the town, which consisted of several stores, a hotel, and this rum shop.

BRICK HOTEL REMODELED.

OLD GRIST MILL.

In the summer of 1868 a grist mill was built in Denton on the north end of the present Fourth Street on what was known as Saulsbury creek. The joint owners of the mill were, Mr. John Emerson, father of the late Mr. Waldo Emerson, and Mr. Frederick Roschy, a German shoe maker of Denton. Mr. Emerson, however, managed the business and had his office on the site of Mr. Frederick Towers' present home. This mill was run by water power but the first heavy storm that came washed the dam out. At once a new dam was built and a race led back to the turbine wheel which operated the mill.

Further trouble with the power led the owners to discontinue the milling business. Mr. Philip Downes later bought the building and moved it to Towers' Wharf where it now stands.

STREET LIGHTING.

After the streets of Denton had for many years been lighted by oil lamps faithfully attended by Charles Smith, now janitor of the Court House, in 1901 the people were very much pleased with the gas plant which was built for the purpose of lighting streets and homes. But a few years later, as the electric light plant had been started near Denton, the gas plant was discontinued and electricity substituted.

LAW BUILDING.

In 1902, "The Law Building and Realty Co." was incorporated by W. H. Deweese, H. L. Cooper, A. G. Towers and Fred R. Owens and the same year the Law Building was built on Main Street, opposite the Court House, on the site of the old Choptank Hotel. The lower floor is now used for the Post Office, hardware store, and other offices; the second floor, for law offices only; and the third floor for lodge rooms and a Law Library.

THE PAVING OF MAIN STREET.

When Denton's Main Street was paved in 1915 and 1916, as the result of a law passed by the General Assembly the year before, a decided improvement was made to the town. The work done by Mr. C. S. Kauffman, representative of the Holt Construction Co., is made of concrete, about seven inches in thickness, with a six inch curb on either side. The extent of this road is about seven-eighths of a mile, extending from the railroad in East Denton to the foot of Denton Hill, including the causeway and making a total length of a mile and a quarter. The width of the street varies from sixty feet in front of the Law Building, to thirty feet through the main part of the town to Eighth Street, east of which point it is only fourteen feet in width.

The cost of construction was about $22,000, the state paying for one half of the cost, if twenty-four feet in width or less, and if over twenty-four feet in width paying for twelve feet only, the town meeting the cost of the remainder. The individual property owners paid for the construction of the curb, the cost of which was one dollar per running foot.

FIRST PUBLIC SCHOOL BUILDING.

SCHOOLS.

Records of the General Assembly of 1804 show that the parcel of land in Denton now used for a jail was once set apart for the purpose of building thereon a school house, but owing to difficulty in securing funds nothing

MANUAL TRAINING EXHIBIT.

was done for several years. From year to year however, effort was made to get an Academy in Denton, until at last in 1826 the General Assembly made it possible to proceed by paying two hundred and fifty dollars for that purpose and an equal amount yearly for its support. This Academy was then organized, but the building was not erected for several years. In the meantime the Academy was conducted in the Hall, over the old Market House, on the site of the present Masonic Hall.

Finally in 1835 a school building was erected on the corner of Gay and Second Streets in the block in which the Court House now stands. It was a plain but substantial two story building, with a school room and a double entry hall-way below, and a school-room and a cloak room above. For a generation the building stood here, and in the year 1879 it was removed to Low and Second Streets on the site of the present Primary School, and was there used as an Academy until 1883, when it was moved a little west on the same street, and supplanted by the present Primary building. In fact the old building is today used as a dwelling house, and the original slate roof, which was all hand made, is still in good repair, promising to last for generations to come.

The year 1887 stands out in school history, for the County School Commissioners, authorized the first High School in the County. Prof. Chas. W. Bryn was the first principal of this school, which was conducted in the Masonic Hall for two years.

Feeling the need of a new school building, in 1901 the present High School was erected on Franklin Street. It is an attractive and comfortable building and for some years was large enough for every need. In the last few years, however, the attendance upon the town schools has grown so rapidly that the building is entirely inadequate.

CHURCHES.

Methodist Episcopal.

The history of the Methodist Episcopal church in Denton began apparently with Moore's Chapel in 1816, as given in this volume under the heading—Early Churches.

The present brick church was erected in 1867, Rev. John Hough being pastor at that time. Several years ago this church was thoroughly repaired, remodelled and a Sunday School room added.

Presbyterian.

One of the first churches built in Denton was the Presbyterian church which was situated on what is now Gay St. Although no one seems to know just when it was built, services were discontinued here many years before the Civil War. After this time it was sold to the colored people and is now supposed to form a part of the M. E. Church of this place.

Methodist Protestant.

Many years ago an effort was made to establish a society of the M. P. Church in Denton, but it was deferred until the spring of 1897. On Monday night, April 26th, of that year, Rev. H. W. D. Johnson, Rev. W. J. D. Lucas, Rev. C. E. Dryden, and several members held a meeting in the school house and decided to rent a hall and have regular service. Accordingly Downes Hall was engaged, chairs and church literature purchased and on Sunday, May 2nd, the first services were held, Rev. Mr. Johnson preaching. On Sunday, May 9th, Rev. C. E.

Dryden organized a Christian Endeavor Society. On Sunday, May 23rd, a Sunday-School was instituted, Mr. T. Pliny Fisher being chosen Superintendent. On Nov. 25th, 1897, the corner stone of the new church was laid, Revs. J. M. Holmes and B. F. Jester being the orators.

P. E. CHURCH.

Christ Protestant Episcopal.

The little Protestant Episcopal Church in this town was built by Mr. Samuel H. Fluharty, a contractor, in the fall of 1873 and early spring of 1874 and dedicated by Bishop Henry C. Lay on the 30th of April of the latter year, at which service the Rev. Dr. Theodore Barber, of Cambridge, Revs. James Mitchell, of Centreville; George F. Beaven, of Hillsboro; Revs. Hoskins, of East New Market; Watson, of Kent Island and Dr. Stearns, the rector, were present. Little change has been made in its appearance either in interior or exterior since its erection. The picture of it taken many years ago whilst the fence surrounded the Court House square is a good one as it now stands minus the fence, which disappeared years ago. The re-organization of the parish was effect-

MAIN STREET, DENTON.

ed at a meeting held at the office of the late Judge Russum in Denton, on the 11th of February, 1870, at which time the following vestrymen were elected: Dr. John A. McLean, Dr. Charles E. Tarr, Messrs. William G. Horsey, Edward C. Carter, Philip W. Downes, George M. Russum and Robert A. Nichols. The late James B. Steele was secretary of the meeting. Efforts were then made to have Rev. George F. Beaven, then rector of St. Paul's Church, Hillsboro, give a service each Sunday and some services were held in the Court House and at private residences by Mr. Beaven.

When the Rev. Dr. Edward J. Stearns became rector very early in the year 1871, a room on Second Street owned by the late John H. Emerson, was fitted up and used as a chapel. Mr. Stearns worked indefatigably to secure funds to build a church and with such success that in Sept., 1873 the site was secured from Col. J. W. Bryant, and a building committee composed of the rector, Messrs. William G. Horsey, Charles Stevens, Philip W. Downes and James B. Steele was appointed. The name given it at dedication was Christ Church.

Brethren.

About fifteen years ago, member of the Brethren society who had settled around Denton in considerable numbers built a very substantial concrete block church on South Seventh Street.

Holiness Society.

About the same time that the Brethren Church was organized here members of the Holiness Society erected a commodious church building on East Main St.

Roman Catholic.

The history of this church may be found under the caption—Early Churches.

ECHOES OF THE PAST.

(Lines written by Miss Rachel B. Satterthwaite and read before Fidelity Lodge, I. O. G. T., of Denton, on Friday night, February 20th, 1885.)

Would you like to hear a story
    Of the times of long ago,
Long before this place was Denton
    But was Edentown, you know?

Long before the bank was thought of,
    With its walls of brick and sand,
Currency was then tobacco
    All throughout "My Maryland."

Offices were not then fought for
    Postal clerkships yet unknown,
Neither had railroads been talked of
    And much less the telephone.

Long before the tall church steeple
    Showed to travellers on the road,
That there was a place of meeting
    For the worshippers of God.

Long before that cruel fire
    Rampant ran along Main street,
Causing ruin and destruction,
    Making ravages complete.

'Twas before the big camp-meeting
    Sang hosannas neath the pines
That stood then where now the house stands
    Known to all as George Deakyne's.

It was there at that camp-meeting,
    Truth it is, so I've been told,
First met youth and modest maiden
    Now together growing old.

To the camp in quaint old fashion
    (Then the custom of the land)
Seated on an ox-cart rode she,
    While HE walked with shoes in hand

But he now can claim his thousands
    With her yet his reigning queen
"Heart and Home" is still their motto
    As it always thus has been.

While they live to tell their story
    There are those of whom I speak,
Who have answered to the summons
    Which calls forth both strong and weak.

It was then that sheriff Hughlett,
　　So the legend comes to us,
Introduced the common sand-bur
　　As an ornamental grass.

And the grass it grew and flourished
　　Decorating hill and plain
Grieving many an honest farmer
　　As he garnered in his grain.

Well we know our crooked river
　　Curved around the self same bank,
And the shade and herring sported
　　In the waters of Choptank.

That the cold and icy winter
　　Brought some business on the "flats"
To the men who trapped the otter
　　And the boys who caught musk rats.

In the spring no steamboat's whistle
　　Echoed through the neighboring wood
But the croak of frog and turtle
　　To the settler boded good.

Then, perhaps, if you had met him,
　　And inquired for his home,
Quick response, "Pig Point, God bless you,
　　And from there I'll never roam."

But alas! for human nature
　　Gratitude won't always stay,
And the answer differed later
　　When the "bilious" held full sway.

Summer had its birds and flowers,
　　And the roses came in June,
Though no "Guide to Floral Culture"
　　Helped them with their rich perfume.

Autumn came with fruits and hunting,
　　Apples, peaches, grapes and pears,
Chinquapins and ripe persimmons,
　　Squirrels, partridges and hares.

Making this a scene of action
　　As the seasons went and came,
Bringing with them joy and sorrow,
　　As to us? Yes, just the same.

For we know the happy mother
　　Clasped her infant to her breast,
Watched him grow to useful manhood,
　　Ere she laid him down to rest.

Or, perchance, she was not happy,
　　Children sometimes went astray,
Wandered from the path of virtue,
　　Even as they do today.

But we know the Christian mother
    Had an answer to her prayer
When she saw the scales true balanced
    In the Home that has no care.

Yes we know that children prattled,
    In those days of long ago;
Know full well that young men courted,
    And sometimes a girl said "No."

As to who received the mitten,
    Or who was the lucky one,
History remaineth silent,
    And my story can't go on.

GAREY'S.

The first school building was situated close to what is now Garey's canning factory, near the present State road. At that time it was called Piney school, the name taken from the pine woods, presumably. The old school house is still standing and is used as part of a dwelling house in the neighborhood. In 1878 a new school house was built more nearly the center of the district. It was named Greenlee's school at first for Arthur John Greenlee who donated the land, later it was changed to Garey's School as Matthew Garey was one of the oldest settlers in the district and owned much land therein.

This district may claim the credit of having the first court in Caroline county—Melville's Warehouse. By a ferry across the river at this point it seems that this neighborhood was in the direct line of travel from Queenstown near the Chesapeake, at that time an important trading place and county seat of Queen Anne County, and Whitelysburg and Dover. Could we but glance back through these 140 years or more, we could doubtless see this community a busy one—especially with the growing of tobacco and its preparation for shipment to England from the warehouse at Melville's landing nearby.

As early as 1780 some notice in the land records in the Clerk's Office is given a chapel which then stood by Ingram's Creek—the early name for Chapel Branch. Perhaps this building was used later jointly as a church and school for the community. No doubt some of the well known itinerant ministers held services in this chapel at various times.

The present church building was erected in 1879 by the efforts of the local people headed by Thos. F. and Matthew Garey, one of whom gave the land, and the other aided in the building.

The original power plant of the Peninsular Lighting Company was located in this section—the former Garey Mill site. The mill at this place was in operation before 1800, being then operated by Col. Matthew Driver, a prominent man of the time. Somewhat later Col. Driver maintained a saw mill near where the state road crosses Chapel Branch.

OAKS.

Oaks school (which derived its name from the large oak trees, many many years old, standing near the school building) is located about one-fourth mile from Hobbs, and is the second known building on this spot. The oak trees referred to above are several feet in diameter and must be several hundred years old. Who knows but that Indians were holding pow-wows around these trees when Columbus discovered America?

In this general section, near the old Anthony's Mill site, official records show that a school was taught by Andrew Banning previous to 1793, thereby indicating an early development of this territory.

Hobbs, a thrifty village of Caroline County, is situated on the M. D. & V. Railway about three miles east of Denton. The village of Hobbs has about one hundred inhabitants, one general store, a post-office, from which there is one rural route for the delivery of mail, also a general factory which is known as the Hobbs Manufacturing Company, where men, women and children are given employment in mking baskets, crates, and boxes for fruits and vegetables.

Hobbs was named in honor of the late Saulsbury Hobbs, a prominent and highly esteemed gentleman, owning broad acres in this section.

There is a church of the Methodist Protestant denomination, known as Ames Chapel, built in the year 1877, dedicated in 1878, and named in honor of the Rev. William C. Ames, the then present pastor. It has quite a large membership. Ames Chapel is one of four churches of Caroline Circuit, the other three being Thawley's, Piney and Burrsville. The parsonage is also located here.

WILLOUGHBY'S.

The neighborhood of Willoughby's and Ringgold's Green (the latter a cross-roads) near the Delaware line, have been known by some of its inhabitants since Revolutionary times. In this section lived Seth Evitts, who was a militia officer in our first war with England. His house, a brick structure, is still standing on the Andersontown road.

Very early too Thomas Willoughby came into this section and gave the name to the community which it has retained till this time.

Ringgold's Green probably takes its name from the constant "greenness" of the swampy region around.

A story is related that near this cross-roads a fatal tragedy once took place.

Since 1882, the school for this section has been in the present building, though at least two buildings were erected earlier in this neighborhood for school purposes.

ANDERSONTOWN.

Andersontown was so named, because a certain James Anderson many years ago owned considerable land and transacted much business in this vicinity. As early as 1840 this place which lay at the juncture of two main roads, the one leading from Greensboro to Hunting Creek (now Linchester), the other being the direct road from Potter's Landing to Marshy Hope Bridge—had a store, a blacksmith shop, and one or two dwellings. Later on two stores were kept busy. Mr. Tilghman Nuttle succeeded by his sons were prominent merchants of this place for more than a generation.

Before 1867, the school for this section seemed to be Meluney's, which was located about a mile away on the road to Potter's Landing. This building probably not being large enough for the community, Tilghman Nuttle, Tilghman Andrew, and William Stevens were July 3, 1867 named a committee to sell the old building and ground and superintend the erection of a new building on the lot purchased nearer Andersontown. A second school house erected on this site was in 1919 burned and the old Holiness Church nearby purchased, and transformed into the present school building.

Much of the land in this community was formerly owned by General William Potter.

LIDEN'S.

Though having been moved some distance several times, Liden's school as indicated elsewhere in this book, dates among the earliest of the county—probably as far back as 1820 when the building of logs stood near Camp Ground Branch.

Since the establishment of the public school in 1865, Liden's has been continually on the list and for a greater part of this time a rather large school.

The name of Liden's is in honor of Shadrach Liden who as early as 1840 deeded a piece of land for a site of a church and school. Thus for years the old building was also used as a place of worship. In 1890 Zebedial Fountain conveyed a piece of land for a new site and the present building was erected.

Thawley's Church, now in Hickman, was originally built in 1884 on a plot of land deeded to the trustees by Zebedial Fountain, being located near Liden's school, about two miles southwest from its present site.

Nobletown, the community in which it was first erected, being greatly in need of a church, several men of this community, among them Philip and Clement Noble, James F. Fountain, Willis Liden, Tilghman Meluney, George Thawley, Zebedial Fountain and others along with Henry Thawley of Burrsville and assisted by Rev. A. D. Davis of Denton, erected the building and named it Davis' Chapel in honor of the Reverend Davis, indicated above. The intention of the builders was to maintain an independent chapel for a while, at least, but in some way the Wilmington Conference of the M. E. Church took possession of the building and sent a minister. Subsequently its name was changed to Thawley's, in honor of Henry Thawley, and about 1898 the building was moved to Hickman where it stands at present. The corner stone which was not moved with the church was recovered in 1919 through the efforts of the pastor, Rev. G. T. Gehman, and restored to its proper place.

HICKMAN.

The village of Hickman, situated directly on the Maryland-Delaware line, has been a hamlet for many years, and was originally called Hickmantown and later abbreviated when a post-office was established there.

For years simply as a cross roads, the coming of the railroad gave it new life and energy until now it has reached considerable proportions, having a church, school, flour and saw mill, blacksmith shop, barber shop and an automobile garage.

Its name is in honor of a Mr. Hickman, who years ago owned considerable property in this neighborhood.

Until eight years ago, when a public school was started on the Maryland side, it was necessary for the pupils to go two miles to Liden's. A joint school by the two states is in contemplation.

WILLISTON (Potter's Landing).

Potter's Landing, now called Williston, is one of the most historic settlements of Caroline County. The early history of this place dates from about 1750 and is described elsewhere in this volume in connection with the Potter family—the first known settlers.

During the Revolutionary War this place served as a depot for collecting supplies for the soldiers and at the same time, likely served as a drilling place for the militia. Since the earliest date Potter's Landing has been known as a shipping centre and continued as such until about twenty years ago when the Queen Anne Railroad brought death to the steamboat traffic from this point. For some years prior thereto, two steamboats daily left wharves at this place for Baltimore, carrying passengers and freight.

The name of Coquericus Creek (Cokiases Creek) was originally given as the name of the local branch which supplies the Williston mill to-day. The first mill

WILLISTON MILL POND OR LAKE.

was built much nearer the head of the pond than the present site and was apparently in operation before 1778 when official notice of its lease by Nathaniel Potter is recorded.

General William Potter built the present milldam or at least widened it considerably, dug out the mill race and even projected a ship channel to the mill race from the river by means of which vessels could unload grain and receive milled goods directly at the mill. The enormous expense of this operation which only partially succeeded is said to have financially involved the projector. After the mill had exchanged hands several times, it finally became the property of Willard C. Todd, the present owner, who has greatly improved the property by adding the latest milling machinery.

General Potter also maintained a tannery, making leather for the people of this section. Remains of this old tannery may be seen in the pits which lie at the south of the mill dam.

So important was this point at one time that a hotel was built and kept for some years. This building has since been used as a dwelling.

The Williston church about a mile north of the village was built about forty years ago largely through the efforts of Elias W. Williamson, a well known county man of thirty years ago, who resided near this place. After being furnished with ministers from the Methodist Episcopal Conference for many years, it became several years ago, under the active control of the Swedenborgian Church, Rev. J. E. Smith, of Philadelphia, being the present pastor.

The children of this section went to Gravelly Branch or Meluney's schools a mile or two away until 1869, when a teacher for Potter's Landing was appointed by the School Board. This school seems to have been open rather irregularly till 1877 when Dr. J. W. Hignutt deeded a piece of land for a school site, the present building being erected about this time.

The Williston Mill Pond, latterly known as the "Lake," is directly on the State Highway and is perhaps one of the most beautiful sheets of inland water on the Eastern Shore.

WILLIAMSON.

Midway between Williston and Andersontown is a school called Williamson, named for Elias Williamson, one of Caroline's representative men until his death about fifteen years ago. Mr. Williamson realizing that the community was somewhat distant from a public school erected a school building and employed a teacher for the benefit of the children of the neighborhood. A little later a teacher was provided by the county School Board and after Mr. Williamson's death the property was purchased by the Board of Education.

This neighborhood is closely connected with the Williston community, for formerly much of the land of both sections was owned by one or more of the Potters.

Pealiquor, a river site nearby (the Cape May of Caroline) takes its name presumably from the name of the original tract—Pealicker.

THE BUREAU.

Many have inquired the origin of the building commonly called The Bureau, located on the state road leading south from Williston.

At the close of the Civil War an effort was made by the Federal government to provide in each section of the Southern States, a place where religious, educational and civil instruction could be given to those that had been set free. This structure—A Freedman's Bureau—was the one provided for this county as its part of the $1,500 used for such purposes. It is said that the lumber which was brought up the river for this building was intended to be delivered at Denton, but was put off lower down by mistake. The colored people have used the building continuously for both church and school purposes until 1910, when the school-room was declared unfit for school purposes and a building in Pinetown secured.

FREEDMAN'S BUREAU.

HARMONY (Fowling Creek).

This section because of its nearness to the Choptank river and Talbot county was one of the first to be settled in the county.

Fowling Creek is mentioned in one of the earliest surveys made and was doubtless early known far and wide as the haunt of game and fowl.

The earliest mill seems to have been farther down the stream than the present one—probably where the road leading from the state road to Gilpins Point crosses the stream. General Potter was a part owner of the mill when reestablished near its present site.

The name of Harmony was evidently not applied to the village until some time after 1840, about which time the first church was erected, though there had been a chapel nearer Fowling Creek for years before this time.

It seems that a public school was started at this point rather early too, for in 1865 when the public school system was established, Harmony school was included in the provision.

With a one-room school for many years, the population of the community has so increased that a two-room school is now a practical necessity. At present the patrons are much interested in securing a school site of two or three acres and building a model two-room school.

Harmony Methodist Protestant Church was first a church of another denomination. On the 12th day of October, 1840, William A. Barton and wife, by their deed conveyed to Deliha Sparklin and others, trustees, and their successors in office for the use of the members of the Methodist Episcopal Church in the United States of America, according to the rules and discipline of that church, the "parcel of land lying and being in Caroline County and State of Maryland and immediately on the cross roads leading from Fowling Creek and Hog Creek, one-half acre of ground be the same more or less."

On this piece of ground a church was built and dedicated to the service of God and the use of the congregation. For over seventy-five years services were held in this church and from it came a number of ministers who are now prominent in the Methodist Episcopal church, and many other useful and active christian workers. At last through mismanagement and neglect, the congregation went away from the church and it was closed.

During the Fall of 1916 the people of the community desiring religious services, requested Mr. Wm. H. Johnson, a local minister of the Methodist Protestant church of Federalsburg, to hold services in the church. He responded and a gracious revival came in which about 51 persons were converted. These desiring to have church organization asked for help from the Federalsburg church. With the old members of the church who still remained a healthy organization was formed, and on the 5th day of August 1919, for the sum of $250 the people of the community bought back their church and rededicated it to the service of God as a Methodist Protestant church. It is now in a vigorous condition and doing the great work for which it was first deeded by William A. Barton and wife.

GROVE.

This section made famous on account of its furnishing the birthplace of Charles Dickinson who fell in a duel with Andrew Jackson as recorded elsewhere in this volume and lying directly on the colonial thoroughfare from Potter's Landing to Hunting Creek (now the Harmony-Preston road) was cleared and settled very early.

A few years before this county was organized Charles Dickinson, the grandfather of the later duellist, and who had been a prominent resident of Dorchester County as evidenced by his being for awhile the chief jurist of that county and the chief of the committee in the construction of her first Court House, secured by grant and purchase several hundred acres of land in the Grove neighborhood and had settled there, moving from Lower Dorchester. This Mr. Dickinson was the man who presided over the well known meeting held at Melvill's Warehouse in 1774, when resolutions were adopted urging resistance to Great Britain in her treatment of the colonies.

Henry Dickinson, the son, acquired possession of nearly 2000 acres of this land at the death of his father, together with other valuable property including many slaves. During the Revolutionary Period Henry Dickinson was active in the affairs of his county and at one time collected and headed a troop of horsemen for the war. A member of the first Constitutional Convention he became later one of the judges of our County Court.

Possessed with broad acres and many slaves to do the bidding of the family it seems only natural that the home of Henry Dickinson was the centre of social activities. In this home the boy Charles Dickinson and his brother Philip along with the two sisters Elizabeth and Rebecca were reared and evidently in accordance with their opportunities and the customs of the day, these young people were among the leaders in the various social functions of the county at the time.

It seems that the family were Episcopalians and attended the Hunting Creek Chapel (near Hynson).

Henry Dickinson died about 1790 and left his large estate probably worth $50,000 to his children. Reared in luxury for the time it seems only natural that the call of the city should be strong to them. Not long after the reaching of manhood by these boys, Charles and Philip, do we find them selling their land, Philip in small sections, while Charles made larger sales. Elizabeth who had married William Richardson of Talbot County, soon disposed of her interest as did Rebecca who became the wife of Thos. B. Daffin and resided in Tuckahoe Neck on the farm now known as the Thawley Farm.

Thus in 1803 we find Charles Dickinson who had married Jane Erwin of Tennessee, conveying the remainder of his real estate in Caroline County to his father-in-law for the sum of about $12,000. Shortly after this he relinquished his citizenship in Maryland and moved to the vicinity of Nashville.

In this connection may it be said that Andrew Jackson, then a rising young man of Tennessee and slightly older than Charles Dickinson, had been elected to Congress then held in Philadelphia (about 1796-1797). Going to Philadelphia as he did on horseback over the well established trail via Baltimore, it seems likely that Jackson met in the latter city prominent men of this state and section. Col. William Richardson, a relative of Charles Dickinson, was one of these. Naturally enough, he was, on one of these trips invited by Col. Richardson, the owner of a fast sailing sloop, to visit the Eastern Shore and accepted, staying while here at the Richardson, Dickin-

son, Daffin and Potter homes in this county. Charles
Dickinson, with whom he was apparently much associated while on these visits, was a very good sport and
proved a very interesting man to Jackson with the result
that Jackson invited him to his home and associations in
Tennessee, an offer which Dickinson clearly accepted.

For years Grove has been the site of a church and
the parsonage of the Caroline Circuit of the Methodist
Protestant church—American Corner, Choptank and
Smithson comprising the remainder of the charge.

The first public school in this section seems to have
been taught by Mr. Peter James Patchett shortly after
the Civil War in a dwelling house provided by Mr. Perry
Taylor. Shortly afterwards a new school building was
erected near the site of the present one and Miss Annie
Hains was the first teacher. This building was used for
school purposes until 1887 when the present school was
erected.

After awhile a cannery was erected on one side of
the school to be followed in a few years by another cannery on the opposite side of the school. Hence the origin
of the term sometimes applied ''Cannery Grove.''

LAUREL GROVE.

Erected as a school site in 1870 when Ager Andrew
gave one acre of land to the School Board, this school
has been in operation ever since. After the decay of the
old building about twenty years ago, the present structure was erected.

Like the church which is immediately across the
county road, this school takes its name because of the
fact that formerly the pine woods completely surrounding the school abounds in laurel, which in bloom is indeed very pretty.

The church here was formerly in the Southern Methodist denomination, Easton charge, but latterly has
been the worshipping place of the Holiness Society.

To the general section hereabout the name of Pinetown is given, and doubtless to many of the older residents the school is better known as Pinetown than by its
official name.

FRIENDSHIP.

The first church built in this community was made of logs and located near the site of the present building.

The present edifice, the third one built, was completed about 1880 and is ministered to at present by a pastor from Williamsburg, in which circuit it is located.

The first school building in this community was erected about one-hundred years ago and was likewise made of logs. It was burned in 1851 because of a defective stove. School was kept in a shack for awhile until the first of the present building was erected. In 1911 a new room was added, making Friendship a two-room school.

About three hundred yards from Friendship on the Hynson road may still be seen some walnut trees which mark the site of the polling place of this district fifty years ago.

PRESTON (Snow Hill).

The founding of Snow Hill, the forerunner of Preston, likely took place about 1845 at which time trees were cut and a clearing made where now stands Preston. It seems that the Willis family, later well known in this section and county, was the holder of the land hereabout. Philemon Willis the ancestor of Peter Willis who was an officer in the War of 1812, deeded very early the site of the present M. E. Church. William Gootee, one of the first inhabitants of the new village, kept a store and included the postoffice to which for miles around the people would come once a week to get their mail if any there be and do their shopping.

As Snow Hill grew and the quantity of mail increased, frequent delays in the service were made because of their being another Snow Hill in Maryland, a much older and larger village. Hence it became necessary to change the name. This was done in 1856 while Mr. J. R. Stack of this section was a member of the Legislature. Why the name Preston was selected seems to be unknown, unless to memorialize some prominent family in Maryland at that time. The name, however, was well selected and continues to add dignity to the charms of this favored section. Before 1890, the growth of this town was slow due to the lack of transportation facilities, Medford's Wharf, now Choptank, being the shipping point of this section at that time. However in this year the railroad was constructed and Preston began to grow.

In 1908 electric lights were added and in 1916 the state road was completed thereby putting the town on the main artery of traffic up and down the peninsula.

In educational matters and sentiment this section has always ranked high—explained no doubt in part by the settlement of the community by Friends, a Society which has always stood for education and enlightenment and latterly by the persistent influence of the once famous debating society of this section. No one can deny the fact that these two factors have been important elements in the educational strata of this community.

The first school was said to stand on the road to Friendship, but later the building was moved to a site

PRESTON SCHOOL.

near the present German church. After a few years the front room of the old school building recently sold was built and later from time to time a room was added as the attendance increased until the building became entirely inadequate to meet the demands of a modern school. In 1918 after repeated efforts on the part of several of the leading citizens of the town a handsome brick building was erected on a lot of six acres which had been previously provided for. The building committee was N. H. Fooks, chairman; Chas. B. Harrison, Esq., and Walter M. Wright.

A clipping from the *Denton Journal* explains the disposition of the older school property located in what is now the church grove:

"The Rev. Thomas A. King, pastor of the New Jerusalem Church in Baltimore, and chaplain of the Grand Lodge of Maryland Masons, has brought the old academy building and the grove in which it is situated in Preston. He will re-model the house, which is a large one, and make it a summer residence for his family. It is in a magnificent grove of large primeval white oaks, so few of which now remain on the Eastern Shore. The wood covers 90 square perches of land. The house was built in 1863. Last year a new school house was erected in another part of the town. The first principal was Prof. R. O. Christian, who had just come out of the Confederate army and had no possessions but a battered suit of gray."

Because of the larger German population that had gradually come in the community a parochial school was established here years ago. In this school both English and German languages as well as church forms were taught by the pastor of the church who had charge. As many of the German patrons had become interested in the public school for one reason or another this private school was closed about three years ago.

CHURCHES.

The history of the Friends Society in this community may be found elsewhere in this volume under the heading—Early Churches.

Years ago a German Lutheran Church was established here and is well attended. Service was formerly held in both the English and German languages.

PRESTON M. E. CHURCH.

PRESTON'S EARLY CHURCH.

Among the earliest Methodist records in our county appear the names of William Frazier and Bethesda Chapel. Largely due to the efforts of Captain Frazier was the erection of this chapel on the present site of the Preston Methodist Church. In July of 1797 Thomas Foster, James Andrew, David Sisk, James Sisk, Jacob Wright, Benjamin Colliston and Daniel Cheezum, trustees of the Church, purchased from Philemon Willis for the sum of 10 shillings the half acre of land on which the chapel stood. Frazier, although not one of the trustees, probably arranged for the purchase of this land and his name with that of Thomas Weir Lockerman is given as testator of the deed. In 1810 the church was incorporated in accordance with the provisions of the Maryland Assembly with trustees forming the body politic.

In the Bethesda Record Book, kept since 1810, there are several interesting items concerning the Chapel. A colored people's class was held there on Sunday morn-ings preceding the regular preaching services, a custom not unusual at that time. The duties of the sexton as as outlined in the minutes were as follows:

"Chop wood, make fires, keep house clean and in order, the benches and pulpit well dusted, with a pitcher of water on the pulpit with a tumbler during church hours, keep lamps trimmed and clean, windows to be kept clean and shutters closed during the week, the premises kept clear of incumbrances."

The carpets were to be taken up and the house scoured twice a year. For all this the sexton received the princely sum of twelve dollars a year.

With the growth of the little town then known as Snow Hill a larger church was needed. It was built about 1847 from which time it became known as Bethesda Church. Ten years later the church yard was enclosed as a burying ground for Methodists of that section.

Repairing and remodelling done in 1888 and 1903 have greatly enlarged and improved the building, which is at present an up-to-date church of considerable size.

LINCHESTER.

This village, formerly called Murray's Mill, is on the site of one of the first settlements within the boundaries of Caroline County.

During the Revolutionary War, this mill still in existence, did its share towards furnishing food to the soldiers not alone in this section but for a very large territory. Large scows could at that time come direct to the mill and be loaded with flour and meal to be reloaded on larger vessels on the Choptank River.

There must have been a store or two kept here at that time. Likewise an ordinary (boarding house) which was licensed by the County court. Before 1775 people from this section attended the old Episcopal chapel that stood on the road leading from what is now known as Ellwood camp to Hynson and near the latter place. This church like others of the same denomination was practically closed by the Revolutionary War, and as its successor in this community the meeting at William Frazier's home was organized.

Through the influence of Robt. D. Bradley, once a member of the Maryland Legislature, the name of the place was changed to Linchester—Lin being taken from Caroline and Chester likewise from Dorchester, these two counties forming a boundary at this point.

LINCHESTER AT PRESENT.

CHOPTANK.

This name, given to the most southern village of Caroline County on the Choptank River, dates back to about 1889 when it was known as Medford's Wharf and even then was in daily communication with Baltimore by two lines of steamers. Later on, three steamers daily left its wharves for our Metropolis.

About 1882 or 1883 the Wright brothers located here, along with some earlier settlers, and started some enterprises which caused the settlement to grow rapidly. The postoffice was established about the time the name was changed to Choptank.

Formerly the children of this section attended a school called Hunting Creek located some distance away. About 1892 a large school building was erected at Choptank.

A little earlier two churches were erected—Methodist Episcopal and Methodist Protestant.

The village is noted for its fisheries, perhaps, the best in the county. As many as 60,000 herring and shad are said to have been caught in a single day.

The inhabitants number about 200.

BETHLEHEM.

Situated on the main thoroughfare leading to Easton, this village has had a commanding location for years.

Just when the settlement began is not known, but suffice to say that Bethlehem has been on the map for a long time.

Both a church and school have long contributed to the religious and social wants of the community.

In 1865, the school which had heretofore existed as a subscribed, or community school, was turned over to the county and became a part of the state school system. For years the present building was located on the church lot in the village, but the great need of more room for play-ground led to the school's being moved a few years ago to its present site.

One of the largest tomato canneries on the peninsula is located here—the property of Mr. A. J. Messick.

The road leading to the river called Dover Road, was long ago so named because of its leading to the ancient town of Dover on the Talbot side of the river.

The earlier enterprise of the locality may be seen in the announcement of a fair to be held hereabout as per the following clipping:

CAROLINE'S FAIR.

"The Bethlehem Fair to be held on the second, third, and fourth of next month, will probably eclipse all others ever held in the County. The programme comprises almost everything that contributes to make such occasions interesting and amusing. Prof. Faux, the champion pedestrian, will make a novel race during the Fair with a fast trotting horse. He is to walk one-half mile in less than the horse can trot a mile. Sportsmen ought surely to see this. As there is no entrance fee to be paid on the property exhibit, come and make the Fair what it deserves to be, a success. The Ladies of Harmony are making a flag and streamer to present to the Fair Association."

SMITHSON.

In the year 1873 the school was built at Smithson. The name Hog Creek was first given to the settlement and the school, probably, by the settlers who lived along Hog Creek branch. As there was no church near, religious services were held in the school for a while. Three years later, a church was built and named Smithson Chapel for the first minister, Rev. Rumsey Smithson.

The name of the school was then changed to Smithson, by which it is still called.

In 1895 a post-office was established. It was suggested that the post-office be called Newton in honor of Mr. Newton Andrew, who was postmaster. When a few years later the post-office was discontinued, this name was dropped and the village now goes by the name of Smithson.

INDIANS.

In the early part of the eighteenth century there were Indians in Smithson vicinity. One tribe lived at Yellow Hill. Besides their wigwams they had several caves, the remains of which can still be seen.

A story is told of a family by the name of Willoughby that lived near where MacCarty's wharf now is. One day, when their little son Richard was only a few weeks old, the father being in the field and the mother hanging out clothes, the Indians crept in and stole the baby. They took him to Yellow Hill and kept him six weeks. The father, with a band of his neighbors, went to the camp and brought the little boy home.

There seems to have been some Indians along the Hog Creek branch. One tribe went far up the branch and remains of their camp and medicine pit were found only a few years ago. Others lived near Blairtown, for we know they had a large burying ground there and their caves have been found along the banks. Still others lived near what is now the Hog Creek Mill dam. When the dam was being rebuilt several things which the Indians had buried were dug from the banks.

Blairtown referred to above was clearly a settlement of slaves belonging to Charles Blair about 1790. The site of this settlement was just below Hog Creek branch on the road leading from Harmony to Smithson. In 1825 much of the land in this neighborhood was purchased from the heirs of Blair by Short A. Willis, the father of Col. A. J. Willis, who died at Williston a few years ago.

Over one hundred years ago a brick grist mill was built along Hog Creek. Perhaps the bricks for this building were brought up the Choptank from some point below where bricks were then made. It is not likely that any of them were brought from England.

In this section, several militiamen for service in the Revolutionary War were secured.

Contributed by Pupils.

HUBBARD'S.

Hubbard's or the Fraziers' Flats region as it is more generally known, was one of the earliest settled portions of what is now Caroline county. Tradition has it that this settlement was intended to be made in Talbot county from which section the early settlers came. This seems quite plausible and perhaps, is true. In those times grants of land were not as definitely outlined as now by degrees and minutes. It seems that the grant included territory above the "second turning of the Choptank river," hence a mistake in the number of bends in the river from its mouth would easily place this site on either side of the river.

Then too the soil in this region is very clayey and similar to that of Talbot county. Under these conditions it was only natural that persons from the former county would locate in the new territory and bring with them their religious worship. This, it seems, is what happened as a Friends' meeting was very early established—perhaps shortly after 1700.

The Flats' territory is really included by two creeks —Skillington on the south and Edmonson on the north. These two streams take their names from Thomas Skillington and John Edmonson, natives of Talbot county, who were referred to above as taking up the land in this section.

It seems, too, that the ferry across the Choptank was in this section, connecting the roads that led from Easton to Hunting Creek (now Linchester), thereby making this way a thoroughfare.

Later on William Frazier, a prominent citizen, churchman, and soldier, acquired much of this land and erected thereon a handsome brick residence as referred to elsewhere in this volume. In this house church services were held for years; these were sometimes attended by Bishop Asbury.

It seems likely, too, that these people, many of whom were Quakers, had used their meeting house doubtless as a school in the early life of the colony. The public school for this section which was in operation prior to 1865 was at that time turned over to the County Board of Education. About 1872 the present site was acquired and a building erected thereon. This building was enlarged in the year 1919.

About twenty-five years ago a colony of Dutch people from the Northwest settled here and named the territory "Wilhelmina" after the Dutch Queen. Several farms were made and for a time the people prospered, bidding fair to dyke some of the marsh area in that region according to the plan followed in their mother country.

The Frazier residence was again used as a place of worship by these Hollanders after a period of one hundred years. Several years ago, however, these colonies began to move away and at present there are only a few of the former families living here.

FEDERALSBURG (North West Fork Bridge).

ORIGIN AND UNIFICATION OF THE TOWN.

The first inhabitants of the county around Federalsburg were the tribes of the Nanticoke Indians. Although they were not so fierce as the Susquehannoughs of northern Maryland, neither were they so friendly as the Piscataway tribes of the western shore. Whether this attitude toward white people delayed the settlement of the county we cannot say; but as early as 1682 James and William Wright, who came from England (probably Bristol) with one of William Penn's colonies, settled on Marshyhope Creek, the headwaters of the Northwest Fork of the Nanticoke River. When Caroline County was formed in 1774, this land fell within its boundaries. By an act of the General Assembly of 1792 the southern boundary was extended to Noris Ford (a corruption of Northwest Fork Ford), because the newly erected bridge at that spot had taken the place of the one which had marked the Caroline-Dorchester division line before it had been washed away.

Already the possibilities of this point where cross-country traffic forded the river had been foreseen by a Mr. Cloudsberry Jones, who built a store, and began to sell groceries and liquor there about the year 1789. This was the nucleus of a small village which so patently owed its growth to the bridge that it was called "Northwest Fork Bridge," or "The Bridge" until early in 1812 when politics took the naming of the little town in hand. By this time the Federalist Party had reached that stage of decline which is characterized by a fever-heat of loyalty and enthusiasm. The party was strong on the Delaware-Maryland peninsula, and a rousing mass-meeting was held at "The Bridge." People came from far and near; the militia drilled and paraded with all the pomp and ceremony of military glory; drums beat and fifes shrieked; the Stars and Stripes, together with the party flag, were cheered to the top of an immense flag pole; prominent speakers of the day used all their gifts of oratory to foster the pride, and kindle the enthusiasm for party and party principles. Something must be done, such emotion demanded an outlet; of the patriotism, enthusiasm, and party loyalty of that day was born a new name for the town—Federalsburg. The few Republicans of the locality voiced their protest by still referring to "The Bridge"; however, though Republican principles finally triumphed, the Federalist name was held and Federalsburg it has ever remained.

The road following the river had been made the boundary between Caroline and Dorchester counties through that section which is now the site of Federalsburg; but as the line of houses which grew up along it developed into proportions of a village, this dividing line threatened the peaceful existence and growth of the town. People living on the west, or Dorchester, side of Main Street, sent their children to the village school. Those living on the East, or Caroline, side sent them to the district school at Tanyard Branch, a mile and a half distant. The residents of the same town paid their taxes into separate county treasuries, and were more or less attached to separate interests. Offenders against the law could baffle and embarrass its officers merely by dodging from one side of the street to the other. Moreover, voters in Caroline County had to go to Linchester to cast their ballots, while the Dorchester population went either to East New Market or to Crotcher's Ferry according to the section of the village in which they lived.

So great and so general had the dissatisfaction over these inconveniences become by 1880 that a petition signed by every voter in the Dorchester part of town, seventy in all, was sent to the Legislature asking for such a change in the boundary between the two counties that the town and its suburbs might be wholly within Caroline County. This request was granted, and upon the payment of $614 into the Dorchester treasury by the transferred tax-payers, the change was duly authorized and made. Thus, with the wiping out of the dividing line, Federalsburg became a unified whole.

EARLY INDUSTRIES.

Probably Federalsburg's earliest industry, and certainly its most picturesque one, was its ship-building. The surrounding white oak forests furnished the material, but as this industry ante-dated the saw-mill, the old-time whip-saw had to be employed to convert it into lumber. To operate this saw a trestle was erected; one man sawed from the elevated position while his co-laborer at the other end of the saw worked on the ground. As the water was too shallow for these ships to be launched at Federalsburg anyway, it was not important that they be built at any definite place; hence keels were laid at many different points in the southern part of the town.

Upon the completion of a ship, it was conveyed on a scow, or lighter, to Brown's Wharf, a landing four miles farther down the river. From thence it was launched, laden, and sent upon its career as a bay and river trading vessel. The same landing was naturally the shipping-point for Federalsburg merchants, although boats of lighter draft ascended as far as Chimney Landing, a distance of less than two miles from the town. Twice yearly, in spring and in fall, the local store-keepers loaded a boat with tan-bark and cord-wood, and returned from the Chesapeake cities with a miscellaneous supply of city needfuls for their country trade.

The first ship built at Federalsburg was "The Clipper." This was followed by the "Richard Tull," the "Eggleston Brown," the "Mary Havelow," the "Jacob Charles," the "Pearl," and the "Annabelle." Of these the "Pearl" was the largest and best equipped, and the "Annabelle," built by Mr. Jacob Covey, and named for his two daughters, was the last. The industry ceased at Federalsburg some time before the Civil War.

Exclusive of ship-building, the work of the town centered around the mill-dam at its northern extremity. Mr. John Elliott owned and operated the mills there. At these mills, later known as the "Idlewild Mills," logs which had been floated up from considerable distance downstream while the tide was coming in, were converted into lumber, in which form they made the return trip down the river and on to Baltimore. To the Idlewild mills also came the fleeces from the country-side, there to be carded and combed, and made into "rolls" for the spinning-wheels of thrifty housewives. Thence, too, came the wheat, destined eventually to be molded into the smoothe, round "Maryland Biscuit," and the corn for the quick batter-bread. Smelting iron-ore obtained from the valley of the town was tried for a time, but it proved unprofitable. As a means of furnishing power for grinding wheat and corn, and for generating electricity the dam was used continuously until the last mill was burned in 1916.

Fifty years ago, and more, all the merchants bought tanbark just as they buy butter, eggs, and other farm products today. The bark was cut into slabs and sold by the cord. Spanish oak bark commanded the higher price. It was shipped in the slab form in which it was bought at the country stores. Black oak bark, however, was shredded after the coarse, sapless part of the bark had been removed. Mr. Henry Mowbray, who kept a store at "The Point," was the only person who shredded the bark. Prior to the year 1840 there had been a tanyard of some importance on the farm of a Mr. Wright, one and one-half miles east of town. By that time, however, the tan-pits had fallen into disuse, and the building in which hides had been stored was being used as a schoolhouse. The industry, thus abandoned, has never been revived in the vicinity, but the name, "Tanyard Branch,' still marks the site of the activity.

THE FEDERALSBURG TAVERN.

In the days before the Civil War there was located in Federalsburg an old-fashioned tavern, originally owned by a man named Perry. It stood on the east side of the bridge crossing the North West Fork, about ten or fifteen feet back from the road on the meadow land adjoining the late T. O. Jefferson property. The structure was mounted on the slope of the hillside, so that while the rear of the building rested on the ground the main entrance was reached by a steep flight of steps. Rectangular in shape, having two stories topped off with an ample garret under the roof, this old tavern was similar to the colonials inns of the time of George III.

Like them, its first proprietors were dispensers of liquor. Later in its history it became a stopping place for negro traders on their way to Patty Cannon's at Johnson's Cross Roads.

In later years this old inn was used as a private dwelling by various Federalsburg families. It was while being occupeid by Mr. Hill Smith that the building was finally destroyed by fire.

NANTICOKE BAKERY-FEDERALSBURG MD 1920

The rivers and bays of a new country are its first routes of trade and transportation. Hence river traffic with Baltimore, as well as with some smaller towns of the Chesapeake, began at an early date. Cordwood, lumber, tanbark, and wheat, as well as less bulky products were loaded on to heavy scows and pushed down the river by four or five muscular men using long poles. At Brown's Wharf, four or five miles below Federalsburg, these commodities were re-loaded upon schooners or other sailing vessels and sent up the bay.

Before the Civil War there was little cross-country transportation for anything except mail and passengers. For these, there were the picturesque old stage coaches. Even after the war, they made daily trips from Bridgeville to Federalsburg, and thence to Cambridge and Easton. These lines were operated by Mr. Wesley Moore and Mr. James Finsthwaite.

The Seaford and Cambridge division of the Pennsylvania Railroad was opened for traffic on Oct. 12, 1868, although at that time it extended only from Seaford to East New Market. This date marked a new era in the history of Federalsburg, for it is that railroad, with its refrigerator car accommodation, which has made New York, Philadelphia and other northern cities the markets for the perishable products of our gardens and orchards.

Union Methodist Episcopal Church.

This church was organized in 1785, in a house owned and occupied then by Jacob Charles. This house stands near the bridge which spans the North West Fork of the Nanticoke river which flows through the town, and is at this date, 1919, occupied by Mr. and Mrs. John Smith. The first church building was erected in 1815, and stood within the bounds of the present cemetery. The ground was purchased from one Eccleston Brown and his wife, for the consideration of sixty cents. Upon this ground a frame building was erected for the use of the Methodists as a place of worship. The trustees were Paul Conaway, Constant Wright, Joshua Wright, Ferdinand Griffith, and William Frampton. This building was occupied as a place of worship for both colored and white people until 1850, when it was sold and moved to a point

UNION M. E. CHURCH, TO THE LEFT.

about one hundred yards south, and on the East side of
Main street, where it was occupied as a carpenter shop
for a number of years. Later it was sold and a part of
it moved to the rear of the residence now occupied by
Charles M. Davis and wife, and still serves as a part of
his outbuildings. The present church building, that is
the main part, was built in 1850, on ground bought from
Jacob Charles and wife. Again the consideration was
the sum of sixty cents. At this time the board of trustees consisted of Paul Conaway, Jacob Charles, Charles
Willis of E., John Elliott, Joseph L. Kenney, Curtis
Davis, and William M. Wingate, M. D. In the years
1901 and 1902 the building was repaired, and enlarged
by the addition of an annex on the south side. The cost
of the improvements was $3375.00. The building was
reopened for worship on the 29th day of June, 1902. At
this time the Rev. Thomas S. Holt was the pastor. In
the year 1912 the building was again repaired and enlarged by the addition of a room in the rear for the ac-

commodation of the Beginners and the Primary departments of the Sunday school. The cost of these improvements was $1400.00.

In 1914 a pipe organ was installed at a cost of $1700.00. These last improvements were made during the pastorate of the Rev. T. E. Terry, from 1912 to 1914. For many years the church was a part of a large circuit, during which time preaching on the Sabbath was done by local preachers, the pastors preaching only during the week. Later it was made the head of a smaller circuit, with preaching by the pastor on the Sabbath. In 1902 the charge was made a station.

By Rev. F. C. MacSorley.

Christ Methodist Protestant Church.

The present structure, now known as Christ Methodist Protestant Church of Federalsburg, was originally Federalsburg Presbyterian Church, therefore, any sketch or history of Christ church in order to be in any way complete must include the history of the Presbyterian church which was the beginning of it.

In the year 1871 under the leadership of a Rev. Mr. Boing a congregation was assembled and October 6th regularly organized as a Presbyterian church. Mr. H. P. Chambers was elected Secretary and Messrs. Jas. A. Sanders, Edward R. Goslin, John Wilson, Jacob Rhoads, and H. P. Chambers were the Finance Committee. The original trustees were Edward R. Goslin, H. P. Chambers, W. C. Logan, R. Mitchell, J. Rhoads, J. A. Sanders, Dr. W. D. Noble and John Wilson.

A hall was rented and properly seated and the services proceeded regularly until the present fine structure was erected. The lot on which it stands was bought from Dr. Noble and the building erected during the years 1872 and 1873.

Regular services were held after this until the year 1897. At this time most of the congregation had moved away or died and it was decided to abandon the work and leave the property in the hands of the New Castle Presbytery. The last meeting of the session was recorded on Sept. 30th, 1897 by S. A. Logan, Clerk. Rev. Mr. Blackwell was Pastor at Bridgeville and served this church in connection with that charge.

For about five eyars after that the church remained closed.

NEW MASONIC TEMPLE.

In 1902, a number of Methodist Protestant families having moved into the town and vicinity, it was decided to form a Methodist Protestant church. Mr. James B. Wright, a loyal Methodist Protestant, seeing the need, bought the church building from the New Castle Presbytery and advanced the money until such time as the congregation should be able to repay him. Rev. Herbert F. Wright, who was then Pastor at Reliance, opened services in the church building and June 12th, 1902 Christ Methodist Protestant church was duly organized.

Since that time services have continued to be held continuously and the church has gained until it has reached its present strength and usefulness and has become one of the strongest powers for good in the community.

By Rev. J. L. Nichols.

Schools.

The first school in Federalsburg was situated on the west side of Main Street midway between Academy Avenue and the M. P. Church. One of the first teachers was Mr. Thomas Brown, who settled here in the latter part of the eighteenth century. This building was accidentally burned during the term taught by Miss Lizzie Goslin. It, as well as its successor, built near the point where Main Street became the Preston road, was under the management of Dorchester County. The first Caroline County school within town limits stood adjoining the present site of the M. E. Church.

Following these came the Academy, at first a one-room frame structure over which Miss Augusta Paine first presided as school-mistress. With the growth of the town, however, other rooms were added until, when last used, it comprised six rooms. Even the conversion of an adjacent machine shop into a primary school failed to meet the growing demands of the town and community; a more commodious building was an imperative necessity.

One of the last public acts of the Hon. E. E. Goslin, who had championed the Academy and donated the first five hundred dollars to it, was to obtain the passage of a bill appropriating money for the erection of the present High School building, first occupied in 1915. This building is a large stucco structure of two stories and basement. Its thirteen class rooms, auditorium, lunch-room, library, text-book room, office, and rest room, are heated by steam. Electric lights, bells, telephones, and running water are other mdoern conveniences which help to make it one of the finest and best equipped schools on the Eastern Shore.

PUBLIC SCHOOL BUILDING.

Colored Schools.

Standing where Main Street curves to form the "Point" is a little shop where Mr. Richard Tull (a white man) did carpenter work by day and taught the colored inhabitants by night. Somewhat later a school house was built for them at Quaker Branch, where the Houston's Branch road leaves town. A part of the old color-ed church opposite Mt. Pleasant Cemetery also did ser-vice as an institution of learning until the erection of the attractive new building on the Nichols road met ex-isting needs.

(From material collected by Federalsburg Pupils.)

OLD BETHEL CHURCH, SINCE RESTORED.

HICKORY HILL.

In the year 1872 a piece of land was bought from Mr. Alfred Davis and Mr. James Willis on which to build a school.

The school was built in a hickory grove on a small hill, so they decided to call it Hickory Hill. In 1916 the school was burned, then for two years the children of this section went in a hack to Federalsburg school.

In the year 1918 the people in the vicinity of Hickory Hill School met and subscribed a certain amount of money to erect a new school. At the end of the year the new school was completed. Two miles away from Hickory Hill School is a church by the name of Liberty that was built in the year 1907.

In the year 1863 the slaves of the United States were freed by our president, Abraham Lincoln. Many of the slaves of the United States were badly treated. There were many kidnappers in the east. Kidnappers caught the negroes wherever they went and then sent them south and sold them for a good price. The greatest kidnapper near Hickory Hill neighborhood was Patty Cannon. She was as strong as a man and lived where Reliance now stands. She went around in a one-horse wagon trying to catch negroes. She would invite them to take a ride with her, and when they were in the wagon would throw them down and tie them hand and foot. Then she would take them to her home and put them in her slave pen, until she had enough to send south and sell.

Pupils of Hickory Hill School.

NICHOLS.

The old school house built of logs many years ago, stood near where Mr. Cohee's house now is. It was named Midway because it was about half-way between Friendship and Federalsburg.

The present school site was purchased from James A. Nichols in 1896, since which time it has been known officially as Nichols School.

A sorgum mill was also built in this section long ago. Mr. Corkran built it.

HOUSTON'S BRANCH.

Houston's Branch is the name applied to a small stream emptying into the North West Fork a few miles above Federalsburg. It was eivdently named for James Houston who came to this section from Sussex County about 1800 and became one of the most representative citizens of this section and well known in county affairs. Mr. Houston was probably the earliest miller in this neighborhood.

As English and Scotch people settled this community largely, their descendants naturally clung to the Episcopal church—so much so in fact that a church of that denomination was established here years ago. For lack of support, however, it ceased to thrive and finally was closed.

After the Liberty school district was divided about 1871, the Houston's Branch school district was laid off and a building erected. With the exception of one or two years when the school was closed because of poor attendance, it has been in operation ever since. To this school belongs the honor of having the first concrete steps in the county, built by the patrons during the incumbency of Mrs. S. E. Parsons, teacher.

SCENE AT CONCORD CAMP.

CONCORD.

Concord was given its name about 1804, at which time John Mitchell, Isaac Collins, Sr., Horatio Short, Francis Elliott, Peter Causey, James Jenkins, and James Sullivan, trustees, appointed by the society that was then meeting at Abraham Collins house (near Potter's Mill Pond) and approved by the preacher in charge bought from Abraham Collins for $15, one and one-twentieth acres of land for a meeting house to be called Concord. There had apparently been no name given to the region up to this time as the records simply speak of the intersection of the two roads, one leading from Greensboro to Hunting Creek and the other from Potter's Landing to Marshyhope Bridge.

The first church at Concord was built near the site of the present one. Both white and colored people attended this church. The latter entered by a separate door which led directly up to the gallery. The present church was erected and dedicated shortly before the Civil War. The building committee consisted of Peter

Sullivan, Gootee Stevens, Wingate Neal, William M. A. Liden, and Tilghman Nuttle. No account was given of the dedication. The building was done apparently by Thomas Murphy. There is a receipt from him dated Jan. 10, 1857 which together with other papers indicate a total of $1861.82 which most likely represents the cash outlay for the building—a considerable sum for a rural church edifice at that time. The church membership in 1847 was one hundred and five divided into three classes. The leaders of the classes were Peter Sullivan, Richard Lockerman and Gootee Stevens. The colored members numbered seventy-seven.

The first camp meeting at Concord was held in 1857 under the joint pastorate of Revs. W. W. Warner and Daniel George. Before this time the local camp had been held at Meluney's woods near Andersontown.

Rev. William Taylor, afterward a bishop, preached the Sunday the money ($60) was raised to pay for four acres of land for the camp ground. At this time Concord church was included in the Denton circuit.

Some years ago the Concord church was completely remodelled and about 1906 a parsonage was built, since which time Concord has been a circuit and continues the seat of the county's largest and most noted camp ground.

Trustees for a public school at Concord were first appointed by the School Board in 1865, before which time by many years a school was apparently maintained. In 1876 the present school site was purchased from Joseph Mowbray.

HOWARD'S.

Howard's takes its name from several families by that name who live in the community. The last generation of these people came from England about forty years ago and proved themselves worthy of their native and adopted lands by becoming enterprising and leading citizens.

In this community as early as 1804 some of the residents planned the establishment of a church and received a visit from Bishop Asbury.

Being rather too distant to public schools the local citizens in 1909 contributed several hundred dollars towards the erection of the present school building.

AMERICAN CORNERS.

For several years the polling place of the famous Eighth district, this village is located on the state highway about five miles from Federalsburg.

Years ago one or two stores, a few dwellings and a tomato cannery seemed to be the equipment of the town. Later, however, the inhabitants of the section succeeded in building a church which belongs to the Methodist Protestant denomination and is attended by the minister from Grove.

About this time the people tired of sending their children so far to school, joined in building a school and finally succeeded in getting the county to take over the responsibility. This latter transaction took place in 1889.

SMITHVILLE AND COMMUNITY.

Days have come, days have gone;
    People have lived and died;
No longer the woods seems to be
    Where once we played "hide."

Houses spacious now are standing,
    Fields of grain and fruits galore
Where once the folks of this community
    Lived several years before.

In the morn the flowers bloometh,
    All its beauty fadeth soon;
In the spring the birdies call,
    But winter calms their tune.

Changes! Ah, yes, there are many more. We, even change in our dress, appearance and habits as the years roll by. Places change too. How surprised our forefathers would be if they could see the little village where once they lived and helped to build; buildings where once their dead were laid away; and roads where years ago were nothing but acres and acres of trees. Since those days many changes have taken place.

Instead of the pleasant country and the little village which we now see, in the years long ago, there were only Indians camped here and there. If we were to take a walk down the pond now we would see many kinds of flowers blooming on tall bushes. Some of these were probably planted by the Indians. We can also find their curious looking darts scattered over the country which they shot from their arrows, and bricks which they made their floors of can be seen yet, thus indicating that a tent was once there. Now, some people wonder what has become of the Indians. But, we can soon tell.

When the white settlers first came over here they wanted the land for their own. They knew that they must get rid of these red faced people, so they kept driving tribe after tribe away until at last all left.

Mr. Richard Liden was the first man to come from England who helped drive them away.

The white people had come to a beautiful land; a land rich in valuable woods, bountifully supplied with game and streams abounding with myriads of waterfowl. Many years went by, each year bringing more people to this country. What were they to do? Make it a place suitable to live in and to support themselves. So they began to clear up the land by cutting down the trees, using what they could and destroying the rest.

The next question which arose was—the building of homes. Where were they to build? The Indians selected their site on the bank of a stream. This stream led up to a place called old Bloomery where there were several shops. Yet, many years elapsed, people lived and died, between the time the first homes were built and the beginning of these shops. But, John and William Douglass about 1800 came to this section and bought land, presumably for the purpose of erecting iron works, since it has been supposed there was a bright prospect of iron ore, and one of these men was an excellent iron master. They were successful with their work for a while and thus before their coming the place was without a name, but when all the pits got on fire they called it "bluming," naming the place "Blumery." The term Blumery was also given to the tract of land from which the iron ore was thought to be found. In late years the "oo" has taken the place of the "u" now spelled Bloomery.

This country was very thinly populated then. Following the stream, it led to a place where one brick building and two small one story houses stood. A Mr. Dukes lived in one of the two small houses. It seems that Peter Jenkins once lived in the brick structure and kept a little store. Later Mr. Wheeler occupied the same building and was the owner of several acres of land surrounding his home. About the year 1840 Samuel G. Smith bought the land and property from Mr. Wheeler. In 1869, Robert Bullock bought it and lives there at the present time. Mr. Smith was a very industrious man, always thinking or carrying out some plan for the betterment and improvement of the community. He was the one that built the first saw mill at this place, although there were mills there before he came, namely, James Houston was the owner of a grist mill where the road from Federalsburg to Blumery leads across Brights Branch—which is the outlet of the millpond. James Wright, also, at one time owned the mill and probably Levin and Isaac Smith before him, that was before 1800. Mr. Samuel G. Smith bought the same mill site about 1849 and conducted an up and down saw mill, but later discontinued it and carried on a grist and bark mill there. It was he that built the brick mill now standing but remodelled by Mr. William T. Hignutt, he being the owner of it for several years.

The coming of that man, Samuel G. Smith, to our village gave it the name of Smithville which name has never been changed.

He was interetsed in the spiritual welfare of the people as well as the industrial. He hadn't been located here very long before he started tent meetings near old Bloomery where the church now stands. After some time they built a small meeting house. This was used for religious worship until the people were able to afford better, which was in the year 1854, when they constructed a new church which has always carried the name of Bloomery.

The first school in this section was apparently located between Brights Branch and Old Bloomery. In 1798 James Wright sold to several persons a lot of land, one acre, and provided a small house thereon to be used for a school reserving unto himself and his heirs one twentieth of the rights of the school. We presume he intended to reserve the privilege of his children attending there. The consideration was one pound, or five dollars. The children probably went to this school until they began to think it was too far to walk and the way was somewhat sandy. For a while they sent them to Liden's School, but still it was too far away. This belief caused a school to be built in a more central place near the crossroads by the big hickory tree. This was called Hickory Hill. It did not stand many years before it was burned. William Edward Liden and Bennett Todd were the chief instruments in the construction of the next school. Mr. Liden giving a corner of his land near the cross roads for it to be built upon. After some years they discontinued its use, and Caroline County bought almost an acre of land from Thawley not quite midway between the big hickory tree and the village of Smithville for a new school to be erected. This remains to the present day.

By this time, mail had become a very important matter. About 1850 the people in this community drove to Denton after it. Later their post-office was at Federalsburg. There wasn't any way provided for them to get it only when they went to town, which was not very often as travel was not only slow but rude in those days. To improve upon this method the government established a post-office at Smithville. After the post-office was built drivers were appointed to bring the mail from Federalsburg to certain named centers as, Smithville, Concord, American Corner. It was delivered once about every two weeks, later once weekly and eventually every day.

NABB'S.

Nabb's school, erected in 1909, was named for T. D. Nabb, who was the prime mover in the enterprise, and gave much of the lot upon which the school stands. Miss Myrtle West was the first teacher.

Another Story of Patty Cannon.

One day Elgin Russell, a colored boy, and his sister were out looking for the cows. Patty Cannon upon passing by thought this was a good chance to get some money, so she got out of her gig and caught the two children, carried them home with her and put them in a closet; she told them not to say a word; the people came in search of the children for they knew that Patty Cannon was kidnapping people. These people demanded Patty to give them the key to the closet for they had searched everywhere else but the closet; she told them that she had lost the key. Just at that moment Elgin put his finger through a knot hole in the closet; the people then told her that if she did not give up the key they would burst the door open; she gave them the key which was around her neck.

Contributed by Pupils.

CHESTNUT GROVE.

Chestnut Grove is in the Eighth Election district of Caroline County. However it has not always been known as Chestnut Grove. For a long time it was known as Chestnut Woods and it is on the map now as Agner.

There are three different groups of buildings in Chestnut Grove: the school house, church, and store buildings, besides several farm houses around. The most important one to us children is the school house. Its name is Chestnut Grove School and like the place used to be called Chestnut Woods. It got its name from the many chestnut trees growing around it. The school was not always where it now is. At first it was on the other side of the road and while there the pupils sat on slab benches. In 1874 the Board of School Commissioners purchased a school site from John Lehman and Robert Rooks. Then the people around Chestnut Grove subscribed enough money to build the school house which now stands on the Chestnut Grove road. The building was put up in 1883 and shows its age quite a good deal.

The Methodist Episcopal church standing by the school house was built about 1885, by subscription.

About thirty years ago a camp was held here. It was called Chestnut Woods Camp.

Besides the school house, church, and store building there used to be also a grist mill, saw mill, and postoffice, about one half mile from Chestnut Grove known now as Morgan's mill pond.

Years back a certain William Morgan, for whom the place is now called, bought real estate and built a saw mill, also adding a corn mill thereon. He also built a store house and kept store for some time. After that it changed hands several times until at last a man by the name of John Agner purchased it and continued keeping store there.

The mill was run by water-power and was the only one for miles around. All the people came here to mill and as Mr. Agner also had the post office, it was of course quite a thriving place at one time.

Later the mills were discontinued and the store moved to Chestnut Grove the postoffice, however, keeping the name of Agner until rural delivery came along.

Contributed by Pupils.

HILLSBORO (Tuckahoe Bridge).

This town located on the Tuckahoe River in Caroline County at the point where the Queen Anne and Talbot counties meet the river on the opposite side, is on the site of one of the oldest settlements of the county.

Official records show that before the year 1750, an Episcopal Chapel was located directly across the river from what is now Hillsboro and further that a bridge had also been built before this time. Located as it is in a region conductive to good farming operations, it was only natural that the community should have been settled very early.

In those early times land was usually granted to representative people and families by the Lord Proprietor. Thus it was that John Hardcastle of Talbot county became the owner of large tracts of land in this section.

Aside from the occasional repair and rebuilding of the Chapel and bridge, but little is known of the settlement which was known as Tuckahoe Bridge later called Hillsboro in honor of Lord Hillsboro of the Calvert Family, until the close of the Revolutionary War when Francis Sellers, Esq., who was born in Glasgow, Scotland, had located here and married Elizabeth Downes the daughter of Henry Downes, who was a well known and influential citizen of the county of that time.

Mr. Sellers it was who had built the large brick house still standing near the eastern terminus of the bridge, as well as a brick warehouse along the river nearby where he evidently conducted his mercantile business. Someone has ascertained that the bricks in these two buildings as well as those in the Old Academy were of the same type and quality, indicating that Mr. Sellers was active in the building of the Academy as well. With the natural characteristics of a Scotchman, Mr. Sellers was energetic and thrifty in business and active in the advancement of his community along educational and religious lines. It seems that he must have amassed a considerable fortune in his business as indicated by his various benevolences. By ancestry, likely a Presbyterian, it seems that he was foremost in the councils of the local Episcopal church.

Whether Mr. Sellers prepared at Hillsboro the well known Sellers' Medical Compound that has for a long time been made in Pittsburgh by his descendants, is not definitely known but it seems very likely that he did, because of the records which show the great amount of fevers in this section at that time. In fact Mr. Sellers and several of his children succumbed to a fever which was epidemic in Hillsboro about 1804. A few years afterwards in 1816, Jesse Lee, a well known minister and close friend of Bishop Asbury attended a camp meeting near Hillsboro, was stricken with a fever and a few days later expired at the home of Mr. Sellers, a son of the late Francis Sellers.

In 1831 the first newspaper in the county was established here, being printed by Lucas Bros.

For some time Hillsboro was the site of the Tri-county Fair and frequently was the meeting place of Congressional Conventions.

A record has been found indicating that Charles Wilson Peale, one of America's greatest painters, and the son of Rembrandt Peale who lived for a time in Queen Anne county, resided once in or near Hillsboro. Thus it seems that this place must have attained considerable prominence in religious and literary circles, as well as having been of much commercial importance, the latter characteristic being indicated by the establishment of a shoe factory, cannery, tobacco warehouse, tavern and one or more general stores.

The Old Hillsboro Academy.

In 1797 a brick school house was erected in Hillsboro, the land having been donated by John Hardcastle, Jr., of Talbot County, and deeded in trust to the following men: Francis Sellers, William Smith, Valentine Green, Henry Nichols, of Caroline County, and Samuel Barrow of Talbot. For over seventy-five years the building remained on this lot known as part of "Hackett's Garding." Provisions of the deed prove the school to have been purely local. In the next year plans were made for one liberal school in each county, and this school became known as Hillsboro Academy.

Private subscriptions provided the money for the school building and was furnished not only by men from Caroline but from Queen Anne's and Talbot as well. Francis Sellers, a well known business man living near the Tuckahoe bridge, was largely responsible for the success of the school. He not only made generous subscriptions to the enterprise but endowed the school for the benefit of orphaned children.

The first board of trustees were Francis Sellers, William Smith, Henry Nichols 3rd, Samuel Barrow, Henry Downes, William Richardson and George Martin. These trustees were "on the job" from the start; in fact the Legislature of 1806 placed the village government in their hands. They appointed a bailiff to collect taxes which were laid upon persons who kept dogs, also fines imposed upon residents who alarmed their neighbors by permitting their chimney to catch fire, and fines upon persons who enticed away or harbored any of the charity children in charge of the teacher or Trustees.

OLD HILLSBOROUGH ACADEMY.
Founded 1797.

The course of study included the classics as well as the elementary subjects. In recognition of the high standing of the school the General Assembly of 1812 made the school a donation of $500, which custom was kept up for nearly twenty years. In 1823 the following report was sent to the Assembly:

One teacher.
Five free students.
Eight classical students.
Nineteen students in English and Mathematics.
Total number of pupils, 27.

Hillsboro Academy held indisputable sway in Caroline until 1827 when half of the State's annual donation was taken from it to give to the Denton Academy, not then erected. For a few years after this the type of teaching at Hillsboro was unchanged. Then came a period of struggle when it alternated between a private school and a local county school according as it enrolled the fifteen subscribing scholars necessary to receive the State donation. Later years saw the revival of interest in the Academy but only for a brief period. In 1878 the school was taken over by the County Board of Education, who replaced the old building by erecting a more modern two room structure for a graded school.

Episcopal Church.

A history of the Episcopal church will be found elsewhere in this volume under the caption—Early Churches.

Methodism in Hillsboro and Vicinity.

In the year 1776, the Rev. Mr. Ruff, was then preaching on what was then known as Kent Circuit. For some reason he was called away for a short time from his work, and at his request Freeborn Garretson came over to take his place while he was away. Garretson preached in Queen Anne's County, and came into Caroline, first at Greensboro, then traveling southward, he visited the upper parts of Tuckahoe Neck near where Hillsboro now is. He was the first Methodist preacher the people heard in these parts.

Garretson says:

"I was wandering along in search of an opening for the Word in deep thought and prayer that my way might be prosperous, when I came to a gate, where I had a sudden impression that I ought to turn in, which I did and went up to a house and told the mistress who came out to meet me, that if she wanted to hear the word of the Lord, to send out and call her neighbors, which she did, and I preached that evening and the next day".

This was at the home of the step-father of the Rev. Ezekiel Cooper, who was an officer in the American Army, and as it was a day of great mustering, Garretson, sitting on his horse, preached to the soldiers, many of which were converted and became Methodists.

A Methodist Society was formed in the year 1776 or 1778 and between 1780 and 1784 the first Methodist Meeting House in Caroline County was built near the Meeting-house Branch and was known as "Ebenezer Chapel."

This was a rallying center for Methodists for more than a quarter of a century. Quarterly Conferences were held with Bishops Coke and Asbury presiding. On his first visit to this community in 1784 Bishop Coke said, "The people here are the best singers I have heard in America."

Several prominent Methodist itinerants came from this section. Among them were Ezekiel Cooper, Solomon Sharp, Stephen Martindale, and Thomas Neal.

About the year 1838 the church was moved from the Old Meeting-house Branch into Hillsboro, where it has occupied its present location ever since, and it still bears its original name "Ebenezer."

From its earliest beginnings to the present time Methodism has had a prominent place in the Religious life of the community, and has always helped to bear the burdens of the denomination.

Contributed by REV. E. W. McDOWELL.

THE HOME OF FRANCIS SELLERS.

FRANCIS SELLERS.

1.

In the old brick mansion down the hill,
Lived Francis Sellers a man of will,
He came from Scotland far across the sea,
And settled Hillsboro, dont you see?

2.

He was very honest, steadfast and true,
And his fellow citizens knew it, too.
Now as to slaves he had many (?)
But never was known to ill treat any.

3

Old Hillsboro Academy owes its origin to him,
Which goes to show he was a man of vim;
He donated much money to help the poor,
And had he been richer he would have donated more.

4.

Miss Downes of Caroline became his wife,
And they lived an ideal married life.
Seven beautiful children God gave to them,
Two of which became noble men.

5.

In the Seller's graveyard upon the hill,
He lies buried but we honor him still,
We know that in Heaven he is at rest,
His friends mourned his death but God knew best.

KATHERINE KLINE.

THAWLEY'S.

On the eastern bank of the Tuckahoe midway between Hillsboro and the Choptank is located a colonial
type of house which is best known, perhaps, as the Thawley House, but earlier as the home of Rebecca Daffin,
who was a sister of Charles Dickinson that fell in the
duel with Andrew Jackson at the beginning of the 19th
century.

A member of the well known family of Daffin of
Dorchester county came to Caroline early and constructed a very handsome residence of brick. Evidently
no expense was spared to make this an elegant home
with large rooms, high ceilings, beautiful stairways and
elaborate mantel pieces. It is said that the great cost
practically led to the financial failure of the builder.

Here one may easily imagine the goings-on of that
period—the stately minuet, the joyous game, the elaborate feast, and the exciting hunt and chase so much indulged in in that day, with all cares left to the disposition of the faithful slaves that made up the household.

The Daffin farm apparently includes the present
Thawley farm as well as the Clark land extending as far
as Thawley's church. This tract seems to have been the
gift of Henry Dickinson to his daughter Rebecca.

It seems that this section was early cleared and developed as a good farming community. The mill nearby, known now as Knott's or Elben's mill, was standing in 1804 as per a plat filed in the Clerk's Office in Denton. At this time it was known as Morgan's mill and was included in a tract of 1500 acres of land belonging to Henry Nichols and extended much of the way towards Hillsboro.

It seems likely that the Hillsboro school served for this community until about 1870 when a local building was erected. This was burned about 1885 when the present one was erected on land purchased of J. W. Clark.

TUCKAHOE NECK.

This section of Caroline County lying between the Choptank and Tuckahoe rivers and the main road leading from Denton to Hillsboro has for a long time been almost as well known by name and reputation to the inhabitants of Maryland and Delaware as the famous "blue grass region" of Kentucky.

Endowed by nature with two crowning attributes— location along the river and fertility of soil, it is of little wonder that this section early attracted settlers from other counties. Until about 15 years ago, this region was inhabited almost entirely by the land owners themselves, a situation which meant that the buildings and fences were in first class condition, and the land in a high state of cultivation. Travellers from other counties to Caroline County at that time would not easily miss a trip of inspection to this beautiful section. Some of the most important families of the county and state have lived at one time or another in Tuckahoe Neck. Joshua Clark, one of the largest landowners, and one of the county's earliest court justices, lived during the Revolutionary War period at Lyford, an estate even well known at the present day. Later on John M. Robinson who became a distinguished jurist in this state was born and raised in Tuckahoe Neck. Suffice it to say that several worthies have come from this section.

It seems that the earliest inhabitants of this neighborhood either attended the Quaker meeting near Denton or went to Tuckahoe Chapel which was located near Hillsboro.

In 1842 Isaac Harris then a prominent resident of this section deeded to Edward Carpenter, James Nichols, George W. Wilson, William Williams, John Nichols, Benjamin Atwell and William Cade, trustees, land to be used as the site of a church which was established under the Methodist Episcopal control. Thus the name of Harris Chapel most likely originated. It was provided in the deed that in case of a vacancy among the trustees the remaining ones should fill the vacancy provided the applicant be at least 21 years of age and a member of the church for at least one year previous. For a long time this church was served by ministers from Denton, but for the past 20 years from Hillsboro. At present, service is conducted by the Southern Methodist minister at Queen Anne.

Owing to there being a large pond nearby where wild geese on their annual trip south formerly alighted for food and rest, this church, the school nearby and in fact the general section has long been known as Goosepond.

The earliest school for this section of which we have any record was located near the junction of the road to Lyford with the Tuckahoe Neck road. Z. P. Steele, Esq., of Denton, recalls having attended this school and perhaps, as a very small boy, to have seen the original school building which seems to have been constructed of logs. Because of the crowded condition of this school in 1870, the School Board appointed a committee consisting of James B. Steele, G. W. Collison, and Edward Saulsbury to consider the advisability of dividing the school district. Their report was favorably accepted by the Board and Upper Tuckahoe and Lower Tuckahoe districts were formed. Since this time public schools have been maintained in these two districts—the one Saulsbury's in honor of Edward Saulsbury—the other Cedar Grove because of its being surrounded by a grove of cedars. In 1885 an exchange of sites was made by means of which Cedar Grove school acquired a lot of two acres.

AGRICULTURAL HIGH SCHOOL—RIDGELY.

RIDGELY.

The Founding.

Ridgely did not happen into existence like the typical cross-roads settlements which gradually extend along the turning highway until they suddenly discover themselves to be full fledged villages or towns. Ridgely was fully conceived and definitely planned before one building was erected on its site.

RIDGELY'S FIRST HOUSE, OCCUPIED BY MR. FRED RIDGELY AND FAMILY, RECENTLY TORN DOWN.

When the Eastern Shore of Maryland was undergoing a transformation because of the approach of railroads, a body of men from Philadelphia heard the call of the city and under the name of the Maryland and Baltimore Land Association, started forth with the dream of planting a city on the site of our present town, which should unite the Maryland and Delaware Railroad and the Choptank River. Without the cooperation of Reverend Greenbury W. Ridgely and Mr. Thomas Bell, the Maryland and Baltimore City LandAssociation could not have caried out its plans. The general understanding is that Messrs. J. R. Renzor, Thomas O. Hambly and

George N. Townsend, the three important men constituting the Association, were friends of Rev. Greenbury W. Ridgely and through his large land interests at this point and their common interests in the construction of the Queenstown and Harrington Railroad, these three men were drawn to this community. Under the circumstances, it was natural that the Reverend Mr. Ridgely should give them his hearty cooperation in their city building project, and that they should reciprocate by naming the city in his honor. After the negotiation of the Land Association with Mr. Ridgely and Mr. Bell, in which they secured the use of the Ridgely and Bell farming lands for the promotion of their town and city scheme, they made their survey of Ridgely. Mr. Sisler, a Philadelphia civil engineer, was employed by them for this special part of the work. He was assisted by Mr. Theophilus W. Smith, then a young man living at his father's home farm, near the prospective town. They surveyed not less than two hundred acres lying within and around the town.

This whole survey resulted in the production of a most interesting map of Ridgely, showing the beautiful streets and avenues planned. Copies of this were used freely in attracting settlers to the contemplated city. The dream city, founded May 13, 1867, was born too early in this section of the state to become a reality, and it soon died. The reason for this was that the financial resources of the Company were not sufficient to enable them to accomplish their great undertaking. As the summer advanced, signs of this were much in evidence. Unpaid bills were accumulating and dissatisfaction was heard from lumber dealers, builders, painters, and day laborers. The city that had been started vanished with only a few buildings and a map left behind to record the unrealized dream.

After the failure of the Maryland and Baltimore Land Association, the real estate firm of Mancha Brothers united its activities in promising the growth of Ridgely; but for the first decade the most apparent growth lay outside the boundaries of the village. New settlers bought farms in the surrounding country where land was plentiful and cheap, and thus gradually the agricultural interests outside the hamlet and the commercial interests within, developed Ridgely into the busy railroad center it has increasingly become throughout its fifty years or more of history. Faith in the railroad was the great factor in holding Ridgely together and in promoting its growth.

The following are some of the earliest settlers in Ridgely,—James K. Saulsbury, a merchant; J. Frank Mancha, and Henry S. Mancha, real estate agents, who were instrumental in bringing northern settlers into this community; Sylvester Smith, who established a fruit evaporating industry, and James Swann, Ridgely's first teacher and later Superintendent of Schools of Caroline County. Other early settlers were Isaac J. Sigler, John A. Sigler, and Thomas W. Jones, Sr.

REV. GREENBURY W. RIDGELY.

The Reverend Greenbury W. Ridgely, in whose honor the town of Ridgely was named, was born in Lexington, Kentucky, May 12, 1798. He attended the Transylvanian University, from which he was graduated, with honor. He then attended the law school at Litchfield, Conn., where he formed a life-long friendship with John M. Clayton, of Delaware. On Mr. Ridgely's return trip to Lexington he visited the families of his uncles, Judge Richard and Henry Ridgely of the Western Shore. Here he was induced to remain and study law. After passing a successfuul examination, he became a member of the bar of this state. After a brief period of legal practice in partnership with Henry Clay, Mr. Ridgely decided to enter the ministry of the Protestant Episcopal Church, and with this idea he entered the Theological Seminary at Princeton, from which in the course of time he was graduated.

While rector at Newtown he married Miss Worth, of that place. His wife died in 1841 and shortly afterward Mr. Ridgely became rector at Chester, Pennsylvania. While at this place he gradually extended his ministerial work in building up new churches in the vicinity. The churches at Marcus Hook and Claymont were the outgrowth of his labors. In 1853 Mr. Ridgely came to the Eastern Shore of Maryland to live. He settled in Caroline County where he made large investments in real estate, purchasing from four to five thousand acres of land. Although he was not assigned to any parish, he constantly held services at places which were destitute of churches. His last years were spent near our town at the residence of his son, William S. Ridgely. In August, 1893, Mr. Ridgely suffered a stroke of paralysis from which he rallied; but a second attack shortly afterward caused his death. He lies buried in the Episcopal churchyard at Hillsboro. He left three children, none of whom are living today. His second son, William S. Ridgely, was for many years one of the most prominent citizens of Caroline County.

BIRDS EYE VIEW OF RIDGELY.

One of the leading men in this section of Caroline County at the time of the founding of Ridgely in 1867, was Mr. Thomas Bell. Mr. Bell was a large land owner with an attractive home near the proposed city; therefore it was natural that he should play an important part in the city's inauguration. Since his land joined the extensive holdings of Mr. Ridgely, he agreed to unite with him in selling enough property to enable the Land Association to carry forward its city scheme. By this agreement it fell to Mr. Bell to give the right of way at this point for the Maryland and Delaware Railroad, in its extension from Greensboro to Oxford. It also fell to his lot to provide sites for the railroad station and hotel built by the Land Association. Thus, in a very real sense, Mr. Bell started the town on its way. But the item of greatest interest that has to do with his share in the founding of Ridgely, is that he suggested, in the sale of lots, that if any ardent spirits were ever made or sold upon the premises, the owner of the lot should forfeit it with all its improvements to the parties from whom it was purchased; thus the town of Ridgely has been blessed throughout its years in being number- ed among the ranks of the "dry."

EARLY CONDITIONS.

The early conditions of Ridgely, as far as schools and churches were concerned, were poor, the settlers having had to go to Boonsboro for both. The first school of Ridgely was built in 1872 and was called "Sedge Field Academy." This was a one roomed school of which Mr. Swann was the first teacher. It is said that this was the first school in the county to have desks built with reference to the size of the pupils. This one-roomed building is now a part of a dwelling on Second Street. Church services were held in the school house until 1877, when the Methodist Church at Boonsboro was taken down and rebuilt on the site of the present Methodist Church, the land being given by Mr. Ridgely.

ADDITION OF CHURCHES.

As time passed and Ridgely grew in population, more churches were added and better buildings planned. The second church in Ridgely was St. Paul's Reformed

Church built in 1880, Mr. Hannebury having been its founder and first minister. Later this church was remodeled. In 1895 the present Methodist Church was built, the former house of worship having been moved back on Maple Avenue to become a dwelling. Then came the Catholic Church in 1896, the Brethren in 1898, the Baptist in 1909, and the Dunkard the same year.

DEVELOPMENT OF SCHOOLS.

Just as many churches were added, so school conditions improved with population. The little one-roomed school was found inadequate; hence in 1888 the present Primary School was started. It, at first, had but two rooms, gradually three more were added. In 1910 this became a high school. After much careful consideration in keeping with the advancement along industrial and commercial lines, a delegation of representative citizens of Ridgely met the County School Board at Denton during April 1910, for the purpose of discussing plans relative to the establishment of an agricultural high school in their community. Courses in agriculture, chemistry, animal husbandry, and manual training having been added to the school curriculum, and many pupils having come in from the surrounding country to avail themselves of the privilege of them and of a high school training, it was pointed out how necessary it was to have a well equipped modern building in which to teach these practical subjects. Due to the untiring efforts of such men as W. W. Seward, Hon. T. A. Smith and others, the money necessary for such a building was pledged and a tract of land was secured which would provide a convenient and suitable site for the school as well as furnish types of soil for a successful demonstration farm. It was hoped that the State would eventually become interested in starting an Eastern Shore Experimental Station here. The school building was completed July 1912 and formally opened with appropriate exercises September 12, 1912.

THE STATE FARM.

At the request of the Caroline County School Board there was introduced into the Legislature in the session of 1914 a bill to transfer fifty acres of the land purchased for the Ridgely Agricultural High School to the Maryland Agricultural College; this passed and the State re-imbursed the Caroline County Board for the amount which the farm had cost them. The farm has been used largely to supplement the investigations being conducted at the Maryland State College so as to check up results and make them applicable to Eastern Shore soil and climatic conditions.

FRONT VIEW OF THE GREAT ARMOUR PLANT AT RIDGELY.

INDUSTRIES.

On account of Ridgely's many industries the population greatly increased. The Armour Plant, one of the largest strawberry preserving factories in the world, was located here because it seemed the most favorable region from which to secure large yields of this fruit. However many carloads are also purchased and shipped in from other states to be preserved here. This plant employs a thousand people during the strawberry season, the majority of whom are foreigners. The company has settlements of its own where foreign help is housed. Everything about the settlement and building is kept in a thoroughly approved sanitary condition.

Swing & Company's Factory is one of the leading canning enterprises of the kind in the county. This factory packs tomatoes exclusively, using the yield from three or four hundred acres of ground. In connection with this, Swing & Co. have a basket factory which has gained a reputation throughout Maryland and New Jersey. Millions of baskets, crates, and strawberry cups are manufactured, thus giving permanent employment to many.

The Saulsbury Brothers also own and operate a large canning factory here, putting up tomatoes, corn, and peas. A large acreage of these crops is put in each year to supply this factory. Foreign as well as local help is employed.

Summit Poultry Farm.

The Summit Poultry Farm of Holsinger & Son covers sixteen acres, being one of the largest in the East. It has a hatching capacity of 17,000 eggs and as many as 7000 day-old chicks are shipped daily to different parts of the United States. Eggs and chicks of frying size are also shipped.

Improvements.

During Ridgely's later years many improvements have been made, chief among which are:

A water works system having a capacity of 65,000 gallons;

A town sewerage system with a sewerage disposal plant.

Scene when strawberries are ripe on the home farm of the late William W. Seward, near Ridgely. Mr. Seward was "Strawberry King," on the Eastern Shore of Maryland, having when this plate was made in 1908 over 125 acres in bearing. It required 300 pickers to gather the fruit daily.

A fire department well equipped with a power house and pumping station.

A library with a splendid collection of books.

Compiled from the History of Miss Emma Grant Saulsbury and others by the Teachers and Pupils of the Ridgely School.

FURMAN'S GROVE.

Furman's Grove, better known as Jumptown, was one of the earliest settled portions of the county. When the county was formed, the Tuckahoe had been dammed and a mill near the present Crouse mill, was then in operation. This was considerably before 1800.

The Bradleys were prominent residents in this section in those long ago times and in fact influential in the county. Their burying ground is on the Starkey farm across from the school. On some of the rough stones may be deciphered the names or initials of some of these early people.

Bradleysburg was quite a thriving hamlet at this time doubtless. This name evidently continued long after the settlement ceased to be, for a county map made in 1875 by J. B. Isler locates this place.

Following the Bradley family in the neighborhood came the Jumps, one of the earliest and best known of whom was Abraham Jump, also a prominent citizen in the county in his time. He is buried near the Brickyard below Ridgely. Josiah Jump was at one time clerk of the Circuit Court for Caroline County.

Later on a family by the name of Starkey acquired nearly all the land in this section.

Several families of German people came from Baltimore and Pennsylvania and settled not far from where Jumptown church now stands. The houses were built in the meadow near the east side of the branch on what is now Mr. M. C. Smith's farm. The settlement was named Germantown on account of the nationality of its settlers. The houses were all made of logs thatched with mud. One house was built partly in the bank of the stream.

The names of some of the settlers of Germantown were: J. R. Lynch, Otto Gephart, Old Christina, John

Reinhart, known as Dutch John, and a family of Kierschs.

The industries of the German people were basket, cigar, syrup, and cider making. The tobacco for the cigars was not grown here. It was shipped here from the south. The tobacco factory was owned by Otto Gephart. It was a part of his home. The whole family helped make the cigars. They were then peddled around the country.

Willows for the basket making were grown on several acres of land in the meadows. When they were the right height these were cut and stripped of their bark. Then they were sent away to be sold. An old woman, usually called "Old Christina," made very beautiful baskets out of some lighter material. It was probably a sort of straw.

The original church in this section was built at a very early period, judging from some old records. Started as a Methodist church and continued as such for several generations. at one time the Holiness society worshipped within its walls, then again the Methodist took charge and now for several years the Baptist denomination has been in control, the minister living in Ridgely. The present name of Jumptown has clung to the church because of the aid and support once given by Abraham Jump and his family.

A school was early established in this section also, though the earliest official record of same was made in 1865 at which time trustees were appointed by the County School Board.

About 1888 the name of this school was changed to Furman's Grove for a Mr. Furman who donated land for a site. A new building was later erected.

Contributed by the School.

THE PLAINS.

The family connection of Mrs. Bourne, the former owner of the above named estate, was perhaps among the most noted of the Maryland aristocrats. Her father, Isaac Purnell, was a typical southern gentleman and married a daughter of Benjamin Sylvester, a large land holder in ante-bellum times. The Purnell family was very wealthy and maintained all the social customs of the old Dominion aristocracy. Slaves, about 75 in number, were housed in a row of small shanties near the mansion. The master of the plantation was very liberal to the poor, but he had many eccentricities; among which was a dignity and reserve maintained towards his commonplace neighbors. When driving about the country his coachman and footman were dressed in livery, and four coal black horses in silver mounted harness were attached to the family coach. The late Mrs. Bourne, when Miss Mary Purnell, inherited "The Plains" at the death of her grandfather, Mr. Sylvester. The heiress was twice married; her first husband was Allan Thorndyke. Mr. Bourne, her last husband, was very wealthy and at his death the widow inherited several millions to add to her already large possessions. Mrs. Bourne died at Newport in 1881 leaving property estimated at ten million dollars to her children and grandchildren. For many years prior to her demise Mrs. Bourne made an occasional visit to her estate in this county, though never residing here for any length of time. Much of her time was probably spent in Europe. She expended probably one-fourth of a million dollars on "The Plains" estate and her various possessions in all amounted to several thousand acres of the county's choicest land.

Social life surely had a golden era at this Eden of the Eastern Shore, of which many unique anecdotes are extant. One in particular is as amusing as it is unique. A certain member of this ancestral family was passionately fond of sleighing. A longing for this sport seized him at an inopportune season of the year—July. Then, as now, artificial means were resorted to, as this incident goes to prove. A supply of salt was procured to cover the mile-lane drive. Let us hope that our impulsive sportsman enjoyed the jingle of the sleigh bells, since he could not the snow breeze, which would be a boon in such a scorching month. To question the veracity of this anecdote would bring one back again to "Mother Goose" and "Fairy Tale" days. However, it goes to prove that money was not wanting at the Bourne Manor during those days when Maryland's proverbial hospitality had been amicably partaken of at The Plains.

In the course of events Providence ordained other scenes to be enacted on this same eventful stage in which society once held so prominent a part. In the year 1887 a community of ascetic women, known as Benedictine Sisters, purchased this "Paradise of the Plains" from Allen Thorndyke Rice, ci-devant editor of the *North American Review*. The property consists of five hundred and fifty acres of arable and two hundred acres of timber land. It is situated in the heart of the farming region of the Eastern Peninsula. The elaborate buildings were erected by Mrs. M. M. Bourne, grandmother of Mr. Rice, and cost over one hundred and twenty-five thousand dollars. The building material was of the finest. Modern critics say that it could not be purchased in our day at any cost. The workmanship, too, has stood the wear and tear of time, for the buildings seem as substantial now as if they were of modern construction.

The Convent and Academy, St. Gertrude's were incorporated in the year 1896, under the laws of the State of Maryland. The Mother House of this community is located in Newark, New Jersey. where a large branch house is established, with two others in Wilmington, Delaware.

Aims of St. Gertrude's Academy. Harmonious education, while providing sound mental and moral training, must not endanger the growth of the body. Of all places a boarding school in the country is a place to assist the development of the body. The country air is stimulating and has health giving properties that are lacking in most city schools, whose environments are usually limited.

Catholic pupils are given a course of instruction in their religion, but no undue influence is exercised over the minds of non-Catholics. For maintenance of order, all are obliged to conform to the external religious exercises of the institution.

Studies. The Academy has four departments: Primary, Grammar, Commercial, and Academic. The branches taught in these departments embrace all that is

NEW BUILDING AT THE PLAINS.

necessary for a thorough and practical education. These courses afford all the advantages of a modern high school. The children's department comprises seven years; namely, four primary grades. one year each, and the Junior, Grammar and Preparatory classes, one year each.

Art. Art is now recognized as one of the essentials of a refined education. Hence, special attention, under a competent teacher, is given to this study. Music and drawing are also made a specialty.

Domestic Science. "Cooking is an art; a noble science." Lectures and experimental lessons in cooking and baking are given to the students who are interested in home economy.

Domestic Art. Every style is taught—both plain and ornamental—from the cutting out and making of a simple wearing apparel, to the designing and embroidering an elaborate shirt waist, center piece, etc.

SPANISH-AMERICAN WAR.

———

While Caroline county furnished no complete companies to the late (1898) War with Spain, her younger
men were active and eager to engage in behalf of their
country and enlisted a score or two of them in outside
divisions.

We have been able to secure thus far only the names
of the following persons who participated, but it is safe
to say that other names could have been added:

Robert S. Garey, of Denton, served with a Balti-
more regiment; Charles G. Griffin with the New York
National Guard, later the gallant Seventy-first; Clayton
Blackison was on the Battleship Indiana; H. B. and R.
W. Messenger of Federalsburg, were included in the 5th
Maryland Regiment; G. H. Jefferson and Thomas S.
Kemp, of Federalsburg, enlisted in a Pennsylvania reg-
iment; Ira Cannon, Fulton Noble of Preston, Jas. F.
Wallace, Wm. C. Dean, and Milton Tull of Bethlehem,
Harvey Jump and S. J. Sneed of Hillsboro enlisted with
a Talbot county company; Thomas Heather, Bernard
Hutchins, and John Shewbrooks of Marydel, enlisted in
Company M. Delaware regiment; R. Earle Fisher was
with the 5th Maryland which went to Tampa. Charles
and Frank McShane of Denton and Wm. Rumbold of
Choptank also enlisted.

While some of our boys did not get into the lines of
battle, perhaps, they suffered even worse in some of the
hot, yellow fever regions, eating "embalmed meat" so
much spoken of at the time.

The following local newspaper account will serve to
show the nature of the charges of one regiment which
lost nearly all of its men in the terrible campaign:

"**Mr.** Charles G. Griffin of the 71st New York Regiment is
spending part of the sixty days' furlough in Caroline. At the expiration of this furlough the regiment will be mustered out of
service. Mr. Griffin is still suffering from the effect of Yellow fever
which seized him, with hundreds of others, while they were in camp

after the battle of Santiago. At that great combat Mr. Griffin's regiment made a memorable rush upon the Spanish breast-works up a hill in front of the city and drove the dons from their trenches. Many of the Americans were killed but Mr. Griffin escaped without injury. When the top of the hill had been gained many dead Spaniards were found. The charge was a desperate one but Mr. Griffin explained it had to be made because our men were under fire and did not propose to stay at the foot of the hill and take it; consequently without orders they made the dash. In doing so they were protected by gattling guns, which poured a steady stream of lead along the top of the hill. Had any Americans been without guns most of them would doubtless, have been killed before the top was reached."

COUNTY NEWSPAPERS.

Early Papers.

The earliest newspaper in the county was printed at Hillsboro in 1831 by Lucas Bros. Its name was the *Caroline Intelligencer.* It seems only natural that the first paper should have been started at Hillsboro, for two reasons: 1, It is one of the oldest towns of the county and probably the one best developed during that period; 2, Hillsboro being the seat of the Old Academy it may be readily assumed that more letters and culture prevailed there at the time.

Shortly afterwards, a paper was started at Denton. It was called the *Caroline Advocate* and was published from 1835 to 1837 by Henry Vanderford, who later removed to Westminster and became one of the best known editors of Maryland. Judge Carmichael, then a rising attorney at Centreville, upon visiting Denton, persuaded Vanderform to remove his printing establishment to Centreville. Thus Denton was left without a paper.

Another early Denton newspaper, *The Pearl,* which appeared in September of 1840, during the administration of Martin Van Buren, was pubilshed by Mr. John H. Emerson. It was printed for sometime in Centreville. Later when the paper had shown that it would pay, Mr. Emerson purchased a horse tread press, and printed his paper in Denton. It was issued weekly at the price of two dollars a year; one dollar of which had to be paid upon the receipt of the first issue, the other dollar due at the end of the year.

Mr. William Stewart has an issue of *The Pearl* printed January 19, 1841. The paper is given largely to advertisements, among which are Joseph Evitts, General merchandise; Charles W. Smith, Coach, Gig, and Harness. The Union Hotel advertises its bar where the choicest liquors might be obtained. A Baltimore shoe shop advertises a "pair of the handsomest slippers ever made," for one dollar shinplaster. Reference was made to the financial distress of the day including the failing of the Franklin Bank of Baltimore.

The American Union of today is really the successor of the old *Pearl.*

FEDERALSBURG COURIER.

On February 7, 1872, the first number of what is now called the Federalsburg Courier was issued. It was started under the name of the Maryland Courier and published by George D. Baker, who moved here from Stamford, Conn. Mr. Baker did the practical part of publishing it, assisted by Thomas H. Chambers, in the capacity of "devil." Mr. Baker published it for about three years when he disposed of it to James Powers, who in turn sold it to Dr. W. D. Noble a few years later. In 1879 Thomas H. Chambers purchased it of Dr. Noble, and continued it until 1885 when he sold it to Heffron Bros., who published it until 1890, when it passed to H. P. Chambers, who continued it up until the time of his death in October 1897. Under the ownership of H. P. Chambers it was printed by J. W. Stowell, who took over the publication at that time and has continued it without any changes since. The present publisher served his apprenticeship under Heffron Bros. from 1887 to 1890 and since then has been connected with The Courier in some capacity, either as "devil," compositor, printer or publisher. The Courier started out as a 4-page, 6-column paper, and under Heffron Bros. it was increased to a 7-column paper. In 1910 it was again increased to an 8-column 4-page size and in 1913 to an 8-column 8-page size, in which form it is at present publihsed.

The Courier was started as a non-partisan paper. Under Heffron Bros. it was published as a prohibition organ, and under H. P. Chambers in the interest of the Democratic party. At present it is an independent paper.

THE CAROLINE SUN.

The Caroline Sun, published at Ridgely, was established March 15th, 1902, by Dr. W. W. Goldsborough, now a leading practitioner at Greensboro. Dr. Goldsborough knew but little about the publishing business, and in September, 1902, sold his interests in the paper to Mr. L. R. Beauchamp and Mr. Henry Wilkinson. Six months thereafter Mr. Beauchamp decided there were other wider fields of labor for him, and as a consequence he sold his interest to Mr. Wilkinson, the paper's present publisher and editor. The Caroline Sun is an 8-

page, all home print newspaper. The office is equipped with all modern machinery, including a two-magazine linotype machine, with four faces of type at command within ten seconds. These machines are very costly and will do the work of five men. *The Sun* is recognized as one of the leading newspapers of the Eastern Shore. Established under difficulties, the paper has gradually won its way to the front, and now boasts of 1500 subscribers, something unusual for a county paper published in an inland town. Mr. Wilkinson, who came to town with the first issue of the paper, was born in Caroline County, and began his newspaper career in the office of the *American Union* at Denton twenty-eight years ago. He has had wide experience in the publishing business, and ranks among the foremost printers in Maryland.

THE ENTERPRISE.

The Greensboro Enterprise was established in March 1915 and is now a solid business paying good dividends.

From March, 1915 to June 20, 1918, the plant which now prints the *Enterprise* was simply a job office and was named "The Model Printery." Mr. W. Thomas Thornton, the owner, editor and publisher of the paper was and is sole owner of the plant. The job business was such a success, that the idea of establishing a paper soon became lodged in Mr. Thornton's mind, and while he knew he was taking chances he went to work and issued *The Enterprise*. The venture was a success from the outset, the people of this section of the county feeling the need of a good home paper at once supporting the new publication.

Thornton is a Greensboro boy, born and reared, and learned his trade and served his time on the *Free Press,* formerly the organ published here, and for a long time Mr. Thornton did the bulk of the work connected with the job office and the paper himself. After getting on his feet, so to speak, with the business, or getting it to the place where it payed Mr. Thornton was able to hire help, and since that time has had his brother, Mr. Wallace Thornton, helping in the work.

The paper is published on Thursdays and is a neat folio of six columns, full of interesting local and general news matter and is neatly gotten up and printed. The politics of the paper is Democratic.

The plant is rapidly assuming up-to-date proportions. The office is equipped with a cylinder newspaper press and there is also job machinery, all of which is run by electricity.

THE WORLD WAR.

The outbreak of the World War, in August, 1914, came as a terrible shock to the world, especially to the United States. From the beginning of the struggle, the sympathies of the majority of Americans were with the Triple Entente. The atrocities and outrages committed by the Germans together with the violation of Belgium's neutrality and international laws only added to this feeling.

Germany immediately began her terrible submarine warfare upon merchant vessels, which greatly affected American lives and property. She, also, proclaimed on February 4, 1915, a war zone extending around the entire British Isles warning all enemy merchant vessels to keep out of this area. On May 7, 1915, the Lusitania was sunk without warning. Of the 1153 souls, who perished, 114 were American men, women, and children. Immediately following this, the liner, Arabic, was torpedoed. Several persons lost their lives, among whom were two American citizens.

These two incidents brought matters to a crisis, and the United States was kept out of war only by Germany's solemn promise to modify her radical policy. But in March, 1916, the passenger steamer, Sussex, was sunk without warning. A few American citizens were either killed or injured. The German government, immediately, disclaimed all guilt, stating that this conduct was contrary to official orders, which ruse succeeded in quieting the tumult to some extent.

Another cause for trouble was the spreading of German propaganda and attempts at murder and destruction of property not only in the United States but all over the Americas, by German spies and secret service agents, among whom were the attachés of the German Embassy at Washington and the Austrian ambassador. Among these intrigues was the "Zimmerman Note" which was brought to light by United States secret service men on March 1, 1917. It disclosed a plot originated by Germany in which Japan and Mexico were to declare war on the United States and as a reward were to receive large slices of our southwestern states. From this disclosure it was easy enough to prove that Germany had been at least partly responsible for our trouble with Mexico in 1916.

On February 1, 1917, Germany threw all caution to the winds and announced that she would adopt the method of unrestricted submarine warfare. After much discussion and deliberation President Wilson appeared before both Houses of Congress on April 2, 1917, and urged that:

"Neutrality is no longer feasible or desirable, when the peace of the world is involved, and the freedom of its peoples, and when the menace to that peace and freedom lies in the existence of autocratic governments backed by organized force which is controlled wholly by their will, not the will of their people."

Accordingly, April 5, Congress finally declared that a state of war existed between the United States and Germany as indicated in the following resolution:

RESOLVED, That the state of war between the United States and the Imperial German Government which has been thrust upon the United States is hereby formally declared; and that the President be, and he is hereby authorized and directed to employ the entire naval and military forces of the United States and the resources of the Government to carry on war against the Imperial German Government, and to bring the conflict to a successful termination; all of the resources of the country are hereby pledged by the Congress of the United States.

THE DRAFT AND DRAFT BOARDS.

During the extra session of Congress called by President Wilson in 1917, a bill was passed providing for the drafting of men for the army, marine corps, navy, and other lines of service. The bill became a law on May 18. The call for volunteers immediately followed the declaration of war, was admirably responded to, but even so the number of men was not sufficient for the need. For this reason the Selective Draft Law was passed.

This law provided for the establishing of Local and District or Appeal Boards to take charge of the draft. For this purpose the United States was divided into districts, each state consisting of one or more districts, according to its size. Maryland was divided into three districts of which the Eastern Shore composed the third. The members of the Appeal Board in this district were Judge W. Laird Henry, Chairman; Harry A. Roe, Secretary; Curtis E. Crane, Charles F. Rich, and Dr. J. MacFadden Dick, with headquarters at Denton. These men were appointed by the Governor and were under the control of the Adjutant General of the State, who was under the Adjutant General of the United States. The district was composed of smaller divisions, each county being one division with a Local Board at the head. The members of the Local Board for Caroline County, were L. B. Towers, Chairman; Dr. H. W. B. Rowe, and Josiah Beck, with headquarters at Denton. In addition to these boards there was an advisory board appointed to give any legal advice needed. The members of this board were Harvey L. Cooper, Chairman; T. Alan Goldsborough, Frederick R. Owens.

Under the bill all men between the ages of 21 and 31 were compelled to register at their respective voting places. The names were then sent to the Local Board of the county and each one numbered. They were then sent to Annapolis and from there to National Headquarters at Washington. Here each number was put in a capsule and then in large containers to be drawn from. Government clerks, blindfolded, drew the numbers and the men were called in the order in which they were drawn. Every man was notified as to which was his number and when to report for examination. By this method of selecting the men, it was done impartially and they were called into service according as their numbers were drawn. Of course, many of them were exempt from service, and this was attended to by the Local Boards of the counties. Questionaires were sent out to the men, which they were to fill out and return. Many of the men were exempt on account of physical disabilities but many claimed exemption for other reasons. The Local Board decided whether or not a man was to be exempt. Anyone not satisfied with the decision of the board could appeal to the District Board and with these boards rested the final decision except in special cases where the appeal might be taken to the President.

The Local Boards also had charge of sending the men to Camps. In our county all the men had to come to Denton first. If the Government sent out a call for forty men, about forty-eight or fifty were notified, to report at Denton on a certain date. The extra men were sent for as substitutes so that if any of the forty did not appear, there would be some one to send in his place. When they arrived in Denton they reported to the Local Board. This was done in order to be sure they were all there. This always took place the forenoon before they were to leave the next morning. In case of a large number being called there was usually a public meeting at the Court House where addresses were given to the boys by local speakers.

When there were forty-eight or fifty men being sent away a captain was appointed over the whole company, and for every eight men a lieutenant. These were to see that the men arrived safely at the Camps.

The same plan was worked out in the other counties of the United States as here, and before the end of the first year half a million soldiers were training in large Camps all over the United States. These Camps, about fifty in number, each a new city, were largely under officers who had been trained earlier in the year in new officers training camps. When the armistice came a year later we had 3,000,000 men under arms, of which more than 2,000,000 were in France.

War Session of the Maryland Legislature of 1917.

On June 12, 1917, Governor Harrington called an extra session of the Legislature of Maryland for the purpose of enacting necessary war measures. At this session there was a bitter fight between a combination in the House of City Democrats and a majority of the Republicans, against the administration, the object of which was to have written into the Million Dollar War Loan bill the names of those who should control the fund, but they were defeated in their prupose. This combination also attempted to insert a repealer of the Wilson Ballot law into the Soldiers Vote Bill, with the result that the bill was killed.

Among the many important laws passed at this session the following are those that are essentially war measures:

1   Providing for Annapolis Junction Camp site.
2   Creating a Maryland Council of Defense.
3   Providing for a $1,000,000 War Loan.
4   Creating a Maryland State Guard.
5   Amending the militia laws.
6   Compelling idlers to work.
7   Authorizing volunteer firemen to act as county guards.
8   Suspending legal proceedings in favor of persons in Military service.
9   Suspending judgments etc. against persons unable to pay on account of war to apply only to soldiers and sailors.

10   Suspending statues of limitations in favor of persons absent on account of war.

11   Permitting absent soldiers and sailors to register for voting.

The sixth measure named above was the law generally known as the "Work or Fight" bill. It was rigidly enforced throughout the state and in some special sections played an important part, but in our own town and county there were only a few specific cases where the enforcement of the law was necessary, for as a rule our boys and men were either willing to fight or to stick at some worthwhile job.

The President of the Senate and the Speaker of the House at this session were, respectively, Peter J. Campbell of Baltimore City, and David G. McIntosh of Baltimore county. The Legislature adjourned "sine die" on June 27, 1917.

The Council of Defense.

In December 1915 Congress passed the National Defense Act which provided for a regular army of 186,000 officers and men, a federalized National Guard of over 400,000 men, a system of civilian training camps for reserve officers, and the establishment of plants for the production of nitrates and other products used in the manufacture of munitions.

The same Act gave the President authority to create a wonderful organization known as the Council of National Defense. This Council was a powerful combination of officials with experts in science, business and the professions. It included sub-committees on transportation, munitions, engineering, supplies, raw materials, and labor, with numerous sub-committees, including one on women in industry. Under this National Council and working in connection with it were the various State Councils.

The Maryland Council of Defense did much work and a wide variety of work. In the beginning was Maryland's pledge—

"RESOLVED: By the General Assembly of Maryland, that the State of Maryland pledges all its resources to the Government of the United States, for the successful prosecution of the war,"

1.   To consider all problems relating to women and their work which might arise during the war.

which resolution was unanimously adopted by members of the General Assembly.

Therefore the General Assembly passed an act, creating the Maryland Council of Defense, providing that fifty men should constitute said Council, and at the same time it provided legislation for $1,000,000 to be subject to the order of the Council, for its expenditure, with the approval of the Governor. Below each State Council, and in constant touch with it, were county councils of like manner.

The Caroline County Commission appointed by Governor Harrington was H. L. Cooper, Chairman; Harry A. Roe, Thos. H. Chambers, Nathaniel Horsey, and John M. Swing.

This commission had supervision over the following branches of work: Organization, finance, public information, registration, thrift department, educational propaganda, industrial workers, vigilance, liberty loans and war saving stamps, maintenance of existing social agencies.

While the act of the General Assembly creating the Council of Defense provided that it should consist of only men, the Governor appreciating the necessity of securing the full aid of the women in this state, named a like number of women, who organized without legislative act as the "Women's Section of the Maryland Council of Defense."

The purposes of this Council were:

1. To consider all problems relating to women and their work which might arise during the war.
2. To co-ordinate the work and develop the resources of the Women of Maryland in order to secure the highest efficiency for War Emergency Work.
3. To furnish a direct and speedy channel between the different departments of the Federal and State Governments and the Women of Maryland.
4. To ascertain and report the patriotic work that was done by women and women's organizations.

The Council was to be a clearing house for all organizations and for the work of all individuals throughout the State. The Women's Work of the Maryland Council of Defense was the same as the men's except that they took up an additional branch of work, the Social and Welfare Department.

The Caroline County Commission was appointed by Governor Harrington May 3, 1917, and the work of the organization was begun at once. This commission consisted of: Mrs. J. Kemp Stevens, chairman; Mrs. Fred P. Roe, Mrs. Thomas R. Green, Mrs. John W. Stowell, Mrs. J. W. Payne.

There was also appointed by the Governor a Division composed of colored men and a Division composed of colored women, all of whom according to their opportunities did splendid work.

The entire organization did exceedingly useful work in promoting unity, arousing interest, and suppressing possible treason within the State.

LIBERTY LOANS AND WAR-SAVINGS CERTIFICATES.

In order to finance the war, the Federal Treasury Department issued United States Bonds in denominations of $50, $100, $500, and $1000, bearing 4% interest. This was the First Liberty Loan, and was inaugurated in June, 1917. Harvey L. Cooper of Denton was appointed chairman of the committee to sell bonds in the county. All banks became agencies, and each district sent out a committee of local agents. These bonds were exempt from all taxes except inheritance and the normal federal income taxes. With the assistance of the Women's Preparedness and Survey Commission of Caroline County a meeting was held at the Court House June 12, 1917 at which bonds to the amount of over $114,000 were sold.

As the war progressed and it became necessary to arouse the people to a conception of the amount of money needed to carry on the war, each state, county, and district was apportioned its share of the loan to be made. This apportionment was based on the banking resources of the community, usually $7.50 per capita unless the banking resources amounted to more than that amount. Whenever any state, county, or district had subscribed its allotment, it was entitled to display its Honor Flag, a red-bordered banner with a number of blue stripes across its white field corresponding to the serial number of the loan for which it was displayed; thus a community subscribing its quota to the Third Liberty Loan floated a banner bearing three stripes. It was a matter of pride and honor among Carolinians to keep their respective Honor Flags flying regardless of the increasing amounts of the loans asked.

All professional people, all county officials, and all organizations were appealed to to assist in awakening the public conscience in the matter of buying bonds. Ministers spoke at local patriotic meetings everywhere, and held special services in the churches, thus linking the cause of liberty and democracy with that of religion. Salesmen traveling in automobiles were instrumental in posting bills and distributing literature. Public spirited, men and women everywhere were appointed to assist in a house-to-house canvas for the sale of bonds.

In all there were five of these loans, the total amount of money thus raised in the county being $1,905,650. Each time a campaign of speaking, exhibiting war souvenirs, martial music, etc. preceded or accompanied the drive for funds. The Second Liberty Loan drive was the occasion for a big mass meeting at Denton in October 1917. A crowd of 3000 or more assembled on the Court House square listening to addresses by Albert G. Towers, Judge Harry S. Covington, and Samuel S. Watts. A Scotch Band in national costume and performing on bagpipes furnished a picturesque and unusual element to the occasion, while the songs of the Naval Reserve Quartet gave the touch and atmosphere of soldier life. County subscriptions to this fund amounted to over $300,000.

The Third Loan, for which the county allotment was $305,200, was launched April 6, 1918 and closed May 4, 1918. These bonds bore 4¼% interest and became due Sept. 15, 1928. Subscriptions were payable outright or in four installments. American and Canadian soldiers (the latter of whom were wounded men returned from the front) figured in this campaign for funds. Caroline's subscription was $353,350.

The Fourth Loan was opened Sept. 28, 1918. The ban on using gasoline for Sunday automobile rides was lifted in order to encourage the big meeting at the county seat on "Heroes Day," Sunday, Sept. 29. James W. Chapman, Clarence Perkins, Simon J. Block, and Rev. C. T. Wyatt were speakers on this occasion. During the campaign the government loaned patriotic films for display in motion picture parlors. These shows were open to all who displayed the button showing that they had bought bonds of the Fourth Liberty Loan. Later in the campaign they were open to all. $612,900 were raised for this loan.

The Fifth, or Victory Loan, as it was called, was made in April 1919, after the armistice had been signed. A special inducement to buy these bonds was offered in allowing 4¾% interest. A rousing meeting was planned for this final campaign. Between 5000 and 8000 people from the county attended the meeting at the county seat April 27, 1919. "Jerry's Coffin" and "Verennes Taxi," two war tanks from overseas, divided interest with an airplane from Washington, the first to come to land in Denton. A thirty-piece band of the Seventeenth Infantry, as well as the presence of several returned soldiers from Caroline County stirred the patriotism of the crowd assisting in a glorious over-the-top subscription of $525,300.

Another means of raising money by government loans was the sale of Thrift Stamps and War-Savings Stamps. This sale was directed by the Treasury Department under authority of the same act of Congress which floated the Second Liberty Loan. It was designed to encourage thrift at a much-needed time for that virtue, and to enable those to participate in war loans whose means would not permit them to buy even the smallest bond,—$50. Thrift Stamps cost twenty-five cents, could be purchased at any time and, when sixteen had been collected, could be exchanged for War Savings Stamps which bore interest compounded semi-annually at 4% and were "absolutely and unconditionally free from all national, state, and local taxes."

Every War-Savings Stamp could be registered at any postoffice, thus insuring the owner again loss. Any purchaser might sell his Stamps back to the government through any postoffice on 10 days written notice. These conditions put and kept W. S. S. within the reach of all who could have anything at all, and made them popular investments. The amount of this loan ($2,000,000,000 for the United States) was reserved for those of small means by limiting the amount purchasable at one time to $100 and by one person to $1000.

The campaign began Jan. 1, 1918 and closed Dec. 31, of the same year, by which time about $400,000 had been collected through W. S. S. sales. Harry W. Davis of Federalsburg was chairman for the county; post offices, banks, stores, and public school teachers were authorized agents or agencies. As far as possible Thrift Stamps and War Savings Stamps were sold through the schools and school children, in order to give training in the formation of thrift habits, and to give the citizens of tomorrow a chance to participate in the duty and the privilege of maintaining liberty as a world standard.

Throughout the war various benevolent and philanthropic organizations made numerous "drives" for funds with which to carry on their efforts to bring something of the atmosphere of home to the boys in camp, in the field, and in the trenches. Acting on the suggestion of President Wilson, seven prominent organizations, the Young Men's Christian Association, the Young Women's Christian Association, the Knights of Columbus, the Jewish Welfare Board, the War Community Service, the American Library Commission, and the Salvation Army instituted a joint drive in the proceeds of which each organization shared in proportion to its membership. Mr. T. Alan Goldsborough was made chairman of the Caroline County committee to raise its quota of $12,900 of the fund for the United War Workers, as they were jointly called. Sub-chairmen were appointed for each district, and the work carried on in the same manner as in previous campaigns. $15,434.26 was the actual amount raised.

As an auxiliary to the United War Workers, bands of Victory Boys and Victory Girls were organized in all parts of the county, pledging themselves not only to *give* a stated amount to the fund, but to *earn* it by their own efforts. Hundreds of children were busy several months in earning money with which to meet their obligations. Interesting, indeed, were the many ways in which children made themselves of use to their parents and other employers.

Approximately 600 boys and 700 girls signed pledges varying amounts from one to five dollars. All of these Victory Boys and Victory Girls were under twenty years of age, and most of them were enrolled in the public schools. The results were most gratifying, and, in fact, little short of remarkable, the total amount pledged being over four thousand dollars, much above the county's school quota.

Following is a list of schools and their respective pledges:

Marydel	$ 40.00	Garey's	40.00
Henderson	50.00	Camp Grove	15.00
Goldsboro	215.00	Burrsville	13.00
Moore's	65.00	Liden's	5.00
Lowe's	29.00	Central	25.00
Greensboro	225.00	Caroline High	867.25

Denton Primary	73.00	Saulsbury's	24.00
Andersontown	53.00	Cedar Grove	10.00
Harmony	14.00	Ridgely High	325.00
Preston	714.00	Ridgely Primary	72.00
Choptank	35.00	Furman's Grove	12.50
Poplar Neck	15.25	Laurel Grove	28.00
Hubbard's	45.00	Concord	3.00
Federalsburg	757.55	Smithville	2.00
Nichols	21.60	Chestnut Grove	23.00
Hillsboro	56.00		

COLORED SCHOOLS.

Mt. Zion	$ 30.00	Federalsburg	58.00
Denton	65.00	Tuckahoe	13.70

Total $4051.20

It was very pleasing indeed to the people generally
to know that nearly $4000 of the amount pledged alone
was actually contributed by the boys and girls and forwarded to the proper source to aid in the successful
termination of the war.

REPORT OF CAROLINE COUNTY MARYLAND CHAPTER OF
RED CROSS.

Prior to the spring of 1917, when we entered the World
War, there had been no Red Cross organization of any
kind in Caroline County, Maryland. There were a few
Red Cross members, possibly six, scattered throughout
the County, recruited by chapters in the neighboring
cities. One Sunday School class of girls in Goldsboro
had begun to make slings, bed-socks, etc. under the direction of thier teacher, who was a member of one of the
Delaware organizations.

Early in May, the Women's Section, Council of Defence for Caroline County, met in Denton to organize
and to apportion the work to be undertaken by the Council to the various members. To Mrs. J. W. Stowell of
Federalsburg, was assigned the department of Social
and Welfare work and the Medical and Nursing department. As these departments were covered by Red Cross
work almost entirely it seemed best to organize that
work throughout the county. Mrs. Stowell immediately
got in communication with the Chairmen of the Baltimore Chapter and it was arranged to organize circles in
the various towns, these circles to belong to the Baltimore Chapter. By the end of June the following circles
were established with the sub-chairmen named:

Denton—Mrs. J. Kemp Stevens
Federalsburg—Mrs. Harry W. Davis
Ridgely—Mrs. John Swing
Greensboro—Mrs. Grace Quigg
Preston—Mrs. Frank Lednum
Hillsboro—Mrs. G. Lawrence Wilson
Goldsboro—Mrs. J. Spencer Lapham
Marydel—Mrs. Harry S. Dailey

The total membership was about three hundred, all working hard to earn money to buy material for the supplies that were required of them.

In June, Mrs. Stowell had a letter from Red Cross Headquarters in Washington, saying that the Baltimore Chapter had no right to organize the counties and urged her to organize an independent chapter in Caroline County. Early in July a meeting was called at the Court House in Denton for this purpose, and after much effort and many communications with Headquarters, the Caroline County Chapter Red Cross was officially recognized. The officers were:

Mrs. J. W. Stowell, Chairman
Mrs. J. Kemp Stevens, Vice-Chairman
Miss Mary Hobbs, Secretary
Dr. M. Bates Stephens, Treasurer

The Chapter, which started with three hundred members, had grown to five hundred and forty-four by Christmas 1917. During the Christmas Drive, by intensive effort of every sort in the way of solicitation, visiting country homes, calling on the town people, booths in banks, stores and postoffices, and by public meetings, the membership was raised to two thousand and fifty-five. At the Christmas Drive in 1918 the total adult membership was counted as twenty-four hundred and eighteen.

The Junior Red Cross work in the County began in earnest in March 1918. At the end of that school year the Chapter School Committee reported a membership of three thousand divided into forty-six auxiliaries. Several schools adopted refugees with the money collected for membership dues, two contributed toward a cot equipment, others wished to buy material and make layettes. A few blankets were knitted—each child making one square. The total amount placed in the treasury by the children was $571.47. On May 18, 1918 over fifteen hundred children marched in a Junior Red Cross Auxiliary Parade, held at Denton. The parade ended at the Athletic field where patriotic exercises were given.

During the summer of 1917, while the membership of the Red Cross in Caroline County was still small, $3784.77 was raised and one thousand dollars was spent in the equipment of a base hospital. By the time the second War Fund Drive had been appropriated the membership had grown until the quota of the county was fixed at five thousand dollars. This amount was more than half subscribed in the Denton churches on Sunday morning, following the pastor's appeal for the cause. At the end of the week a big mass meeting was held on the Court House Square. Speeches were made by Chairman Harry A. Roe, Dr. M. Bates Stephens, State Superintendent of Education, Mr. R. A. Boyd of the Federal Trade Commission, and Corporal Chas. W. Bowlby, a Canadian who was on the battlefield of France for two years. The total subscription amounted to twelve thousand dollars. There was always a plan for raising money for Red Cross and the execution proved in most cases successful. The ministers co-operated heartily, both by speaking at the regular church meetings and by their words at public gatherings.

The colored women of the county felt their sons were going to war and they desired to help the Red Cross. In Ridgely a circle was organized and joined the Chapter. In Preston a group of colored women sewed under the direction of Mrs. Douglas, the sub-chairman of Preston. At Denton, the women formed a club and sewed on caps or aprons which they sold to their friends and donated the money to the Red Cross; they also made comfort kits for their soldiers and filled them. On the whole the colored population responded very well to the call for members, especially when solicited by their own people. They showed their eagerness to aid in many ways, some of the women would offer to launder the linen when hemmed by the white women, saying that they wanted to do something.

CHART SHOWN IN COUNTY AGRICULTURAL EXHIBIT ON NOVEMBER 1, 1918.

CAROLINE COUNTY RED CROSS

Nov. 1, 1917—Nov. 1 ,1918.

Adult Members 2275
Junior Members 3000

Circles 11
Members 2275

In regard to the work done by the county directly for boys in service, there is much to be said. The first Christmas (1917) one hundred and eighty-eight Christmas packages were sent to boys in camp. One town sent to every man in service from their district a fruit cake costing ninety-five cents. Another town made a specialty of collecting Victrola records for camp. Smileage books sold very well too, in the county. The second year, the Red Cross gave all possible publicity to the Christmas cartoon distribution for families who had men in the Expeditionary Force. The custom was established when the first men left Caroline, of furnishing each man with a Comfort Kit. The kit came from his home town and seemed especially appreciated on that account.

The Home Service Section is now the most active of all branches in our Chapter. Since the first of July, 1918, when Mrs. J. Spencer Lapham, the present secretary, was appointed, about two hundred cases were handled. Members of the Volunteer Motor Service Corps have aided in reaching outlying country districts. Emergency calls receive immediate answers. The work has been varied and interesting. Wives and mothers whose allotments do not come regularly report to the Secretary and inquiries are begun at once. Mrs. Lapham has had forty-three of these cases, and all but five have been settled satisfactorily. Three of these families have had financial aid. She also helped relatives get information concerning those reported missing in action or wounded or ill. During the fall of 1918 there were many cases of influenza in soldier's families. In several instances the Home Service Section obtained a few days' leave of absence for soldiers who were still in camp, to return to see relatives who were dangerously ill. In other cases Mrs. Lapham corresponded with the man in service, keeping him in touch with his family until danger was over. Letters have been written to men in service for the wives and parents who were not able to do their own correspondence. The members of this department have helped men in service to get affidavits necessary to release them in cases where there was illness or business difficulties.

The returned soldier comes to the Home Service Section for information concerning compensation, insurance, the sixty dollar bonus and other similar things. Occasionally a day passes when the Secretary does not write a letter, but generally from three to fifteen are written daily. To prove some claims it was necessary to get certified copies of birth certificates, marriage records, and even divorce decrees.

Both during and after the war the Belgian Relief has not been forgotten. Garments were donated for the refugees and new material was made, by the women of the county, into serviceable underwear and outer garments for Belgian children according to directions from Headquarters. The Red Cross will never again show only a handful of members in Caroline County. The altrustic spirit introduced by and through its work is of untold benefit to our people.

ANNIE CARTER SINCLAIR, Sec't.

INTERNAL CONDITIONS.

Food.

Simultaneous with the mobilizing, arming, and equipping of troops for the trenches, another army was being mustered, organized, and drilled to serve in the less spectacular, but not less necessary, war against waste, and for the increased production of life essentials. On April 10 and 11, four days after the declaration of war, Secretary Houston met a delegation of Agricultural Commissioners in St. Louis to discuss the food and fuel situation. During the summer months the general plan of campaign there formulated was worked out in detail so that when the passage of the Food-Control Act of Aug. 10, 1917 clothed the President with unlimited power to control the food resources of the nation, little time was lost in putting those plans into effect.

In general the objects of the Administration were: (1) To decrease the home consumption of wheat, meat, and sugar, (2) to keep up the shipment of supplies to our army and our allies, (3) to prevent profiteering. and (4) to increase production. To do this necessitated the cooperation of each county and state in the Union. Although almost all regulations in effect in the counties were made by the Federal or the State Administration,

and although every possible use was made of already
existing organizations and officers, it was yet necessary
for each county to have an Administrator to issue sugar
permits, to meet local merchants for the purpose of fixing prices within regulation liimts, to keep millers informed as to prices, and to see that government demands were met. Mr. T. H. Chambers of Federalsburg
was appointed Administrator for Caroline County in
June, 1918.

By this time many government regulations had already gone into effect. In November, 1917 cards had
been distributed to and signed by housewives who thus
pledged themselves to one meatless and one wheatless
meal each day, one meatless and one wheatless day each
week, no pork on Saturdays, and a general saving of
sugar and fats. These abstainances were voluntary;
others were mandatory. Only one-half pound of sugar
for each individual in the family could be purchased
weekly. Every grocer was required to keep a record
of date, amount, name of purchaser, and number in
purchaser's family. These records were inspected by
the Administrator. For every pound of wheat flour
purchased an equal amount of some substituute such as
rice flour, corn-meal, oatmeal, etc., must be bought. No
individual in town or city could buy more than twenty-
five pounds of wheat flour at one time. Country residents were allowed fifty pounds. Bakeries, also, were
under regulations. A maximum quantity of sugar and
shortening was fixed, uniform loaf weights were adopted, and the flour used had to consist of one-fifth wheat
substitute. Such bread received the patriotic name of
"Victory Bread." A "Fair Price" list agreed upon at
a meeting of merchants of the county and Administrator
Chambers in July, 1917 gave these figures:

Sugar, per lb.	$ .10	
Flour (wheat), per lb.	.07	
Flour (corn meal), per lb.	.06	
Flour (rye), per lb.	.07	
Flour (barley), per lb.	.08	
Rice, per lb.	.10–	$ .15
Oats (loose), per lb.	.08	
Corn syrup (2½ lb. cans)	.25	
Cheese, per lb.	.30–	.35
Butter, per lb.	.55–	.60
Beef (rib roast), per lb.	.28–	.40
Beef (Sirloin Steak), per lb.	.30–	.45
Lard (Kettle rendered), per lb.	.32–	.35
Smoked Ham, per lb.	.35–	.45
Bacon, per lb.	.45–	.50

Many a half-forgotten recipe for making corn-breads, cottage cheese, etc. was revived; the old-time practice of drying friuts and vegetables came into vogue; and many perishable vegetables were conserved by modern methods of canning. Mrs. Edith Norman, Home Demonstration Agent for the county, was instrumental in disseminating such knowledge. One hundred twelve women were -enrolled in Women's Home Economics Clubs which met regularly during the summer of 1918 for demonstration in canning and drying. Although the amouunt of such work done was limited by a fruit and vegetable shortage due to drought, yet the value of produce thus preserved was approximately $2000. Club work, comprising poultry and tomato raising as well as canning fruits and vegetables, was carried on among the girls also. One hundred eighty-four girls were enrolled; the value of the canned goods amounted to $359.10. Under E. A. Anderson, County Farm Demonstration Agent, boys' clubs were organized, with the result that during the two years of the war 1680 bushels of corn, 384 bushels of potatoes, and 19 pigs were added to the food production of the county.

Fuel.

Conservation of fuel was another problem of the war. Chiefly on account of lack of transportation facilities from mines to consumer, but also because of strikes among the miners, to obtain coal became both difficult and expensive. Hence conservation and use of substitutes became necessary as in the food situation. A campaign of volunteer "save a shovelful a day" was inaugurated by the government. Mr. H. C. Hobbs of Denton was appointed Fuel Administrator to see that coal was properly distributed, to procure it for dealers, and to instruct them in their methods of dealing. The maximum price paid for coal in the county during the war was $11.77. Partly in order to relieve the coal famine in the eastern states, but more to decrease shipment to already congested ports the Federal Fuel Administration ordered practically all factories east of the Mississippi river, unless engaged in the manufacture of war material, to shut odwn for the eight day period from Jan. 17 to 29, 1918. Moreover on Monday for ten successive weeks stores, shops, factories, and public buildings except schools, hotels, and lighting plants were required to close. There were no exceptions to this order in Caroline County. Mondays were "heatless holidays."

For a similar reason, unnecessary travel by automobile in states east of the Mississippi was discouraged during the summer months. Another measure designed to save fuel and lights as well as to promote gardening was the Daylight-Saving Law which became effective May 1, 1918. It provided that clocks be set ahead one hour on that date, and set back again in October. The plan was popular in towns, where a man might have considerable time for gardening after business hours, but the opposition by farmers, generally, was so strong that after two years' trial Congress repealed the law. Further to complicate the heating problem an unusually low temperature prevailed throughout the winter of 1917-1918. Many bushels of potatoes and apples that had been buried in pits of ordinary depth froze. So great was the consumption of coal and so inadequate the available supply that schools were in some cases forced to close for want of it.

Influenza.

The fall of 1918 is memorable as the time of the Spanish Influenza epidemic. The disease probably crept into America through the medium of the army, since practically all of Europe was devastated by it prior to its appearance here. The first case reported in Caroline County was from Preston, Oct. 5. The whole county was quickly involved; schools, churches, moving picture theaters, and other meeting places were closed by state and county boards of health, and remained closed for a period of five weeks. Many places of business closed because of the illness of managers and operators. Whole families were stricken down at once. A total of 1140 cases was reported; 134 deaths resulting therefrom. Although there were cases of the disease during the entire winter, the epidemic was practically over by November.

Armisitce.

Meanwhile, from the battleline of Europe there were coming indications that a cessation of hostilities must be near. Eager anticipation, therefore, speedily gave way to wild demonstration when on the morning of Nov. 11, 1918 word was received that an armistice had been agreed upon. Business was suspended, prayers of thanksgiving were offered in the churches, parades were formed, whistles shrieked, bellsjingled, flags fluttered. Every house showed its bunting; every citizen expressed in his own way joy, relief, and gratitude at the indications of peace.

Flood.

On August 15, 1919 calamity again visited the county—this time in the form of a flood. Heavy rains for a week so saturated the soil and filled the streams that the downpour of the memorable Wednesday of Aug. 15, broke dams, overflowed river banks, swept away bridges, flooded streets, cellars and the first floors of dwellings, and drowned small animals such as pigs and chickens. Electric lines were broken, street lights were out, and railroad traffic was suspended. Crops were either destroyed or badly damaged. Boyce Mill, Bloomery, and Pennypacker Bridges were completely wrecked, as was likewise a bridge on the state road near Federalsburg. Falkner Bridge stood intact with a thirty foot gulley cutting the road each side of it. The total damage to roads and bridges was estimated at $60,000.

LIST OF INDUCTED MEN FURNISHED BY THE LOCAL BOARD
OF CAROLINE COUNTY TO THE ADJUTANT-GENERAL
OF MARYLAND.

Names starred are those of men who died in service either in camp or on the field. No titles of rank are given because of the impossibility of securing all. For a similar reason a few names occur both in this list and in the Roster of Enlished Men when the exact case could not be ascertained.

Adams, Leonard W. (Col.)	Denton	Barcus, Luther	Denton
		Baynard, Norman W. (Col.)	
Aldridge, James N. (Col.)	Preston		Hobbs
Alexander, Oscar	Marydel	Beer, Wilbur Peter	Denton
Allen, Raymond (Col.)	Ridgely	Beel, Noble	Henderson
Anderson, Alonzo (Col.)	Denton	Benson, Arthur D.	Greensboro
Andrew, Harold	Denton	Benson, George W.	Denton
Anthony, Calvin	Denton	Betton, William D.	
Anthony, Howard	Denton		Federalsburg
Austin, Courtland	Ridgely	Beulah, Thomas	Denton
Bascak, John	Hobbs	Beulah, Walter (Col.)	
Baker, Wilbert John	Denton		Federalsburg
		Blackburn, John Henry, Ridgely	

—338—

Blades, Ralph Thos., Bethlehem
Blanche, Raymond B.   Ridgely
Blades, Harlan R.   Denton
Blosser, Orville A.   Denton
Breeding, Thomas Mark
    Federalsburg
Brewington, Solomon H. (Col.)
    Federalsburg
Bridegroom, Alonza L., Preston
Bridegroom, Elmer J.
    Federalsburg
Brown, William D.   Goldsboro
Brown, James Earl
    Federalsburg
Brumbaugh, Andrew I.
    Greensboro
Brumbaugh, Isaac V.   Denton
Butler, Albert R.   Preston
Burgess, William M.   Preston
Burkey, Irvin W.   Denton
Cahall, Edward C.   Goldsboro
Cahall, Alfred G., Federaslburg
Callahan, Samuel C.
    Federalsburg
Cannon, Lacey (Col.)
    Federalsburg
Cannon, Oscar H. (Col.)
    Federalsburg
Carroll, Clinton T.   Preston
Carroll, John Russell
    Federalsburg
Cauley, Harry W.   Denton
Chaffinch, Clarence E.   Hobbs
Chambers, Percy A.
    Federalsburg
Clark, Alfred Carson   Denton
Clevenger, Harland D.
    Federalsburg
Clough, James A.,   Henderson
Clough, Stephen W., Greensboro
Closson, Orland Cecil
    Federalsburg
Cohey, Lewis Kennard   Ridgely
Cohee, Samuel B.   Marydel
Collins, Benj. F. (Col.)
    Federalsburg
Collins, William A. (Col.)
    Federalsburg
Cole, Walter Raymond   Preston
Collins, Wilmer T.   Federalsburg
Comegys, Carroll   Hillsboro
Conner, Emory Claude
    Greensboro
Conley, Henry E.   Henderson
Connor, Roland B.   Greensboro
Corkran, Arthur W.
    Federalsburg
Coulbourne, Ralph E.
    Federalsburg
Covington, Norris E.
    Federalsburg
Cox, Earl Saxton   Choptank

Cox, Jerome R.   Preston
Craft, Herbert Paul
    Federalsburg
Craft, Frank M.   Denton
Cuthberton, Zeb. (Col.) Ridgely
Davidson, George W.   Denton
Davis, Charles N., Federalsburg
Deen, Albert Lawrence   Preston
Dew, Harold James
    Federalsburg
Dhue, Noble J.   Goldsboro
Dickerson, Joshua M. (Col.)
    Federalsburg
Dill, Whiteley W.   Denton
Downes, Marion H.   Denton
Downes, George W. (Col.)
    Denton
Downes, Robert W.   Denton
Downing, Ira J. (Col.)
    Federalsburg
Dulin, Benjamin R.   Goldsboro
Dukes, Levi Reyner   Denton
Dyer, Norman (Col.)   Denton
Eaton, Edw. Herman   Denton
Ebling, Daniel   Ridgely
Edge, William Robert
    Greensboro
Edwards, Charlie   Greensboro
Ellwanger, David Howard
    Denton
Emerson, John H.   Denton
Emerson, Raymond E.
    Greensboro
Everngam, John L.   Denton
Fields, Daniel, Jr. Federalsburg
Fisher, Clarence W. (Col.)
    Ridgely
Fisher, Charles   Ridgely
Fisher, George L.   Ridgely
Fleming, William McN.
    Goldsboro
Fletcher, William L. (Col.)
    Preston
Flowers, Henry   Greensboro
Fluharty, Arthur S.   Preston
Fountain, John W.
    Hickman, Del.
Fuchs, Conrad   Williamsburg
Gadow, Albert B.   Preston
Garey, Edward S.   Denton
Geisel, C. Robert   Denton
Geisel, Owen P.   Denton
Gibson, Gilbert   Preston
Gordon, Roy   Denton
Gould, Harrison (Col.)
    Goldsboro
Gould, James B. (Col.)
    Greensboro
Gray, Robert Hooper
    Goldsboro
Green, Edmond W. (Col.)
    Preston

Griffin, William M. (Col.)
    Greensboro
Griffith, Ernest F.   Denton
Gross, Fred (Col.)   Denton
Gwin, William J.   Denton
Hammond, Silas (Col.) Ridgely
Hammond, Charles W. (Col.)
    Federalsburg
Harden, John Wesley (Col.)
    Hillsboro
Harding, Harvey E. Bethlehem
Harper, James M. Federalsburg
Harrington, Lawrence J.
    Greensboro
Harvey, Charles T.   Denton
Harris, Norman Greensboro
Harris, John J. Henderson
Haynes, Hayward (Col.) Preston
Heather, James T. Marydel
Henry, Robert W. (Col.)
    Goldsboro
Henning, Edward Dukes Denton
Henry, Mitchell F. (Col.)
    Go.dsboro
Henry, Joseph E. (Col.)
    Goldsboro
Hickey, George W. Marydel
Hicks, Clifton R. W. Hillsboro
Hignutt, Elmer E. Federalsburg
Hignutt, Clarence E. Hobbs
Hines, Alonzo (Col.) Hillsboro
Hines, Lee Roy (Col.) Ridgely
holland, Waldon (Col.) Preston
Holland, Gilbert (Col.)
    Federalsburg
Hollingsworth, Henry T. Denton
Holt, William A. Hillsboro
Hopkins, Harry Elmer Preston
Horn, Elmer Francis Preston
Howell, William Robert, Denton
Howell, Rossie M. Ridgely
Hubbard, Chauncey T. (Col.)
    Preston
Hubbard, Veda W. Greensboro
Hubbard, William H.
    Greensboro
Hubbard, Raymond T. (Col.)
    Federalsburg
Hughes, Johnathan L. Denton
Hughes, Milton Wilby
    Goldsboro
Hulliger, Frederick W.
    Federalsburg
Hulliger, Henry H. Federalsburg
Hunley, John (Col.) Ridgely
Hurlock, Milton W. Denton
Hutson, Chester Arthur
    Greensboro
Hynson, William H. Denton
Irwin, Robert Stewart Denton
Jackson, Charles R. Greensboro

Jarman, Clinton B., Jr.
    Greensboro
Jenkins, William T. (Col.)
    Ridgely
Jester, Thomas L. Federalsburg
Johns, Benj. H. (Col.) Preston
Johnson, James H. Denton
Jones, Fred E. Hobbs
Johnson, Richard (Col.) Ridgely
Johnson, Benjamin F. Denton
Johns, Alfred Thos. (Col.)
    Preston
Johnson, Emory (Col.)
    Federalsburg
Johnson, James A. Federalsburg
Jones, John W. (Col.) Preston
Jones, James Fred Choptank
Jopp, Samuel Taylor Denton
Jopp, William Harry Denton
Kauffman, Jacob F. Ridgely
Kemp, William August Preston
Kennedy, John M. Greensboro
Kenton, Hiram W. Greensboro
Kent, Josepu Federaisburg
Kinnamon, Oscar Greensboro
Kinnamon, Albert W. (Col.)
    Denton
Knox, James Henry Denton
Knox, Lawrence Denton
Koeneman, Herbert E.
    Greensboro
Kusmaul, Christian Henderson
Lane, Clarence F. Ridgely
Latshaw Vernie W. Ridgely
Layton, Edward Preston
Legree, John (Col.) Denton
Lewis, Harvey Edw. (Col.)
    Denton
Lewis, James Henry (Col.)
    Ridgely
Lewis, Arthur J., Hickman, Del.
Lowe, William G. Federalsburg
Lynch, William E. Ridgely
Magers, George W. Preston
Magee, Edgar (Col.)
    Federalsburg
Meluney, Wm. Clement
    Hickman, Del.
Marvel, William D. Ridgely
Matthews, Robert L. (Col.)
    Goldsboro
Matthews, Oscar (Col.)
    Greensboro
Merriken, Calvert C.
    Federalsburg
Meredith, Leslie L.
    Wilmington, Del.
Messer, Alton R. Federalsburg
Milby, Charles R. Goldsboro
Miley, James L. Preston
Milleman, John C. Preston

Mills, Marion Earl Federalsburg
Mitchell, Harry Leon Federalsburg
Mitchell, George H. Greensboro
Moore, Harry T. Ridgely
Moore, Wondell H. Preston
Morgan, Edgar Denton
Murphy, Harry J. Hobbs
McNeal, Lewis T. Denton
McKnatt, Alexander, Greensboro
McKnat, Burt Greensboro
McCrea, William V. Federalsburg
McCoy, John W. Federalsburg
Nashold, Walter McK Greensboro
Neal, Luther C. Federalsburg
Neff, Paul James Ridgely
Newell, George Arthur Federalsburg
Nichols, Lee Earl, Federalsburg
Nickerson, Arthur (Col.) Federalsburg
Orrell, Elwood C. Greensboro
Parker, John (Col.) Ridgely
Parrott, William M. Denton
Patchett, Edward I. Bethlehem
Pearson, Thomas C. Preston
Perry, John Arthur Denton
Perry, William M. Preston
Perry, Charles Levin Preston
Perry, Joseph H. Ridgely
Perkins, Huntley E. (Col.) Greensboro
Pettijohn, William H. (Col.) Denton
Pendleton, Edmund T. Ridgely
Pinkins, Roland (Col.) Federalsburg
Pinkine, Edward M. Denton
Plummer, James O. Denton
Porter, Clayton S. Denton
Price, Reuben H. Federalsburg
Pritchett, Enoch (Col.) Hillsboro
Pritchett, Loren S. Henderson
Pritchett, Ralph B. Greensboro
Rash, Thomas Geo. Ridgely
Reaser, Fred (Col.) Federalsburg
Reed, Benjamin E. Preston
Reed, Emmons Harvey Denton
Reese, James Herbert Preston
Reese, John H. Preston
Reichelt, William P. Hobbs
Reynolds, Henry F. Preston
Rhynas, Fred (Col.) Hillsboro
Rickards, William F. Ridgely
Robinson, Alexander (Col.) Ridgely
Robinson, Wright E. Marydel
Roberts, Bion Ridgely

Roe, Thomas Dukes Denton
Roe, William Shanley Denton
Roher, Elmer C. Hobbs
Roy, Cordy (Col.) Greensboro
Royer, Jonas Ridgely
Ross, Arthur (Col.) Federalsburg
Rouse, Benj. F. Goldsboro
Russell, Horsey S. Greensboro
Satterfield, John H. (Col.)
Satterfield, Edwin C. Denton
Satterfield, Allie H. Denton
Satterfield, Chas. S. (Col.) Denton
Satterfield, Nelson M. (Col.) Denton
Saunders, Harry C. Goldsboro
Scott, Fred Houston Denton
Scott, Clint Denton
Scott, Herbert (Col.) Goldsboro
Scott, Manuel (Col.) Federalsburg
Sculley, William A., Jr. Ridgely
Sculley, Arters Ridgely
Sharp, William R. (Col.) Preston
Sheubrooks, Herbert Marydel
Shipman, Stephen P. Denton
Shively, Horace D. Goldsboro
Short, Luther Hillsboro
Sisk, Albert Fletcher Preston
Sisk, Joseph Gilbert Preston
Smith, Olus Erie Goldsboro
Smith, Walter Roy Greensboro
Smith, Wm. Henry (Col.) Ridgely
Smith, Lawrence Greensboro
Smith, Edw. Fields Federalsburg
Smith, Fred Norwood Hobbs
Smith, Earl James Federalsburg
Smith, Norman Earl Federalsburg
Smith, Frank Lewis Federalsburg
Smith, Oscar Denton
Smith, Selby Ray Ridgely
Smith, William (Col.) Preston
Smith, William E. (Col.) Ridgely
Sparklin, Daniel W. Federalsburg
Stafford, Willis Ray Denton
Stanford, Arthur L. (Col.) Greensboro
Stanley, Harry L. (Col.) Federalsburg
Stanford, Wm. McK. (Col.) Preston
Swann, Oscar Greensboro
Thawley, Wesley E. Denton
Theis, Oscar H. Denton

Thomas, Harry (Col.)   Ridgely
Tiller, Aaron   Ridgely
Tiller, Davis (Col.)   Ridgely
Todd, Carlton Ward   Choptank
Todd, Ralph Richson
                                Federalsburg
Todd, Herbert R.   Preston
Todd, Roland Edw.   Preston
Totheroh, William E.
                                Greensboro
Towers, Roland O.   Denton
Trazzare, Clifford T.   Denton
Tribbett, Edwin   Greensboro
Tribbett, Harvey F.   Greensboro
Tribbett, Sherman L.   Denton
Trice, Edwin Haynes
                                Federalsburg
Truitt, Herman H.   Ridgely
Truxon, Elijah B. (Col.) Denton
Turner, Clarence Edw. (Col.)
                                Federalsburg
Turner, Charles (Col.)
                                Federalsburg
Turner, Oscar W. (Col.)
                                Federalsburg
Turner, James Roland
                                Federalsburg
Vickery, Lawrence   Hobbs
Vonwille, Philip F.   Greensboro
Warner, John (Col.)   Ridgely
Ward, Joseph Francis   Denton
Warren, Alonzo (Col.)
                                Federalsburg
Waters, George W. (Col.)
                                Federalsburg
Watkins, George A. (Col.)
                                Greensboro
Waldron, Lee A.   Choptank
Wayman, Henry (Col.)
                                Hillsboro
Webb, Benj. B. (Col.)   Preston
Werner, Ralph   Preston
West, Carlton   Preston
West, Nelson (Col.)   Baltimore

Whiteley, Roy E.   Choptank
Willin, Everett Edw.
                                Federalsburg
Willin, Alton Adkins
                                Federalsburg
Willin, William (Col.)
                                Baltimore
Willin, Mark A. H., Jr.
                           Oak Grove, Del.
Wilson, William R. (Col.)
                                Ridgely
Williamson, Charles F.
                                Choptank
Williams, John H. Federalsburg
Williamson, Emmett McK.
                                Federalsburg
Williams, Silver (Col.)
                                Federalsburg
Williams, Will (Col.)   Denton
Williamson, Ben C.
                                Federalsburg
Williamson, Leonard F.
                                Federalsburg
Wilson, Carroll   Denton
Wilson, Joh W. (Col.)   Denton
Wilson, Joseph (Col.)   Marydel
Wisher, Linwood (Col.)   Hobbs
Woodward, James C. Greensboro
Wright, Clarence A.
                                Federalsburg
Wright, Leonas V. Federalsburg
Wright, Olin B.   Preston
Wright, Leland C.   Preston
Wright, Albert (Col.)   Ridgely
Weight, Clarence (Col.)
                                Hillsboro
Wright, Robert R.   Greensboro
Wright, William E.   Preston
Wyatt, Vaughn Collins
                                Greensboro
Young, Chris Edw. (Col.)
                                Ridgely
Zeigler, Frank D.   Denton

Roster of Enlisted Men From Caroline County Engaged or in Preparation for the European War.

Following is an explanation of the symbols found after some of the names:

(*) Dead	(Ma.) Marne
(a) was abraod	(St. M.) St. Mihiel
(c) served in Champagne district	(M.) Montfaucon
	(C. T.) Chateau Thierry
(v) Verdun	(N.) Navy
(M. A.) Meuse-Argonne	(O. A.) Oise Aisne
(reg.) regular	(H. A.) Haute Alsace
(Arg.) Argonne forest	For lack of information some titles are omitted.
(B. W.) Belleau Woods	

Anderson, Eugene (a) .... Denton
Adams, Howard J. .... Federalsburg
Beall, Arthur C. (N.) .... Denton
Bennington, Robert L. .... Ridgely
Blades, L. J. K. .... Preston
Blades, Capt. Webster, U. S. Navy .... Preston
Blake, Cecil .... Denton
Booker, Byron .... Goldsboro
Breeding, Capt. Earl G., Medical Corps .... Federalsburg
Brownell, Ralph L. .... Denton
Benson, Charles E. (N.) .... Preston
Carroll, John Russell .... Federalsburg
Bunting, Chaplain John J. .... Ridgely
Brooks, 1st Lieut. F. T. .... Federalsburg
Brower, 1st Lieut. C. C. (a) .... Federalsburg
Butler, Raymond L. .... Denton
Closson, Sargt. Eldon H. (C) (M A) (O-A)......... Federalsburg
Coulbourne, Carl N. (a) (V) (M-A) .... Hobbs
Curz, Walter R. (a) .... Federalsburg
Cox, 2nd Lieut. Jerome (a) .... Preston
Carroll, Sargt. J. Russell (a) .... Federalsburg
Closson, Corp. Orland C. (a) .... Federalsburg
Clark, Pierce .... Greensboro
Clough, Stephen (a) (reg.) .... Greensboro
Cortelyou, Clifford (a) .... Goldsboro
Cortelyou, Wilbur (a) .... Goldsboro
Dill, Norman H. .... Denton
Deakyne, 1st Lieut. Luther S. (a) .... Denton
Dulin, Virginia (a) (nurse) .... Preston
Dulin, Carleton (*) .... Preston
Davis, William .... Ridgely
Deen, Sargt. Albert S. (a) .... Preston
Darling, John (a) (A) (Arg.) (V) .... Preston
Duvall, Robert (a) .... Preston
Deen, Norman (a) .... Federalsburg
Downes, 1st Lieut. J. R., Medical Corps .... Preston
Davis, Leon (a) (M. A.) (H. A.) .... Federalsburg
Deen, Levin (a) .... Federalsburg
Drum, James (a) .... Federalsburg
Davis, Henry (a) (*) (B. W.) .... Federalsburg
Dukes, Sargt. Louis R. (a) (H. M.) (V) .... Denton
Davis, Capt. Dudley W. .... Ridgely
Evans, Raymond E. .... Greensboro
Eddington, Sargt. John R. (a) .... Federalsburg
Elderdice, Sargt. James R. (a) .... Federalsburg
Edwards, Thomas (N) .... Preston

```
Fisher, Major Roland P. (a) .........................Denton
Fooks, Herbert C. (a) ..............................Preston
Fountain, Herbert .................................Ridgely
Garey, Sargt. William .............................Denton
France, 1st Lieut. G. H. (a) ..................Federalsburg
Fountain, Sargt. Mag. Sydney (a) ...................Ridgely
Fountain, Sargt. Charles ..........................Ridgely
Fowler, William (a) .............................Greensboro
Fields, Daniel, Jr. (a) (*) ....................Federalsburg
Gray, William J. .................................Goldsboro
Gadow, Carl W. (a) (M. A.) .........................Preston
Green, Capt. J. Woodall (a) .........................Denton
Griffith, Clarence ..............................Greensboro
Harper, Corp. Floyd H. (*) ....................Federalsburg
Henry, Mitchell F. ...............................Goldsboro
Hunt, Corp. Ralph (a) .........................Federalsburg
Holleck, Jerry C. (a) ..............................Preston
Holmes, Luther B. ..................................Denton
Hutson, Corp. Alfred .............................Greensboro
Hurlock, Hosuton (a) ..........................Federalsburg
Jefferson, Sargt. Donald E. (a) ...............Federalsburg
Johns, Alfred Thomas (col.) (a) ....................Preston
Jarman, Christopher ...............................Ridgely
Jeavons, Allen ................................Federalsburg
Johnson, Corp. J. Arthur (a) ..................Federalsburg
Jones, Noble (a) ................................Greensboro
Jarman, Clayton (a) .............................Greensboro
Klotz, William (a) ................................Ridgely
Kabelka, Otto (a) (M. A.) (St. M.) ...............Henderson
Keehan, Howard (a) (Arg.) (B. W.) (A. M.) .........Ridgely
Kelley, Elmert T. ..................................Preston
Kornrumpf, James A. .............................Greensboro
Lednum, Ralph C. ...................................Preston
Ludwig, J. Henry (*) (N) ..........................Ridgely
Lynch, Lee Henry ..................................Ridgely
Long, James D. .....................................Denton
Lankford, Corp. Claude (a) .........................Preston
Lord, George (a) ..............................Federalsburg
Lane, Irvin (aviation) ............................Ridgely
Medford, Corp. Frank P. (a) ........................Marydel
Medford, Lieut. Wm. Tyler (a) ......................Marydel
Mowbray, Alderson .............................Federalsburg
Madera, Maj. Dr. J. C. (reg.) .....................Ridgely
Morris, Capt. Irvin (reg.) .........................Preston
Miller, Bugler Joseph (a) .....................Federalsburg
McConnell, Corp. Vaughn (a) (Toule Sector) .........Preston
McConnell, Corp. Philip (a) (C) (Ma.) (A. M.) ......Preston
Merriken, 2nd Lieut. Wilbur (a) ...............Federalsburg
Mowbray, 2nd Lieut. C. Brown (*) (a) ..........Federalsburg
Meredith, Sargt. Alvin (*) (a) (C. T.) ........Federalsburg
Meredith, Leslie (a) .............................Henderson
Magnus, William (a) .............................Greensboro
Neal, William H. ...................................Preston
Nichols, Sargt. Winfield T. (a) (A) (C) (St. M.) (Arg.)...Denton
Noble, Maj. John W. (a) ............................Preston
Noble, Capt. Houston (marine) (a) (arg) .......Federalsburg
Noble, Corp. Robert K. (a) (Houte) (A) ........Federalsburg
Noble, Lieut. Wm. D., Medical Corps ................Preston
Nuttle, Harold C. (a) (St. M.) (C.) (M. A.) ........Denton
Neal, Corp. Francis W. (a) ....................Federalsburg
Noble, Brig. Gen. Robert H. (a) (reg) (arg).....Federalsburg
```

```
Novak, Roland (a) ...........................Federalsburg
Perry, Joseph H. (*) ..............................Ridgely
Pells, James N. ...................................Denton
Plummer, Charles ..................................Denton
Pearsaul, Edward (N) ..............................Ridgely
Pinder, Frank ..................................Greensboro
Pippin, Lieut. Noble ...........................Henderson
Poore, Lieut. Goodwin (a) ......................Greensboro
Poore, Byron (a) ...............................Greensboro
Pritchett, Lorain (a) ..........................Henderson
Rice, Robert J. (a) (Ma) ..........................Denton
Ring, Frank J. ...............................Federalsburg
Ricketts, Loyd (a) ...........................Federalsburg
Ross, Ailtrum ................................Federalsburg
Saulsbury, Sargt. Irvin T. (a) ....................Ridgely
Schlegel, Ernest F. ...............................Denton
Slacum, Louis H. .............................Federalsburg
Smith, Walter R. ...............................Greensboro
Spence, Clarence E. ...............................Denton
Stevens, Lynne E. (a) (c) (St. M.) (Chat.) ........Denton
Summerfield, Maj. J. Henry (a) (St. M.) (Arg) (V) .....Denton
Sisk, Edwin K. (a) ...............................Preston
Shepherd, Pierce (a) .........................Federalsburg
Sharp, Preston (*) (N) ............................Ridgely
Smith, Ernest (Y. M. C. A.) .......................Ridgely
Spence, Percy (N) .................................Ridgely
Smith, Alexander, Jr. (a) (Arg) (B. W.) ...........Ridgely
Swing, Thompson (a) ...............................Ridgely
Schrieber, Sargt. John B. (a) ..................Greensboro
Trice, Clyde ......................................Denton
Travers, Floyd (N) .............................Greensboro
Taylor, 1st Lieut. Dr. F. F. (a) ..................Ridgely
Trice, Corp. Arthur (a) ..........................Preston
Vonwelle, Philip (*) (a) .......................Greensboro
Wright, Clarence ...............................Hillsboro
White, Albert .....................................Ridgely
Willoughby, Richard Maurice ..................Federalsburg
Wright, Walter T. ..............................Greensboro
Wright, Charles P. ...........................Federalsburg
Wilson, Henry (N) .................................Denton
Wyatt, Sargt. William W. (aviation) ...............Ridgely
Wilson, Alice (nurse) .............................Ridgely
Waterson, David (*) (a) ........................Greensboro
Waterson, Joseph (a) ...........................Greensboro
Weaver, Henry ..................................Greensboro
Wheatley, Wilbur (a) .........................Federalsburg
Wheatley, Guy (a) ............................Federalsburg
Wright, Kemp (*) (a) .........................Federalsburg
Wright, Lenos (a) ............................Federalsburg
Williams, Perce ..............................Federalsburg
White, Sargt. Everett (a) (V) (A. H.) ........Federalsburg
```

HONOR ROLL

THE GREAT WAR

List of Caroline County men and women who either in service or in preparation made the Supreme Sacrifice.

MARY TODD
NORMAN WESLEY BAYNARD
HENRY DAVIS
WILLIAM CARLETON DULIN
NORMAN DYER
DANIEL FIELDS, JR.
WILLIAM McKNUTT FLEMING
JOHN GREGG
JOHN WESLEY HARDEN
JAMES HOLLAND
IRWIN JOPP
FRED R. JUMP
J. HENRY LUDWIG
ALVIN MEREDITH
CHARLES BROWN MOWBRAY
WALTER NASHOLD
JOSEPH H. PERRY
WILLIAM PUSSE
PRESTON SHARP
NORMAN EARLE SMITH
NORMAN THOMAS
ROLAND EDWARD TODD
PHILIP F. VONVILLE
DAVID WATERSON
KEMP WRIGHT
VAUGHN C. WYATT

THE FLOODS OF 1919.

(From local newspapers.)

Not within the memory of our oldest inhabitants were such incessant rain storms recalled as swept our country in 1919. The local weather official H. B. Mason reported that practically a normal year's rainfall fell within the space of three months, with unusually heavy rains the remainder of the year. Some idea of the enormous loss sustained everywhere may be gathered from the following taken in part from one of the county news papers issued in August.

"Death rode the flood of Wednesday night and Thursday morning, one young man losing his life on account of it. The victim was John Brown, fireman on a work train which ran into an unsuspected washout about a mile west of Denton about seven o'clock on Thursday morning. This work train was on its way to repair a cut in a road near Hobbs and was traveling at a good rate of speed. When the danger spot was close at hand Engineer Julian Bryan saw it, told the fireman, and jumped. Brown remained and in a moment was killed. The engine went through the trestle, the tender falling on it. The caboose also left the track and fell into the swollen stream.

For months the big rains had been coming, but it was on Wednesday last that the floods descended—fell as they had not fallen for many years. The rain of Wednesday and Wednesday night was the heaviest, according to some of our citizens who remember well, since the celebrated downpour of June, 1862 when all the mill dams in the county were swept away. All agree that it was terrific in its volume and in the damage that was done. On nearly every farm in Caroline county heavy loss has been sustained in crops injured.

The county suffers much in the havoc wrought to roads and bridges in many sections. One of the greatest losses was that near the Boyce mill, on the road from Greensboro to Delaware. The roads engineer says the cost of a new bridge here will be from $6000 to $8000. There are many bridges damaged, some very badly, and there are scores of washouts along the public roads.

The floods left the road in a bad way at Faulkner's bridge, near Federalsburg. In Tuckahoe Neck Pipe bridge is carried away, and at the Sparklin or Elben mill the road is impassable on account of a big cut. There is also a bad washout at Mason's bridge, on the headwaters of the Tuckahoe river. At Bunker Hill branch, north of Denton, on the west side of Choptank river, the big pipe has been swept away.

The tremendous fall of water inundated a vast area in the vicinity of Adamsville, Delaware, the Marshy Hope stream, the headwaters of the Northwest Fork river being spread over many hundreds of acres of land under cultivation. At the point of the M. D. & V. railroad bridge the waters were several hundred feet wide and so deep over the structure and the track adjacent for a long distance on each side that Engineer Polk, of the road, said Thursday night that there was then no immediate prospect of making repairs at the point where the wreck occurred, because a wrecking train with the big derrick could not pass over the road. The flood would have to be allowed to subside. Two washouts are to be repaired, one near Hobbs and the other between Denton and Tuckahoe Station. Train service will likely be resumed on Monday.

From 20 to 30 feet of the dam of Williston mill—that portion from the State road to the mill—was washed out, causing the shutting down of business and involving the owner, Mr. Willard C. Todd, in a considerable loss, and the manager, Mr. C. E. Abbott, in considerable trouble.

The dam at C. C. Deen's mill, Fowling Creek, was carried away Wednesday evening, and there was a great flood about the millhouse. A thousand bushels of wheat, 500 bushels of corn and 50 bushels of meal were overrun and badly damaged.

Corn fields and tomato fields suffered great injury from the heavy wind and rains. Tomatoes especially are hurt. The prospect is that the pack will be the smallest in many years. A dispatch from Federalsburg on Thursday said that place experienced the worst storm in its history. The Main street was a foot deep in water in some places. A number of merchants had to move stock and other things to save them. Boats were propelled about the streets in this Venice of Caroline. There was an eighty-foot washout on the Cambridge and Seaford road and passenger and freight trains were stopped.

Owners of traction engines are warned by Engineer Waldorf that many of the bridges may be in unsafe condition, and caution should be exercised in going over them. Autos should travel slowly and drivers should be exceedingly careful."

INDEX

INDEX

Evans, Raymond E., 343.
Richard, 171.
Eveland, Ethel, 217.
Everngam, John L., 339.
Evitts, Joseph, 316.
Seth, 245.
Farley, John, 173.
Faulkner, Thos., 171.
Fauntleroy, Capt. John, 61, 68, 187.
Faux, Prof., 263.
Fiddleman, Philip, 56, 62, 71, 74.
Fields, Daniel, Jr., 339, 344, 346.
Finsthwaite, James, 272.
Fisher, Charles, 339.
Clarence W., 339.
Earle R., 314.
George L., 339.
John, 15, 183.
Dr. P. R., 133.
Purnell, 130.
Roland P., 344.
Stephen, 131.
T. Pliny, 238.
Thos., 106.
Fitzhugh, George, 8.
Fitzhughes, William, 8.
Flanagan, John, 173.
Fleetwood, William W., 173.
Fleming, William McKnutt, 346.
William McN., 339.
Fletcher, William L., 339.
Flowers, A. W., 6.
Alcaid N., 173.
Henry, 339.
Wesley, 173.
Fluharty, Arthur S., 339.
Daniel R., 172.
Samuel H., 238.
Fooks, Herbert C., 344.
N. H., 258.
Ford, John, 75.
Wm. H., 171.
Forman, S. E., 161.
Foster, Thomas, 259.
William, 74.
Fountain, Andrew, 67, 222.
Charles, 344.
Herbert, 344.
James F., 246.
John W., 339.
Marcy, 143, 189, 222.
Massy, 74, 149, 150, 151, 205.
Nehemiah, 225.
Robert, 137.
Sydney, 344.

Fountain, Zebedial, 246.
Fowler, Willian, 344.
Frampton, Chas., 172.
William, 272.
Wm. E., 172.
France, G. H., 344.
Frazier, Alexander, 103.
Capt., 114, 115.
Henrietta Maria, 104.
Sarah, 103.
Wm., Capt., 88, 94, 103, 104, 259, 260, 265.
Froume, John, 74.
Fuchs, Conrad, 339.
Furman, Mr., 310.
Gadd, Alexander, 169.
Frank, 169.
Luther H.(Col.), 169.
Gadow, Albert B., 339.
Gannon, Perry, 74.
Garey, Edward S., 339.
Matthew, 243, 244.
Robert S., 314.
Robt. J. W., 173.
Thomas F., 244.
William, 344.
Garretson, Freeborn, 114, 292.
Garrison, Freeborn, 213.
Gehman, Rev. G. T., 247.
Geisel, C. Robert, 339.
Owen P., 339.
George, Rev. Daniel, 282.
Dr. Enoch, 161.
Joseph T., 175, 177.
III, King, 74.
Gephart, Otto, 309, 310.
Gibson, Charlie, 182.
Chas. W., 171.
Gilbert, 339.
Ginn, James, 124, 125.
Godow, Carl W., 344.
Godwin, Henry M., 200.
Preston, 110.
Goetchious, John, 172.
Goldsboro, Robert, 14.
Thomas, 131.
Goldsborough, Mrs. Angeline, 213.
Dr. G. W., 187, 213.
Greenbury, 71.
Rev. Robert, 107.
T. Alan, 322, 329.
Thomas, 14, 55, 70, 88, 157, 166.
Dr. W. W., 317.
Gootee, Kelly, 172.
William, 256.
Gordon, Chas. L., 173.
Roy, 339.

Goslin, E. E., 161, 276.
Edward R., 274.
Miss Lizzie, 276.
Gould, Harrison, 339.
James B., 339.
Graham, Walter D. D., 220.
Gray, Robert Hooper, 339.
William J., 344.
Wm. L., 173.
Green, Edmond W., 339.
J. Woodall, 344.
Thomas R., 13.
Mrs. Thomas R., 325.
Valentine, 290.
Greenlee, Arthur John, 243.
David, 191, 192.
Gregg, John, 346.
Griffin, Charles G., 314.
William M., 340.
Griffith, Clarence, 344.
Colonel, 73.
Ernest F., 340.
Ferdinand, 272.
John H., 173.
John S., 174.
Gross, Fred, 340.
Gwin, William J., 340.
Hains, Miss Annie, 254.
Hall, James H., 171.
William, 175.
Hallingsworth, Clarence, 184.
Hambly, Thomas C., 299.
Hammond, Chas. W., 340.
James R., 172.
Silas, 340.
Thos. L., 173.
Hand, James, 226.
Handy, George, 74.
Levin, 74.
Hannebury, Mr., 305.
Hardcastle, Ann, 134.
Edward, 96.
John, 134, 162, 165, 290.
Mary Ann, 96.
Peter, 131.
Robert, 95, 224.
Thomas, 10, 17, 62, 88, 95, 106, 120, 165, 186, 187, 213, 289.
William, 131.
Wm., 157.
Harden, John Wesley, 340, 346.
Hardin, Edward, 74.
Harding, Harvey E., 340.
Harford, Henry, 8.
Harper, Floyd H., 344.
James M., 340.
James S., 171.
Shadrach, 171.
Wm., 171.

INDEX

INDEX

INDEX